Police Use of Force

POLICE USE OF FORCE

A Global Perspective

JOSEPH B. KUHNS
AND JOHANNES KNUTSSON, EDITORS

FOREWORD BY DAVID H. BAYLEY

Global Crime and Justice

Graeme R. Newman, Series Editor

 PRAEGER

AN IMPRINT OF ABC-CLIO, LLC
Santa Barbara, California • Denver, Colorado • Oxford, England

Library of Congress Cataloging-in-Publication Data
Police use of force : a global perspective / edited by Joseph B. Kuhns and Johannes Knutsson ;
foreword by David H. Bayley.
   p. cm. — (Global crime and justice)
  Includes bibliographical references and index.
  ISBN 978-0-313-36326-9 (hard copy : alk. paper) — ISBN 978-0-313-36327-6 (ebook)
1. Police—Attitudes. 2. Police brutality. 3. Police misconduct. I. Kuhns, Joseph B. II. Knutsson,
Johannes, 1947-
  HV8069.P65 2010
  363.2'32—dc22   2010000171

ISBN: 978-0-313-36326-9
EISBN: 978-0-313-36327-6

14   13   12   11   2   3   4   5

This book is also available on the World Wide Web as an eBook.
Visit www.abc-clio.com for details.

Praeger
An Imprint of ABC-CLIO, LLC

ABC-CLIO, LLC
130 Cremona Drive, P.O. Box 1911
Santa Barbara, California 93116-1911

This book is printed on acid-free paper ∞
Manufactured in the United States of America

Contents

Series Foreword

THIS FASCINATING AND diverse book in the Global Crime and Justice series follows an earlier title, *Human Trafficking, Human Misery*, a book that highlighted this crime's international proportions, and the challenge it posed to police who were faced with the problem that often the offenders they apprehended (illegal immigrants) were also victims (trafficked into prostitution or forced labor). They were both innocent and guilty at the same time. As this book shows, however, the problem of the innocence and guilt of suspects is a universal, indeed core problem that faces all policing, at least modern policing. It is deeply tied to the use of force by the State. It is a philosophical and political problem that is played out in the daily actions of police as they perform their duty.

Force, and the use of it, is rather like water. Without it, we could achieve little. We could not build houses, roads, or skyscrapers. We could not transport ourselves to faraway places. Indeed, without it, societies would collapse. Great philosophers have tried in vain to construct ways in which societies could function without force, and revolutionaries have, contradictorily, tried to impose these grand political visions on people in many lands. The thinkers of the 18th century enlightenment following Hobbes, particularly Rousseau, Locke, and Hume, finally had to acknowledge that the State was a necessary, though distasteful, body for imposing peace and order in societies. It was Locke, following Montesquieu, who first clearly recognized though that force had itself to be controlled, and this could be achieved by the "separation of powers." This principle has become the linchpin of the rule of law, embedded in the United States political system and Constitution (i.e., the legislative, judicial, and executive branches). Indeed, it is embedded in the constitutions or systems of law in just about every country of the world—though its actual application varies considerably.

Yet this separation of powers does not go far enough, because police, who have become the tool of the State's use of force, find themselves uneasily, in some countries, embedded within the executive branch, and in others in the judicial branch of government. And their link to the legislative branch continues to be ambiguous. A clear line between police and military is also difficult to maintain, and is not so drawn in many countries. It is a great irony that the force used to maintain peace and security in a society may also be used to undermine it.

The principle of separation of powers also applies within the judicial system. In modern judicial systems this is achieved through legislation that preserves the rights of the accused—the right to remain silent, to face one's accusers, to conduct a defense, *nullum crimen sine lege,* and so on. This would seem to suggest that police, in apprehending, questioning, and processing suspects, cannot presume their guilt because it can only be determined by a court of law. That is the rule of law, is it not? This seemingly irresolvable contradiction is sometimes defended by those who advocate the inquisitorial system of justice (probably the most widely adopted system throughout the world in which magistrates investigate and prosecute crimes, not police) by arguing that they use their techniques of interrogation and investigation in order to ensure that *no innocent person is ever brought to trial.*

This contradiction runs through every chapter in this volume. Part I asks what force is, whether it is physical or psychological, what are its limits and application, and who are its masters? Part II simplifies the political aspect of the question addressed in Part I: Should police be allowed to use firearms (the traditional tools of the military, after all) or not, and, if so, under what conditions? The contradiction here is stark, for if police officers shoot a fleeing suspect, they must assume he is guilty. And what if he is not? Even in the face of well developed rules and regulations concerning use of a firearm by police, shootings of innocent persons still occur. The police shooting (five times at close range) of a Brazilian man in 2005 (innocent, as it turned out) in the aftermath of the terrorist bombings of London, is a prime example. Police defend their actions in such circumstances by arguing that they must protect themselves (and us), and that they often have no alternative.

If such mistakes or tragedies of judgment occur even in the best regulated police organizations, why not use non-lethal weapons to apprehend a suspect? It is easy to anticipate the difficulties: what non-lethal weapons are available and are they really non-lethal? Furthermore, an entirely new set of rules is needed to cover their use, because, as can easily be imagined, if they are truly non-lethal, there exists the temptation to use them in more situations to solve more problems. The popular use of pepper spray to quell disturbances at football games—which itself may create a bigger disturbance—is a prime example of the problem. And of course, there is the problem that non-lethal weapons, such as nightsticks or batons, can be used lethally. Of greater concern perhaps is what the future holds. New technologies often bring with them unanticipated consequences. The easier and safer are the new technologies of control, the more rules and regulations there must be to control their use. This will be particularly important should techniques of control be invented that are not easily recognized as using force at all.

This outstanding book deals with a particular slice of the "Justice" side of this Global Crime and Justice series. It cannot cover every country or region of the world, but it does reveal the diversity in approaches and solutions to police use of force in many different regions and police forces, and the sophistication in its use, pitfalls and shortcomings as well. The contributors, well known experts in this field, bring to this topic their extensive experience and research. Every police executive should read this book. So should every politician.

Graeme R. Newman
University at Albany, United States

Foreword

THE POLICE IN any country are given an extraordinary power. They, almost alone, are authorized to lay their hands on people's bodies and to compel obedience, even to the point of inflicting grievous harm and death. In most countries, few others are granted this authority, whether public or private persons. Not doctors, lawyers, judges, prosecutors, legislators, prime ministers, or presidents. In many countries, military personnel are also prohibited from doing so with respect to the domestic public. Police uniquely are allowed by law to take a person by the scruff of the neck immediately and deprive them of their freedom. They don't need to apply for permission. They decide on their own at the moment amid the confusion of often turbulent events. Holding police to account for their use of force is generally difficult. Moreover, resistance at the moment is considered a reason to use additional force.

Is it any wonder, then, that people everywhere are concerned and apprehensive about how police use force; that every country has its "scandals" about police abuse of force, either publicly revealed or at least widely believed to be true?

Sadly, the public's fear is often justified by events. There are not more than a handful of police forces into whose hands I would feel safe from the illegal and unprincipled use of force. Out of 192 countries that are currently members of the United Nations, there are only 15–16 whose police I would not fear in this regard. These are the police of the English-speaking democracies (Australia, Britain, Canada, Ireland, New Zealand, the United States); the stable democracies of western Europe (France, Germany, Belgium, Italy, Netherlands, Switzerland, Denmark, Norway, Sweden); and Japan. This should not be treated as an exhaustive list, although I believe it comes very close. There may be other countries that readers think would qualify for inclusion. Even in these countries, however, eternal vigilance is, as Thomas Jefferson said, the price of freedom. The fact is that police in the overwhelming majority of countries today frequently, if not systematically, misuse their power to physically coerce.

Therefore it is entirely appropriate that one volume of a series devoted to global crime and justice should focus on the police use of force on a comparative basis. Its coverage is ironic, however, but at the same time instructive. As is customary in comparative international scholarship, the essays over-represent experiences in countries that offer best performances with respect to the topic. Of the eleven countries discussed here, only four are from the less developed, less stable democratic world: Latin America (Brazil and Guatemala) and Asia (China, India). These regions, along with Africa and the Middle East, have the most dismal records of police abuse of power. The reasons for the skewed distribution of cases examined are obvious: lack of access, transparency, and institutional accountability.

This imbalance of knowledge has a profound effect on analysis. Scholars are unable to adequately document the true global state of affairs with respect to police use of force. Moreover, analysis inevitably concentrates on variations with respect to what is right rather than focusing on the reasons for what is wrong. Because the samples lack controls, it is difficult to pinpoint the conditions that are truly necessary for acceptable performance. This hampers efforts to facilitate reform in places where reform is most sorely needed. In effect, non-representative samples may lead to overvaluing Western prerequisites and misunderstanding what is required in non-Western countries.

Nonetheless, the excellent essays in this volume compellingly demonstrate global variation in the police use of force with respect to legal and normative standards for the use of force, levels of armament, and rules concerning warning shots and targeting. This foundation should enable scholars to take the next step in understanding police use of force; namely, pinpointing factors that shape these variations. In an insightful concluding essay, Ed Maguire makes some intriguing suggestions.

There is, however, an important caution implicit in Maguire's discussion of what scholars need to do next. It is important to distinguish continually between normative and empirical assessments of the police use of force. Police abuse of force may be assessed in terms of normative conceptions of fundamental rights or empirically in terms of its impact on political development. It would not be contradictory to favor particular standards for the police use of force on normative grounds while simultaneously concluding that insisting on such standards in some cultural contexts might hamper desired political objectives, such as stability and even eventual democracy. In short, practices that make the police legitimate in one place may not make them so in other venues. Western norms for the police use of force may not contribute everywhere to governmental legitimacy. This suggestion will probably make readers uneasy. At the same time, it raises the core question for comparative analysis—in developing humane governments, are there universal standards for the police use of force?

David H. Bayley
University at Albany, United States

Acknowledgments

WE ARE INDEBTED to the numerous authors from around the world who contributed their time, effort, and expertise in preparing, editing, and finalizing the individual chapters. Obviously, without their substantial contributions this book would not have been possible. We are also grateful for the extraordinary assistance of Diana Summers and Tammatha Clodfelter, who both worked diligently to prepare and format the individual chapters and the final manuscript. Finally, we are thankful for the guidance and wisdom of Graeme Newman, who skillfully guided us through this project.

Joseph B. Kuhns
University of North Carolina at Charlotte, United States

Johannes Knutsson
Norwegian Police University College, Norway

PART I

Police Use of Force

Introduction

Joseph B. Kuhns and Johannes Knutsson

POLICE USE OF force remains a vitally important, and yet continually controversial, area for scholars, law enforcement leaders, and policymakers around the world. When used legitimately, respectfully, consistently, and lawfully, police use of force is a functional and necessary aspect of living in a safe and healthy society, regardless of the form of government, culture, or society. But when police use of force is considered illegitimate, disrespectful or unlawful, real or perceived, it can quickly erode the confidence of citizens in their government, increase crime and violence, and generate wider dissent and dissatisfaction across communities and countries. However, there are considerable differences regarding what constitutes legitimate, respectful, reasonable, excessive, and lawful police use of force across different countries. The first section of our book focuses on the broader context of police use of force and considers these substantial variations in defining force, officer training, and implementing use-of-force policies across a number of countries and among a variety of situational settings.

William Terrill and Eugene Paoline begin with an analysis and draw attention to the complexities associated with clarifying what constitutes proper versus improper force by exploring this issue from different perspectives (e.g., public, legal, organizational, and officer). This opening chapter is a particularly important starting point, given that the rest of the book provides a wide variety of country-based case studies that illustrate these differences in how and why police use various forms of force in their law enforcement activities. Emil Plywaczewski and Izabela Nowicka focus our readers' attention on the police use of force in Poland, analyzing the legal and historical basis that provides for, but still attempts to balance, the need for police use of force while respecting citizen rights and protections. This chapter, supported with empirical data, suggests that most often, but not all of the time, police do act with force in accordance with Polish law.

Kam Wong next provides a rare glimpse into Hong Kong policing practices, focusing specifically on firearms (further discussed in Part II) as one method of force and relying on a case study approach to document some of the challenges with training and implementing use-of-force policies. This chapter also draws attention to the nuances associated with defining what is meant by "reasonable" force. John Buttle then narrows the focus to officer training specifically, using Victoria, Australia as the setting and illustrating the urgent need for training that emphasizes adoption of non-lethal options (which is further discussed in Part III of our book); emotional control among officers; and adherence to law and policy within the context of citizen-officer situations that require force. This chapter further debates the differences between emphasizing "reasonable" force versus "minimal" force and the impact of those decisions on officers and training protocols.

The next three chapters of Part I share a common theme—the concerns associated with unlawful use of force by police. First, Mark Costanzo and Allison Redlich turn a critical eye toward the historical and contemporary use of force during military and police interrogations of suspects or criminals, within and outside of the United States. This type of inquiry is particularly important, given that broader use of force policies may benefit from greater situational specificity. In addition, officers would likely benefit from improved scenario-based training protocols in many countries, but particularly those that still rely on force (reasonable or excessive, lawful and unlawful) to extract criminal confessions. Jyoti Belur then provides a candid and critical assessment of police "encounters" in Mumbai, India. The term "encounter" refers to the many situations where hard-core criminals are killed by police, not uncommonly under questionable circumstances. In India, such police encounters are not only "prized" internally by police organizations (and sometimes rewarded with one-rank-promotions, bravery medals, and/or other privileges) but also enjoy some level of societal approval in various parts of the country. This organizational and societal positive reinforcement may explain, in part, why encounters tend to be less scrutinized in some countries of the world.

Marie-Louise Glebbeek examines the social and political context of *mano dura* (excessively tough or zero tolerance) public security policies in Central America, focusing in particular on the contradictory consequences for police forces, policing, and police reform initiatives in the region. This chapter recognizes that while such approaches have been carefully designed and arguably successful in certain countries, such as the United States, Latin American police forces often lack adequate funding and resources to effectively implement comprehensive zero tolerance strategies. More to the point, none of the Central American countries have reported that these policies have reduced crime. On the contrary, when compared to the year that *mano dura* approaches were systematically implemented in Honduras, El Salvador, and Guatemala in 2003, overall crime levels actually increased. Finally, Martha Huggins draws on a combination of official and unofficial statistics to indicate that on-duty Brazilian police are responsible for up to 70% of all civilian murders in Brazil. This important chapter explores four sources of lethal violence by Brazilian police: extreme societal inequality that encourages and excuses it; pervasive societal violence that justifies and hides it; organizational institutionalization that enables and legitimizes it; and a public-private social control fusion that fosters and conceals lethal police violence. This chapter, using original and secondary research on police violence in Brazil, illustrates the difficulties with separating police claims about lethal shootings from external data used to assess the legitimacy of such claims.

Non-Lethal Force by Police in the United States: The Various Lenses Through Which Appropriateness Is Examined

William Terrill and Eugene A. Paoline, III

ABSTRACT

POLICE LEGITIMACY IS invariably linked in large measure to the manner in which the police go about engaging in forceful tactics to accomplish their mandate. Police officers are expected to use individual judgment in applying force, while at the same time working within the appropriate legal and organizational parameters. In the end, when police misuse force it challenges public trust and thereby threatens legitimacy. The present chapter examines the application of police use of force from a variety of angles in an attempt to more fully appreciate the complexities surrounding the mechanisms used to determine public, legal, organizational, and street-level officer standards.

INTRODUCTION

Public trust of the police is borne from legitimacy (Tyler and Huo 2002). On the whole, in the United States most citizens trust the police and thereby view the institution as a legitimate (and necessary) governmental entity. Nonetheless, any number of police actions can erode the public's trust (e.g., the use of a speed trap to supplement local municipality coffers, an officer on routine patrol exceeding the speed limit, an officer parking her patrol vehicle illegally while having lunch, an off-duty officer displaying his badge to secure a special privilege such as getting out of a speeding ticket [e.g., a professional courtesy]). Despite such examples, short of widespread serious economic

William Terrill, Michigan State University
Eugene A. Paoline, III, University of Central Florida

corruption (e.g., an officer shaking down a citizen for a payoff), the greatest threat to the core of legitimate policing comes in the form of questionable use of force. This can range from egregious excessive force such as the repeated beating of an already handcuffed suspect with a police baton to verbally berating and threatening a compliant suspect with physical harm because the officer felt disrespected. In short, public trust and goodwill can be undermined quickly when the police rely on coercive tactics that are perceived to be, rightly or wrongly, inappropriate in some manner.

Determining what constitutes the nature of police use of improper force is a difficult proposition. Many scholars have struggled with different terms to describe varying forms of inappropriateness including: excessive use of force, use of excessive force, brutality, unauthorized force, wrongful force, unjustified force, misuse of force, and unnecessary force. While these phrases are interchangeable to some, others note fine distinctions. For example, use of excessive force can be defined as more force than is needed to gain compliance in any given incident, while excessive use of force may be defined as using force in too many incidents (Adams 1996). James Fyfe (1997) makes the distinction between brutality (a willful and knowingly wrongful use of force) and unnecessary force (force used by well-meaning officers ill-equipped to handle various incidents). Robert Worden (1996) also distinguishes between different types of force. He defines excessive force as that which is more than required to subdue a citizen, and unnecessary force as that which precedes a citizen's resistance or continues after citizen resistance has ceased.

In this chapter, rather than attempting to distinguish varying forms of excessive, unjustified, or unnecessary force, or any of the other such characterizations noted by scholars, we focus on what constitutes proper versus improper force by exploring this issue from a variety of different perspectives (e.g., public, legal, organizational, and officer). Specifically, we attempt to more fully appreciate the complexities of what may be considered appropriate or inappropriate non-lethal force behavior, and how such a determination ultimately depends on the lens through which it is viewed.

APPROPRIATENESS AS VIEWED FROM DIFFERENT PERSPECTIVES

Regardless of the time period in American history, one can easily uncover examples whereby use-of-force incidents stirred controversy and challenged public trust. For instance, during the 1960s, amid growing civil unrest over a variety of reported police abuses, many urban areas experienced outright rioting often sparked by questionable police use-of-force tactics. In the early 1990s, the Rodney King incident in Los Angeles brought the issue front and center to the public consciousness again, as did other high-profile incidents in New York City in the late 1990s (e.g., the Abner Louima and Amadou Diallo incidents). Presently, with an increasing number of police departments equipping officers with Conducted Energy Devices (CEDs), most commonly the TASER, there appears to be an enhanced public concern with the manner in which police use force. The proliferation of this law enforcement tool combined with other ever-expanding technological advancements such as the Internet, cell phone picturing, and any number of recording devices all with instant communication capabilities, means that rarely a week will pass when an alleged incident of police misconduct is not captured and disseminated globally. While questionable police behavior involving the use of force historically may have been kept out of the public consciousness on the whole, with only the police version of it being officially documented and given credence, contemporary technological changes have brought the issue of force to the forefront of public attention. As a result, citizens, legal experts, police administrators, and street-level police officers are increasingly asking the question: What is the framework from which we should draw to determine appropriate use of force? One only needs to view the latest YouTube video posted on the Internet and query a handful of people to glean an understanding that determining appropriate force is not so simple, but rather depends on any number of orientations and standards being applied in different ways by different people. All have insight regarding what constitutes the appropriate use of force in a given incident depending on the varying perspective or standard applied. There are public standards, which vary along any number of dimensions (e.g., class, race, gender, prior experience with the police, political ideology). There is a legal standard (e.g., objective reasonableness), which is vague at best. There are professional or departmental standards, which can and do vary from one police organization to another.[1] And there are standards that street-level patrol officers utilize, which differ from (but must also consider) all other viewpoints, given they are the ones actually responsible for discharging force within what can be unstable and rapidly changing scenarios. What follows is a synopsis of the varying orientations and standards these different actors emphasize and apply based on our conceptualizations and research experiences.

THE PUBLIC PERSPECTIVE

Most U.S. citizens are satisfied with the overall services provided by the police (Tuch and Weitzer 1997). However, within the context of police use of force, satisfaction levels drop off. For instance, findings from a national survey of citizens by the Bureau of Justice Statistics (BJS) in 1999 show that a large percentage of citizens involved in forceful encounters with the police believed the force used was excessive. Specifically, about three-quarters of the 422,000 persons involved in a police force incident characterized the force as excessive (Langan et al. 2001, 3). What might help explain such a finding is that all cases resulted in a bad outcome for the subject (e.g., the officer using force on him or her). Nonetheless, as noted by Seron and Kovath (2004, 666), the public in general has a rather low tolerance for police misconduct, particularly the unnecessary use of force.

Public perception of police use of force is not just reserved for those *directly* involved in a force incident, as citizens can be indirectly or vicariously connected to them by viewing or reading about them through various media outlets (Kasinsky 1995).[2] Such media depictions may lead to one of two outcomes, both of which have implications for public confidence in the police. First, media depictions of police non-lethal force often fail to capture the entire sequence of events (e.g., citizen and officer actions from start to finish) and instead focus on the end result by police. Such depictions can lead citizens to inaccurately deduce that the police are not behaving appropriately in exercising their coercive authority, despite the fact that the officer may have been operating within appropriate legal and organizational parameters. Second, where officers are acting inappropriately, overexposure of isolated events by the media can further work to distort public perception that such behavior is the norm rather than the exception. If citizens (either directly or indirectly) involved in forceful events often feel that the force used by police is improper in some way, and the general public is displeased overall when officers resort to force deemed to be inappropriate in some manner, then the question becomes, on what basis are members of the public citizenry basing their views as to what is right or wrong?

Seron and Kovath (2004), in a study employing a factorial survey design, presented citizens with varying scenarios of police misconduct to examine what factors influence public perceptions. They found that citizens often employ a somewhat complex mix of legal and extra-legal factors to determine the appropriateness of force. Respondents indicated that they want officers to rely on legal cues before using force (e.g., resisting an officer's attempt at control, a weapon present, subject flees, etc.), but also understand to some degree the unpredictable nature of police work that may require officers to preemptively employ forceful tactics (e.g., physically restraining a suspect for fear that he is going to flee, using disparaging language in the process of verbally threatening a suspect, etc.). Put succinctly, citizens expect officers to behave professionally, or by the book, but with a recognition that street-level discretion has its place in an officer's toolkit (Seron and Kovath 2004, 665). The researchers also found that other factors such as a citizen's race or political orientation can affect their view of misconduct. For instance, racial minority respondents and those with more of a liberal persuasion are more critical or less accepting of police extra-legal factors. In other words, officer behavior not predominantly based on legal cues (e.g., the suspect assaulted the officer) is deemed inappropriate, despite extra factors that may be in place.

THE LEGAL PERSPECTIVE

The legal standard for assessing the legality of police use of force was set in *Graham v. Connor* (1989).[3] The court ruled that the use of force by police officers must be judged under a standard of objective reasonableness. More directly, the Fourth Amendment "reasonableness" inquiry is whether the officers' actions are "objectively reasonable" in light of the facts and circumstances confronting them, without regard to their underlying intent or motivation. The "reasonableness" of a particular use of force must be judged from the perspective of a reasonable officer on the scene, and its calculus must embody an allowance for the fact that police officers are often forced to make split-second decisions about the amount of force necessary in a particular situation (396–397). Given the court's finding, legal experts concentrate on the concept of reasonableness when attempting to reconcile the appropriateness of force. Thus, legal scholars, judges, prosecutors, and defense attorneys all seek to determine if a case can be made for whether force used by an officer may be considered objectively reasonable. Of course, applying this standard still requires a subjective interpretation. Moreover, there is no legal specification mandating that the police rely on or apply the *least* amount of force necessary to control a citizen, but rather just what may be classified as *reasonable*. Thus, appropriateness from a lawful perspective (e.g., within the realm of objective reasonableness) and the use of "good force" do not always equate. There are certainly situations where force used by a police officer could be classified as "lawfully awful" (e.g., an officer who prompts a suspect to physically resist and then uses such resistance for justification to apply more aggressive force). This presents a challenge for police administrators attempting to chart a policy course. On one hand, administrators need to be conscious of how juries interpret the objective reasonableness standard set in the *Graham* case. There are very real consequences if they do not. However, there is anecdotal evidence (Terrill and Paoline 2006) indicating that some jurisdictions have become so worried about liability that the issue of good policing squarely takes a backseat. In fact, several agencies that employed a "use-of-force continuum" in the past have now reversed course and cut any mention of a continuum approach in their policy, or the use of language specifying officers use the least amount of force, solely for fear of liability.

THE ORGANIZATIONAL PERSPECTIVE

Despite direction from the high court, determining force that is objectively reasonable is not an easy task. As a result, police departments rely on use-of-force policy and training to help establish parameters for the application of force and to offer more explicit direction to officers about what may be considered appropriate force. In general, little systematic empirical evidence exists concerning the nature of force training or the manner in which police

are instructed on policy. Outside of deadly threats or the handling of physically assaultive suspects, it appears force training has primarily centered more
on *how* to use various weapons as opposed to *when* and the *type* of force that
should be used.

As noted previously, many police agencies rely on use-of-force policies
that are linked to a force continuum. A standard force continuum policy ordi-
nally ranks varying levels of force and resistance in terms of severity, with
the explicit purpose of offering officers guidance on how to respond to specific forms of resistance.[4] Complicating matters, however, is the fact that there
is no commonly accepted ranking of force, either by researchers or practitioners. A continuum policy in one department can be completely different
than another. Some agencies employ a more linear type of force continuum,
while others opt for a wheel type design. Some departments have non-specific
types of policies whereby force and resistance are referred to only in vague
terms and not categorized into specific levels, while others offer very detailed
policies that articulate many levels of both force and resistance. There is also
wide variation as to where specific types of less-lethal technologies should be
placed on the continuum scale (Terrill and Paoline 2008). For example, one
department may place the TASER lower on the continuum (e.g., right after
verbal direction), while another may place it higher on the continuum scale
(e.g., just before deadly force). In a related manner, placement of less-lethal
tactics and technologies also varies in relation to different types of citizen resistance. The result of this type of variation is that appropriate force in one
department can be viewed as completely inappropriate in another department
(e.g., using a TASER on a verbally resistant suspect is within policy in one
city but not another). Thus, the field of policing, as a whole, views force
appropriateness different depending on the agency involved. Moreover, as
noted above, from an administrative perspective, the emphasis is not always
on establishing good police practice, but rather on avoiding lawsuits. In this
sense, appropriate force is the kind that does not result in a financial payout,
or in the case of front-line supervisors who, in many instances, are intimately
involved in the reporting of force (e.g., filling out or starting a use-of-force
investigation to determine appropriateness), and acts that do not bring undue
attention or culpability to them or the corresponding officer.

THE STREET OFFICER PERSPECTIVE

Street-level officers, who are directly responsible for engaging in force tactics,
have their own view of what is and what is not an appropriate level of force
given varying situations. Unlike the other perspectives, however, street-level
officers have to take into account each of the other perspectives. For example,
the public lens can work in isolation of considering the legal, organizational,
or officer perceptions but, in turn, helps to shape each of the latter.

Alternatively, the legal perspective is often closely connected to the public perception, but may not have to directly consider the organizational lens in deeming appropriateness. By contrast, street-level officers must consider the legal parameters and organizational policies in utilizing force, as well as the social ramifications of their actions in terms of public perception. As a result, the street-level perspective is more interconnected than the others.

From an operational standpoint, the use of non-lethal force assists officers in carrying out their daily duties. In this sense, appropriateness is gauged in terms of the ability to accomplish a given task (e.g., arresting a suspect, breaking up a fight, removing a baseball bat from a mentally disordered citizen, etc.). Moreover, in varying degrees, officers perceive their occupational world to be a dangerous one, and one way to minimize potential danger is by "taking charge" during encounters with the public (Muir 1977). The balancing act for street officers is to utilize enough force to handle the given situation, but to also neutralize threats in securing their own safety. Perceptions of the situation and the decision to apply force given that situation can vary across officers depending on their experience and skill level. Not surprisingly, more experienced officers use less force, in terms of frequency and levels, than those with less experience (Paoline and Terrill 2007).

While safety issues arise from physical confrontations with citizens, officers must also be aware of potential professional and legal harm as a result of their force actions. Legal standards and organizational policies are geared toward providing forms of guidance and boundaries in the application of force, the latter of which often include supervisory and/or civilian oversight of use-of-force incidents. *Ex post facto* scrutiny by supervisors regarding use of force (e.g., examining and investigating incident reports, early-warning or intervention systems, etc.), as well as possible legal courses of action for improper force utilization, also factor into the assessment of appropriateness by street-level officers. As such, these higher levels work as a secondary filter for officers, as they are often directly accountable for legal (e.g., reasonableness) and organizational (e.g., policy) violations. In an effort to deem the appropriateness of force, officers must manage their individual working concerns on the street (e.g., managing citizens and coming home safely at the end of their shift), but also professional concerns as well (e.g., will I be reprimanded, lose my job, or be prosecuted because of my actions?).

In the late 1990s, researchers conducted a national survey in an attempt to glean insight as to officer views toward the abuse of authority (Weisburd et al. 2000). The findings illustrate the complexity with which police officers attempt to balance operational, working, and professional concerns. Most officers reported that the police were given adequate power to effectively accomplish their mandate and, like the public (see Seron and Kovath 2004), viewed the improper use of force in a negative light.[5] Nonetheless, a substantial percentage ". . . believed that officers should be permitted to use more force than the law currently permits and found it acceptable to sometimes use more force than permitted by the laws that govern them" (Weisburd et al. 2000, 3). In other words, officers with this view believe the law is overly restrictive, thereby hampering their ability to properly get the job done, which then requires them to overstep the legal threshold (and at times a public threshold) to maintain order and ensure officer safety. In addition, findings from the study also indicated a large divide across officer race with respect to how often the police use improper force. In particular, black officers (57%) were much more likely to believe that the police treat racial minorities more harshly (in terms of force usage) than white officers (5%) given similar situational contexts. Such a finding provides yet another example that force appropriateness is viewed within the eye of the beholder and appears to vary widely not only across perspectives or arenas (public, legal, organizational, officer), but also within.

SUMMARY

The aim of this chapter was to shed light on the various perspectives that go into assessing the appropriateness of police use of force. While none of these mechanisms work in total isolation of one another, the degree to which they are interconnected does vary. There are a variety of factors that internally influence public, legal, organizational, and street officer assessments of appropriateness. The unanswered question appears to be the extent to which each lens of appropriateness agrees or disagrees with the others. We know that negative public reaction to the improper use of force by the police can result in changes with respect to legal standards and organizational policies, which, in turn, trickle down to officer behaviors. What we do not know is how citizens view reasonable objectiveness or the varying types of organizational policies currently being used by police agencies (e.g., linear, wheel, etc.). As such, the public gets involved in the back end of decision making (e.g., *ex post facto*), but is not too directly involved in the front end. By the same token, we have no empirical data to assess the degree to which street officers agree or disagree with the type of force policy that their agency employs. Such information would be useful given the diversity of policies that exist, none of which have been deemed better or worse. In this sense, the various perspectives are connected in some manner, but also largely disconnected from one another. This disconnect is discouraging given the relative importance of each of the various groups. Like the obstacles noted in studies of culture conflict (Sellin 1938), more unified conceptions of appropriateness of police use of force will not occur unless each perspective is given the opportunity to look through the lens of the other.

2

The Use of Force by Police in Poland

Emil W. Pływaczewski and Izabela Nowicka

ABSTRACT

THIS CHAPTER, CONCERNING police use of force in Poland, is mainly focused on the rules about the use of coercive measures during the execution of various police duties, including use of deadly force (firearms) by Polish police. Based on the premise that the Polish police is a lawfully created, uniformed, and armed law enforcement organization, established for protecting society and maintaining public safety and order, we analyze the legal basis which entitles police officers to violate citizens' sphere of constitutional rights and freedoms. Most of all, some legal provisions were exposed that, in rigorous ways, described exact rules for the usage of coercive measures, including legal provisions that described the penal responsibility of police officers in cases of infringement of those rules. This chapter also contains information about the instruments of legal protection for Polish police officers during their service. This theoretical approach was reinforced and enriched with statistical data and practical examples and observations resulting from professional expertise of police officers that exercise use of coercive measures in their everyday service.

There is a belief that the Polish administrative structure system includes the so-called administrative police services, whose task is to ensure public security and order. The administrative police services include armed and uniformed formations similar to military units, such as the police and the Border Guard, as well as civilian specialized public administration bodies (inspectorates) and other entities that perform tasks related to ensuring public security and order. The fact that so many entities have powers related to ensuring public law and order is, on the one hand, the result of the complex

Emil W. Pływaczewski, Białystok University
Izabela Nowicka, The Higher Police School in Szczytno

nature of such tasks and, on the other, of the fact that nearly all states, in their preventive activities, strive to better understand the causes of crimes, to mitigate the consequences, and to determine the most beneficial forms and methods of dealing with offenders (Pomykała and Kazimierz 2005). In this system, the police play a special role, serving as the key entity responsible for security and order in the state (Bolesta 1972).

The Police Act, which was established April 6, 1990, states that "the police is established as a uniformed and armed formation charged with the task of protecting the safety of citizens and maintaining public security and order" (Małopolska Policja 1991; Pieprzny 2003). Later amendments of the Act did not affect the core statement that the police are an armed and uniformed organization, but they supplemented the definition of the police with new elements. In its final wording, the Act states: "The police is established as a uniformed and armed formation serving the society and charged with the task of protecting the safety of people and maintaining public security and order" (Małopolska Policja 1991, 1). Consequently, the Police Act sets forth a number of tasks that the formation must perform, which are defined in more detail in executive acts. The nationalized police force also performs tasks under international treaties and agreements, in ways and scopes defined therein. The large number of regulations and overlapping objectives, as well as the mix of values that the police must protect (e.g., citizens' safety or public security and order) by utilizing outlined and stipulated methods, negatively affect the precision in interpreting the duties of the police. Consequently, one may say that it is impossible to identify a situation where the police may not take actions aimed at ensuring public safety and order.

The Police Act defines public security and order as a situation in the state where individuals and the society as a whole face no interior danger (Małopolska Policja 1991). The levels of security are defined in the legal provisions, and any factors that negatively affect the country's security constitute a broadly defined danger. Of course, the state of public security and order is merely an ideal condition, and, one could say, if the ideal condition were to be achieved, the police would be able to focus on other matters. The modern culture in Poland and its societal vices do not allow the police to properly allocate enough resources for campaigns such as "Safe Poland," "Safe Region," etc. The fact that the Act defines the police force as "an armed formation," should be interpreted to mean that officers are authorized to use weapons to perform their duties. The weapons are not limited to firearms, which are only used in extreme situations, but also include other devices that may be used to provide and maintain public security and order. Article 1 of the Ordinance of the Minister of Interior and Administration, enacted on the 15th of November 2000, stipulates which weapons police officers are authorized to employ:

1. Firearms: pistols, revolvers, smooth-bore guns, machine pistols, carbines, rifles, machine guns, and grenade launchers;

2. Items for launching chemical and water subduing agents: gas pistols and revolvers, gas launchers, water launchers, grenade launchers, and tear-gas grenade launchers;
3. Launchers of rubber, deafening, blinding, and shot projectiles, as well as subduing nets;
4. Items for shooting alarm and signal ammunition;
5. Military knives, assault knives, parachute jumper's knives, and diver's knives;
6. Regular, multi-functional, assault, and subduing service batons and truncheons;
7. Ammunition for firearms and projectiles for items and launchers listed in points 2–4 above;
8. Grenades and explosive materials;
9. Chemical agents; and
10. Technical equipment to include electric stun guns, hinged handcuffs, disposable handcuffs, and combined handcuffs to be put on the hands and on the legs, guiding devices, straitjackets, subduing belts and nets, spike strips, and other obstacles for stopping vehicles.

The police are allowed to use these tools as a part of their use-of-force continuum, which means that officers are also able to engage in physical (forceful) action against an individual so as to force him or her to comply. One cannot deny that the use of force breaches the basic civic rights and liberties that citizens are guaranteed by the constitution. As representatives of the doctrine indicate, the essence of most of these methods is to inflict physical discomfort (Goetel 1996). Therefore, both domestic laws and international standards must regulate use of such force by the police. In international law, the means of using direct force and firearms is regulated by the same acts. The most important ones, which have had a significant impact on Poland's laws on the use of force and firearms are: 1) the European Convention for the Protection of Human Rights and Fundamental Freedoms; 2) the Code of Conduct of Law Enforcement Officials; 3) the Basic Principles on the Use of Force and Firearms by Law Enforcement Officials; and 4) the Declaration of the Police.

The Police Act and the Ordinance of the Council of Ministers defines the cases, conditions, and methods which constitute legal grounds for the police to use specific types of force, and defines the detailed principles, cases, and methods of their use, most of all by police officers who make the decisions to use them. The guidelines for using firearms by cohesive units and sub-units of the police are regulated separately by the provisions of the Ordinance of the Council of Ministers.

Regardless of the legal grounds of the regulations indicated above, the use of direct force by police officers requires actual reasons. Any departure from the cohesiveness of the legal and factual grounds for the use of force can result in the appearance of unlawful acts that breach human rights and lead to penal responsibility (Goetel 1996). This is quite important when considered in the context that Polish police officers engage in about four million interventions a year involving means of direct force (Karczmarczyk 2007).

The premise for use of force by police is divided into two main categories: general and detailed. A "general" premise is a circumstance that generally allows for the lawful use of force by police. According to the Police Act, such a circumstance would include a suspect's failure to follow lawful orders issued by police bodies or officers. "Detailed" premises are further defined in executive regulations. The executive regulations also present cases detailing the use of specific means of applying direct force, and precisely define the level of force that can be used to address specific behaviors of an individual. These provisions pertain to the use of force by police officers in ordinary situations (e.g., when the police officer is performing his or her official duties) and in extraordinary situations (such as during the operations of armed units of the police).

Examples of situations where the use of force is permitted include forcing someone to follow an order, overcoming passive resistance, overcoming active resistance, as defense against an active attack, as defense against an assault against human life, health, or property, or countering the destruction of property. The Police Act stipulates the different types of direct force options available to officers, including:

1. Physical, technical, and chemical means for subduing or escorting persons and/or stopping vehicles;
2. Service truncheons;
3. Subduing water devices;
4. Service dogs and horses;
5. Non-penetrating projectiles shot from firearms; and
6. Firearms (of special nature) (Małopolska Policja 1991, 13).

The physical, technical, and chemical means for subduing or escorting persons and for stopping vehicles are: 1) use of physical force in the form of subduing grips and similar defensive or offensive techniques; 2) use of technical devices such as handcuffs, guiding devices, straitjackets, subduing belts and nets, electric paralyzers, as well as spike strips, and other obstacles for stopping vehicles; and 3) subduing by chemical means (Małopolska Policja 1991). It must be stated that, unlike other administrative police services, Polish police officers do not currently have the right to use electric stun guns (Karczmarczyk 2007).

An analysis of the Act and the executive legal acts allows for formulating certain basic principles that must be observed when using any means of direct force (both before deciding to use force and in the course of using it). In this sense, there are some guiding principles for the use of force (Goetel 1996; Karczmarczyk 2007; Podgórski 2007). The most important are:

- **The principle of purposefulness**: the use of direct force in general, or the use of a specific type of force, must be dictated by a justified need (a breach of security or order), or must be aimed at achieving a specific goal (forcing an individual to follow the lawful orders of the police). If the situation requires, several different means of direct force may be used simultaneously.
- **The principle of warning**: consists of the duty of a police officer to instruct the individual to cease the unlawful behavior and to warn them about the imminent use of force when the preceding call has been ignored. This principle is not binding in cases where immediate action is required (e.g., where any delay would result in a risk to life or health of persons and, in the case of use of means other than firearms, also to property).
- **The principle of necessity**: requires that only the means necessary to remove the danger are to be used. Force must no longer be used when the danger is no longer present (the individual is following orders), or when the use of force is not needed.
- **The principle of limiting the effects**: requires that force should be used in a way that causes the least possible pain and, if possible, does not lead to injuries or health disorders.
- **The principle of independence**: states that the person who has committed a crime or a misdemeanor will receive proper punishment for his or her behavior regardless of the use of force, and that various methods of force may be used independently. The use of force does not constitute a punishment for a crime or misdemeanor.

As mentioned above, the use of direct force constitutes a breach of citizen's rights and freedoms and, therefore, Polish law requires that before using force, a police officer must call on the person to cease the unlawful behavior and warn about the application of force (Małopolska Policja 1991). The officer may not perform the above actions if a delay in the use of force could result in a danger to human life or health, or to property.

PRACTICAL RESEARCH AND RESULTS

A study was conducted in the Higher Police School in Szczytno on the topic: "Use of means of direct force and firearms in the aspect of personal safety of police officers and other participants of extraordinary events" (Karczmarczyk 2007). In the course of the study, it was concluded that during the years 1993–2005, police officers used firearms 1,778 times, including 211 cases (12%) where the application of the firearm breached the law. This study is unique in Poland, allowing for a rare quantitative evaluation of the phenomenon. Police information systems do not typically grant access to information about the number of events where a police officer utilized firearms during the course of their duties, and therefore this study gains insight into the actual frequency of firearms use by police.

When an officer does encounter a situation where the use of firearms is required, a set course of action is in place for submitting details of the incident. The process begins with an official note made in writing by the police officer on the use of firearms incident. The note is submitted to the proper supervisor and, depending on the category of the field unit, it is transferred to proper provincial police headquarters. The data is then processed by the police unit in electronic form. This is evident in the examples provided in Table 2-1 from the Provincial Police Headquarters in Szczecin.

These examples show that data on the use of firearms is mixed with data on events where dangerous items were used against police officers or where an active attack against a police officer took place. The Chief Police Headquarters receives data from all the field units on the police at the provincial headquarters level. The National Police Information System includes information on incidents involving police officers using firearms, which can be found in the following categories:

1. Other extraordinary events involving an officer;
2. Against an officer;
3. Caused by an officer.

In many cases, performing regular duties of the police borders on breaching the rights and freedoms of other persons, as well as the police officers themselves. The law, within certain limits, provides protection for police officers by penalizing citizens for such behavior as: breaching the inviolability of a public official, active attack against a public official, active resistance, and insulting a public official (Lexadin, 7–8). Such legal protection is necessary due to the increasing number of attacks on police officers. The Chief Police Headquarters has provided the following data:

A police officer must base his or her actions on information that allows him or her to accurately analyze the event, so as to decide when to use force or firearms without breaching the provisions of law. In the case of improper interpretation, a police officer may commit an offense described as abuse of powers or failure to perform duties (Lexadin). In 2005, police officers used firearms 261 times; in 33 (13%) of those situations they did so without sufficient legal grounds (Karczmarczyk 2007). The Law Department of the Higher Police School in Szczytno also conducted research on the use of force and firearms. This study suggested that abuse of powers or failure to perform duties in relation to the use of force took place in cases involving: an unjustified use of force (five cases); use of force in a way that did not correspond to

Table 2-1 Examples of Incidents Connected with Police Use of Force

Item No.	Date and Time of Event	Description of Event	Effects
1	6 February 2007 17.40 hrs	Due to an attack on a jewelry shop by two masked assailants, blockade and penetration actions were initiated. As a result of these actions, a police officer of the patrol and intervention unit and a municipal guard officer initiated a pursuit of one of the assailants. In the course of the pursuit, the police officer shot three rounds from the service weapon: 2 warning shots in the air and 1 at the offender. The offender was apprehended as a result of this action.	The offender was shot in the left foot.
2	4 March 2007 20.40 hrs	Police officers intervened in the case of a drunk man who was drinking beer in a public place and then threw a bottle on the street and broke it. The police officer called on the man to stop the unlawful behavior, but the man ignored it and began to walk away while responding with abusive language. The police officer again called on the man to cease the unlawful behavior and warned him that otherwise he will have to use force. Then the man picked up the broken bottle and attacked the police officer with the sharp edge by striking the police officer in the left shoulder. Then the assailant began to run away and the police officer called on him to stop in accordance with the principles of use of firearms and fired one warning shot in the air with his service weapon. The man did not follow the order issued by the police officer and, consequently, police officers began a pursuit. As a result, the man was apprehended by the police officer. At the time he was apprehended, the man actively resisted the police and kicked the female police officer in the face as well as used abusive language towards the police officers.	The police officer was cut on the small finger of the left hand. The female police officer had a bone in the nose bruised.
3	6 March 2007	A man who was intoxicated invaded an apartment where he threatened the inhabitants by saying that he would kill and beat them up and refused to leave the apartment despite the demands of the inhabitants. Then he attacked the intervening police officers with a knife.	In the course of the intervention, the police officers had an ankle joint and a left hip joint bruised.

Source: Provincial Police Headquarters in Szczecin.

Table 2-2 Number of Offenses/Number of Police Officers

	2003	2004	2005
Active attack, using weapons or other dangerous items	417/687	430/580	523/835
Causing a grave loss of health of a police officer (in the course of the performance of duties)	119/132	125/120	113/166

Source: Chief Police Headquarters.

the needs of a given situation and was unnecessary to make individuals follow the orders that were given (seventeen cases); breach of physical inviolability when using force (ten cases); beating up in the course of using force (seven cases); causing bodily injuries in the course of using force (sixteen cases); punishable threats made in the course of using force (three cases); and insulting a person in the course of using force (two cases). Further, abuse of powers or failure to perform duties in relation to the use of firearms took place in cases involving the unjustified use of firearms during a police intervention (four cases) and accidental discharge of weapon not related to the performance of official duties (two cases).

SUMMARY AND CONCLUSIONS

Police use of force in Poland describes the methods that police officers use to constrain a person to a definite behavior. The analysis of laws and regulations allows one to formulate certain basic and general rules that should be obeyed when force is used before, during, and after the use-of-force incident. The undertaking of any proceedings by police must be based on such information that allows for proper use of force without breaching the regulations of law and while maintaining the protection of human rights. Independently, from a legal standpoint of the earlier mentioned legal regulations, the use of force by police officers requires the existence of actual grounds for the execution of force. Every defection from the integrity of both legal and actual grounds for police action results in the infringement of legal regulations, which corrupts the dignity of human beings and causes the penal responsibility of police officers. It takes on additional meaning that every year in Poland, police officers are conducting as many as four million interventions that require the use of force.

3

Police and the Use of Force in Hong Kong

Kam C. Wong

ABSTRACT

THE HKP (Hong Kong Police) possesses expansive and pervasive powers. Currently, there is very little literature on HKP accountability, especially bearing on the use of force. This chapter investigates the prevalence of the use of firearms by Hong Kong Police. Next, the administrative supervision, regulation, and control of HKP use of force and the political and legal limitations of controlling use-of-force are examined. Through the use of a case study, the strengths and limitations of past practices are considered and criticized. The chapter concludes with some recommendations for improving future training and investigative processes into use of force incidents.

> "Power tends to corrupt, and absolute power corrupts absolutely."
> Lord Acton (1887)

INTRODUCTION

The Hong Kong Police (HKP) possesses expansive and pervasive powers (Wacks 1993). The HKP also has a long history of police abuse of power (Wong 2000), dating back to the Colonial days when corruption was accepted, coerced confession was routine, and beating up criminals was a way of life. In those days, police were commonly referred to as "licensed thugs" ("有牌爛仔").

In the 1990s, HKP recorded somewhere between 3,000 and 4,000 complaints against police on duty each year, with 50% or more registered as police assaults. However, very few Independent Police Complaints Commission (IPCC) cases were substantiated. For example, IPCC reported in the "Number of Assault Allegations Endorsed by the IPCC by Nature of Injury and by Result of Investigation in the Years 1999–2001," that in documented

Kam C. Wong, Xavier University

injury cases, only one out of 633 cases in 1999, six out of 557 in 2000, and three out of 340 cases were substantiated (IPCC).

This chapter investigates the prevalence, regulation, and control of HKP use of force, which is organized into five sections. The first section contains a brief literature review, which is followed by some discussion and reports on the use of firearms by HKP. Next, the chapter explores the administrative supervision practices with respect to use of force, as informed through a case study. Some review of the political and legal controls over use of force follows and the chapter concludes with some recommendations regarding research, practices, and policies regarding police use of force in Hong Kong.

A BRIEF LITERATURE REVIEW

A comprehensive review of literature uncovers very few systematic studies of the Hong Kong police, especially on the use of force (Lau, Wan and Shum 1999). The few exceptions include *Police Powers in Hong Kong: Problems and Prospect* (Wacks 1993); *Police Powers: Arrest, Detention, and Seizure* (Heilbronn 1998); and a few law reform commission reports on police abuse of powers (e.g., Law Reform Commission 1984; 1992).

In addition, there are two academic papers on police use of force, both of which are these in criminology from Hong Kong University. Both were written by serving police officers. The first, "Use of Firearms in the Royal Hong Kong Police: An Examination of Patterns and Police Attitudes" (Ting 1988), dealt with patterns of attitude toward firearms use in the HKP between 1983 and 1986. Ting's report was based on official HKP data, media reports from January 1983 to December 1986, and interviews of a cross-section of 150 police officers (sample size 200) from all command levels (13). No method of sample selection was detailed, and the findings will be discussed further in the following section. The second, *Police Discretion: Application of Deadly Force* (Chan 1996), focused on the development of HKP firearms policy and determinants of shooting decisions. Chan interviewed ten of his working colleagues at the Regional Crime Unit of New Territories North Headquarters of the Royal Hong Kong Police in 1996, and found that officers have different understandings of the key concepts governing HKP use of force, such as "minimal force" and "reasonableness in circumstances." Officers are otherwise not kept informed of changes to "open fire" conditions or aim to disable vs. kill policy. Finally, the survey revealed salient determinants of use of arms by officers, e.g., suspect intent to harm.

In terms of contribution, both of the above HKP theses were not conducted with scientific rigor, and had questionable validity and reliability. Still, they shed light on HKP officers' understanding (Chan 1996) of and attitude toward (Ting 1988) police use of firearms.

HONG KONG POLICE AND THE USE OF FIREARMS

The use of firearms by officers in the line of duty is rare, with about 20 to 30 incidences a year. Ting (1988) reported a total of 109 shooting incidents from 1983 to 1986: 29 in 1983, 30 in 1984 and 1985, and 20 in 1986. Further, Chan (1996) documented a total of 130 shooting incidents from 1990 to 1995 (31 in 1990, 28 in 1991, 30 in 1992, 27 in 1993, 26 in 1994, and 10 in 1995). In terms of precipitating events, Ting (1988) reported that robberies were most often associated with the use of firearms (38 shootings), followed by vehicle-related offenses, suspicious persons, offenses against persons, and burglaries.

Regarding the reasons for the shootings, threats to life accounted for 241 firearm discharges, followed by preventing escape of a suspect (18 firearm discharges); escaping vehicle (11 discharges); and accidental discharge (7 discharges), for a total of 277 shots fired from 1983 to 1986. Of the 277 shots fired, only 15 rounds by 8 officers were classified as unwarranted.

Finally, during the mid-1990s, in a non-random sample of 200 HKP officers, it was found that 26 officers had drawn their revolvers in the line of duty resulting in six shooting incidents, but only 22 had reported it through the chain of command. When firearms were drawn, they were for protection and arrest reasons (Chan 1996).

ADMINISTRATIVE SUPERVISION OF USE-OF-FORCE INCIDENTS

As a general rule, all use-of-force incidents involving HKP officers are subject to meticulous and stringent internal reporting and review. For example, a use-of-force report is filed following each instance, and shooting cases are subject to the most detailed scrutiny at senior levels, receiving the personal attention of the Deputy Commissioner of Police Operations.

Use-of-Force Continuum

As a general rule, only HKP officers who have been properly trained and equipped are allowed to use weapons or arms of any sort. Police can only use force when, considering the totality of circumstances, it is deemed "necessary" and "reasonable" to do so. This means that any use of force should comport with the use-of-force continuum that is defined as "a series of closely linked and escalating options of force to be considered by an officer" (Hong

Kong Police 2008, 29-1). More specifically, the use of force is considered within the context of the following factors:

1. Level of resistance
2. Perception of threat
3. Officer's ability
4. Minimal force
5. Progressive and proportionate
6. Last resort

Table 3-1 Use-of-Force Continuum—Hong Kong Police

Levels of Resistance	Definitions	Levels of Control	Methods Suggested
Psychological intimidation	Non-verbal manner indicating attitude, readiness or threat	Verbal advice/ control	Officer presence/erection of barriers/verbal direction
Verbal non-compliance	Verbal response showing unwillingness, abuse or threats	Verbal advice/ control	Officer presence/erection of barriers/verbal direction/reinforcement
Passive resistance	Physical inaction designed to obstruct but not threaten	Soft restraint control	Remove by 2 or 4 officers/Soft empty hand techniques (pressure points control/escort position/ transport wrist lock)/quick cuffing
Defensive resistance	Physical action intended to prevent control, might cause injury to oneself or others	Hard restraint control	OC foam/hard empty hand techniques (palm heel strike/stunning/knee strike/ front kick/angle kick)/ straight arm bar takedown/ iron wristlock takedown
Active aggression	Physical assault not intended to cause serious bodily injury	(i) Hard restraint control or (ii) intermediate weapons	OC foam/hard empty hand techniques (palm heel strike/stunning/knee strike/ front kick/angle kick)/ straight arm bar takedown/ iron wristlock takedown/ use of baton
Deadly force assault	Assaults intended to cause death or serious bodily injury	Deadly force	Use of firearm

Source: Hong Kong Police General Orders 29-2.

Investigation Process for Use of Firearms

Following a case that involves the use of firearms, an investigation is carried out by the Division Commander and reported to the Deputy Commissioner of Police Operations by and through the Regional Commander. The use of police firearms principles are contained in the Police General Orders (Hong Kong Police 2008), which mandates that firearms can only be used under the following conditions:

1. To protect any person, including himself, from death or serious bodily injury;
2. To effect the arrest of any person who the officer has reason to believe has just committed a serious and violent crime, and/or who attempts to evade such arrest, or;
3. To quell a riot or insurrection, provided that no lesser degree of force can achieve this purpose (Hong Kong Police 2008, 29-3).

The three main questions to be addressed in an open-fire investigation focus on the purpose of the use of firearms, determining whether the minimum degree of force necessary to achieve the purpose was used and whether the force ceased once that objective was achieved, and whether use of force was reasonable given the circumstances. To facilitate internal investigations and eventual decisionmaking, the police officer who opened fire must make a statement that covers the following:

1. What the officer saw and heard;
2. The sequence of events leading up to the incident;
3. Why and at what stage the revolver was drawn;
4. Verbal warnings given prior to the open fire;
5. How many rounds were fired;
6. Reason for opening fire for each shot;
7. Distances involved and positions of participants;
8. Available cover (if relevant);
9. Obstructions (e.g., passersby, vehicles, lampposts, etc.);
10. Lighting, visibility, and weather conditions;
11. Point of aim (all officers should be aware that it is part of their training to open fire at center body mass and not at extremities);
12. Any action taken immediately after the incident which is directly relevant to the open fire;
13. If the incident resulted from a pre-planned operation, what briefing and instructions were given.

Reasonableness in the Circumstances

There are two kinds of reasonableness tests (subjective vs. objective). Subjective reasonableness requires investigation into what the officer knows, perceives, feels, and thinks at the moment that lead him or her to shoot (Hong Kong Police 2008). Consistent with other countries, the test of reasonableness is subjective in Hong Kong. When determining whether the use of force was reasonable, the following factors are considered:

1. The circumstances leading up to the decision to open fire is important, including any briefings given to the officer and his own observations.
2. What is going through the officers' mind?
3. How the officer saw the incident developing.

As a matter of law, the term "reasonable in the circumstances" came from the Section 3(1), Criminal Law Act 1967 ("a person may use such force as is reasonable in the circumstances in the prevention of crime, in the lawful arrest of offenders or of suspected offenders or of persons unlawfully at large") and has been interpreted as a question of facts to be determined by the jury, but not the judge. The determination of reasonableness includes a proportionality test (the force used should be proportional to the danger or genuinely perceived danger confronted by the officer). Further, the controlling precedent in Hong Kong on the right to use deadly force is the leading authority and the decision of the Privy Council in *Palmer v R. R* (1971) 1 All ER 1077. According to Watson (2001):

> . . . the defense of self-defense is one which can be and will be readily understood by any jury. It is a straightforward conception. It involves no abstruse legal thought. . . . It is both good law and good sense that a man who is attacked may defend himself. It is both good law and good sense that he may do, but may only do, what is reasonably necessary. But everything will depend on the particular facts and circumstances. Of these a jury can decide. . . . If a jury thought that in a moment of unexpected anguish a person attacked had only done what he honestly and instinctively thought was necessary that would be most potent evidence that only reasonable defensive action had been taken. (1088)

Firearms Investigation in Practice: A Case Study

It is sometimes useful to describe an investigative process by using a case study. This example will help to illustrate the issues involved in a firearms investigation. The findings of facts are as follows:

> This is a report of the investigation of an incident of Police Open Fire following a case of Burglary, which occurred at . . . Tin Sin Sight-seeing Trading Co. between 0035 and 0300 hrs. on 3rd May, 1986. Two Chinese males were found loitering at the rear lane of the above building. PC X together with S/Sgt Y was on guard in the vicinity. Then, PC X saw a man coming out from the rear lane and joined with two other men. So, he chased after him. Consequently, PC X fired three shots from his police revolver toward one of the men. He was later arrested. (Ting 1988, 21)

Following this report, the Superintendent in charge submitted the following report:

> I am satisfied that PC. X had the strong impression that a serious crime had been committed when he chased after the men. Considering all the circumstances, the fact that a serious crime had indeed been committed and a third man arrested directly as a result of the chase, I have considered that after the culprit had failed to fire after PC. X fired the first two shots that he might have held back with regard to the third. However, all three shots were fired in a matter of seconds. Any culprit who faces an armed police officer with what appears to be a pistol must realize the chance he is taking. (Ting 1988, 21)

A more senior police administrator added in the report the following:

> Bearing in mind the time of the incident, the fact that the officer was alone and had been engaged in a lengthy pursuit, the young age of the officer (twenty-three years old) and his inexperience of service only a few months had been spent in a land division, and most important of all considering the officer's state of mind, I am firmly of the opinion that no disciplinary action should be contemplated in this case, but that the officer be given suitable advice. (Ting 1988, 22)

If we were to conduct an independent review with the "reasonable under the circumstances" rule, the case raises some unsettling factual and unresolved (applied) legal issues. First, the PC did not have sufficient information to justify a shooting decision. From the findings of facts in the case, it appears that the PC shot the suspect because he was found loitering around an alleged burglarized building at night, and started to run away from the police. At the time of shooting, neither the existence nor the seriousness of the crime has been affirmatively established. More damningly, there was no evidence to directly link the man with the burglary. The only reason why the man was shot was because he ran away from a crime scene when approached by the police officer.

The facts of the case warranted a police inquiry. However, the question remains whether the PC was justified in shooting at a loitering man fleeing from the police under suspicious circumstances.

Further, the PC did not give any warning before shooting, which was in violation of HKP standing orders. Finally, the PC kept firing, even though the first shot may have served the purpose in stopping the suspect. In the end, it seems that the PC had overreacted under the circumstances. It also appears that the senior officers have cleared the PC not (entirely) on legal considerations, but based (mostly) on compassionate grounds (e.g., giving a second chance to an inexperienced but zealous young officer doing his best to fight crime). In doing so, the HKP has confused "subjective" reasonableness with "objective" reasonableness, and can hardly be said to have decided the case based on the totality of circumstances.

The official disposition in this particular case points to a bias in favor of the police. Senior officers in the case were unwilling to second-guess the street officer and were eager to give him/her the benefit of doubt. Reviewing officers considered subjective perceptions, motive, and intention as controlling and personal (in) experience as an additional influential fact.

POLITICAL AND LEGAL CONTROL OF THE HONG KONG POLICE

Thus far, we have focused on HKP internal administrative regulation. Such HKP internal regulation is further subjected to external political supervision, media oversight, and legal constraints. These later measures, developed over time, serve as important and meaningful checks and balances functions in the HKP use-of-force control scheme.

1. *Political control.* Legislative Council (Legco) members are entitled to raise a question or make comments concerning any aspect of HKSAR activities—including the HKP's policy, practices, procedure and individual officers' action—in the Legislative Council (Cheek-Milby 1995). The HKP answer the Legislative Council member's question by and through the Security Bureau. Alternatively the Legco Security Panel can discuss a police matter with the HKP via the Security Branch. For example, in 1999 Legislative Council Member Ho Sai-chu asked the Secretary for Justice the following question: "Will the government inform this Council of: (a) the number of complaints received by the Complaint Against Police Officers about people being treated with violence by police officers during detention at police stations in each of the past three years, and the number of substantiated cases; and (b) the measures in place to prevent the occurrence of such incidents?" (Hong Kong SAR Government. 1999, 1).
2. *Media exposure.* Civic and interest groups could investigate police abuses. For example, in 1993, the Human Rights Commission filed the Hong Kong Human Rights Report (1993), stating: "In February 1993, during a police operation, two off-duty customs officers, for no reason, were handcuffed and beaten up by police in a restaurant and at the police station respectively. The two victims were beaten separately by about ten policemen using electric torches and batons. They were cuffed and kicked into semi-consciousness. They were charged with "resisting arrest, obstructing police carrying out their duties and assaulting police officers" (Chapter 2).
3. *Legal control*:
    (3.1) International law: Hong Kong SAR and the HKP are governed by international conventions by virtue of the Basic Law. For example, the International Covenant on Civil and Political Rights (ICCPR).

The Joint Declaration between the United Kingdom and the People's Republic of China in 1984 on the future of Hong Kong contains the following provision under Annex I, Part XI: "The application to the Hong Kong Special Administrative Region of international agreements to which the People's Republic of China is or becomes a party shall be decided by the Central People's Government, in accordance with the circumstances and needs of the Hong Kong . . ." This means that Hong Kong Police powers, in legislation or practice, must conform with International conventions, such as Covenant on Civil and Political Rights (ICCPR) or subject to challenge in a court of law.

(3.2) Fundamental–domestic laws: The rights of citizens are guaranteed under the Basic Law of the Hong Kong Special Administrative Region (promulgated on 5th April 1990) and Bill of Rights (Hong Kong Bill of Rights Ordinance (Cap 383) and other Domestic Laws of Hong Kong, e.g., Police Force Ordinance and Crimes (Torture) Ordinance (Cap 427)).

(3.3) Criminal law: HKP officers are subject to criminal prosecutions for illegal use of force. In the case of *HKSAR vs. Chuen Lai-Sze et al.*, MA 470/98 (1998), four officers of Special Duty Squad were found guilty of assaulting a drug offender by causing actual bodily harm. The judgment in the case provided extensive discussion of what happened and why the officers ran afoul of the law.

CONCLUSION

This chapter investigates how HKP use-of-force is being conducted and controlled. It finds that the HKP has established a very tight administrative control system in monitoring police firearm use, with a force continuum doctrine as an operational guide, and common law "reasonable under the circumstances" as judicial review norm. In general, the control of HKP use of force is mainly an internal administrative affair.

This study observes several problems with HKP use of force policies and procedures. First, the policies and procedures are *dated*. As currently structured, the Hong Kong Police General Orders do not follow best practices worldwide. Specifically, the orders do not allow for bypassing use-of-force steps based on the totality of circumstances, which might warrant/necessitate such a move. For example, it does not allow for any preemptive use of force for deterrent purposes in crowd-control situations. By comparison, the Federal Bureau of Investigation has moved beyond the sterile, stepwise use-of-force continuum and now relies on the "Wheel Variants of Non-Linear Continuums" scheme based on "Perceptual Continuums" (Joyner and Basile 2007).

Second, *the Police General Orders have not been reconciled with judicial decisions and community expectations.* As currently written, street officers would have a difficult time applying PGO 29-2 (continuum use-of-force framework), because there has been no attempt to reconcile community expectations or PGO 29-2 with Hong Kong court decisions. With the latter, PGO 29-2 is purely an administrative, not a legislative, scheme and has never been tested in court. While PGO 29-2 is designed to provide concrete guidelines on the use of force based on court rulings, following PG0 29-2 will not stop the courts from examining the reasonableness issue as it relates to police officer decisions to use force (Hong Kong Police 2008). As to the former, the Hong Kong population is 98% Chinese and the use-of-force continuum is 100% Western doctrine. It is an open secret that culturally, the East (Hong Kong) and West (United States) perceive criminals and approach the use of force differently (e.g., the Chinese view fleeing from police as more serious).

Third, *PGO 29-2 is not an integrative model.* The use-of-force continuum is built on uniform and unifying legal principles, such as progressive and proportionate use-of-force doctrines. It does not factor in other personal (emotion); operational (tactical); professional (image); cultural (respect for authority); and political (public opinion) factors in an integrated and holistic way.

Finally, *shooting decision reviews are not monitored by the public.* Currently reviewing the shooting incident is in the hands of the HKP alone. As the example illustrated, the HKP is sometimes biased in favor of its officers and more inclined to approve shootings for law enforcement reasons.

In the future, there is a need to study the efficacy of police use-of-force policies and training and on the effect of current gun-control systems on police decision-making processes and outcomes in Hong Kong. There are also research findings indicating that a rule-based approach, however sophisticated and dynamic, is not effective in controlling police decision making in the street.

4 _____

Officer Safety and Public Safety: Training the Police to Use Force in the United Kingdom

John W. Buttle

ABSTRACT

DURING THE EARLY 1990s, the police in England and Wales set in motion a program to allay concerns about officer safety. This officer safety program effectively replaced the traditional "bobby" with an officer who is visibly better equipped to deal with violence. This went mostly unnoticed by the public until 1996 when CS spray (named after Corsten and Stoughton who formulated the CS compound) was introduced. A number of highly publicized allegations about misuse by officers and the possible side effects of being exposed to CS spray ensured that concerns about public safety were also expressed. Also, the introduction of the Human Rights Act of 1998 provided statutory support for the provision of public safety in officer safety training. This chapter suggests that officer safety training needs to succeed in three objectives in order to provide safety for all. First, officers need to be competent in a range of defensive, restraint, and offensive techniques using their bare hands and officer safety equipment. Second, it is important to encourage a calm mind that facilitates the avoidance of harmful mistakes occurring in stressful violent situations. Third, this must all be accomplished within the parameters set down by the laws and guidelines that express a minimum use-of-force doctrine. This chapter will use these three criteria as a means of providing a critique of officer safety training in England and Wales.

INTRODUCTION

Traditionally the police of England and Wales went to considerable lengths in constructing an image of vulnerability that cultivated public consent. The British "bobby" was as unarmed and untrained as other members of the public (Emsley

John W. Buttle, Auckland University of Technology, New Zealand

1996). Policing was to be conducted through the strength of the officer's personality and their ability to embody and project authority. The idea was that highly trained, visibly armed or armored police would not be accepted by the public (Reiner 2000). So, for approximately 200 years, the police in England and Wales relied mostly on their street experiences to inform their use of force. However, this all changed in the 1990s when officers became more vocal about safety concerns and expressed a lack of confidence in the traditional truncheon and handcuffs, leading to a stricter adherence to health and safety at work legislation. It was then the case that chief constables were responsible for providing officer safety equipment and training that allowed the police to safely effect arrests (HMIC 1997).

The provision of officer safety equipment in England and Wales was influenced by the policing practices in the United States (Buttle 2003). Therefore, the police in England and Wales now wear body armor, use rigid handcuffs, have a choice of batons (the expandable side-handled baton and a friction lock baton), and carry CS spray as a matter of routine (Buttle 2006). With all this new equipment, the need to provide adequate training became an important issue.

The initial focus on the building of a training program was one of providing officer safety, while little concern was given to public safety. However, as time progressed, concerns were raised about the safety of using CS spray on members of the public (Rappert 2002b). This issue, along with the introduction of the Human Rights Act of 1998 that emphasized ethical imperatives between individual rights and those of the community (Neyroud 2003), indicated the need for the officer safety program to consider public safety as part of the training.

Against a background of public concern, this proliferation of officer safety equipment raised interesting questions regarding what ethical officer safety training should include. Furthermore, what are the barriers to attaining ethical officer safety training in England and Wales? This chapter will explore these questions and consider current and future officer training needs.

THE IDEAL OF THE HIGHLY SKILLED USER OF FORCE

Training the police to use force in a way that affords officers maximum safety while providing the same for those being arrested, involves an understanding of three distinct but not mutually exclusive areas. The police need to be trained in the physical techniques used to safely effect an arrest, while cultivating a state of psychological preparedness that allows for calm and considered action to be taken. Also, officers need to be indoctrinated in the principles, guidelines, and rules of engagement that are essential to their understanding of when and how to use force in any given situation.

It must be noted that the majority of complaints made about the use of excessive force result from situations where officers make mistakes rather than actively abusing their power (Kappeler, Sluder, and Alpert 1998). Therefore, to achieve ethical policing, officers must be trained to use appropriate levels of force when undertaking arrests. Any officer safety program must focus its training on producing officers who are highly skilled experts in the use of force. Geller and Toch (1996) suggest that highly skilled officers are competent users of force because they have a wider range of coercive techniques to employ during violent and non-violent encounters. Therefore, they can use lower levels of force because they are comfortable using a variety of coercive techniques during arrest. Greater options also provide the officer with a more varied choice of defensive techniques to use in violent situations. From this perspective, a police officer who is only trained to be an expert in the use of a baton will feel comfortable with that weapon and employ it in the majority of situations where force is needed regardless of whether the use of a baton is appropriate. Conversely, an officer trained to verbally negotiate, use wrist-locks, and use a baton has a wider range of options available to ensure officer safety, and the majority of these skills provide the potential for using less severe means of coercion when pertinent to the situation. This allows the officer to make ethical choices about the level of force used while still remaining within the comfort zone of their expertise.

There is more to becoming a skilled user of force than merely learning physical techniques; the mind also has to be prepared to deal with dangerous encounters. This is not some esoteric search for a perfect state of mind, but the development of a practical mindset that facilitates effective and appropriate action on the part of the officer. Neither is this just about making preparation before attending a potentially violent incident (Fyfe 1989), because even a prepared officer will find it hard to function if overcome with fear. When officers are frightened, they are prone to mistakes that result in the use of excessive force (Sharf and Binder 1983). It can also be assumed that fearful officers can make mistakes that threaten their own safety. Therefore, the mental preparation needed involves the inoculation of officers against their fears of being assaulted. This can be achieved by downplaying the often-exaggerated dangers of policing, especially during officer safety training. Furthermore, the production of skilled police officers with confidence in their ability to defend themselves reduces the fears associated with the uncertainty of policing by fostering the belief that no harm will befall them (Bonifacio 1991).

Police officers are often expected to use force with the instruction of how to accomplish this, often consisting of a sermon about being humane and circumspect (Klockars 1996). It is probable that officers who lack an explicit understanding of what is considered an acceptable level of force during arrest may make mistakes. Therefore, the importance of familiarizing officers with the doctrine of force is imperative if officer and public safety are to be served. In this case, a doctrine of force contains laws and policies regarding rules of engagement and specific guidelines regarding the various weapons used by the police. I propose that there are two types of doctrines: the doctrine of reasonable force and the doctrine of minimum force.

The doctrine of reasonable force relies on the word "reasonable" as part of the statutory requirement for the use of force. It can be argued that this term is so ambiguous that even the most egregious of physical abuse may be considered reasonable (Alpert and Smith 1994). This statutory requirement allows for guidelines and rules of engagement that foster this sense of ambiguity by avoiding any form of explicit guidance, which provides room to justify the use of unreasonable force after it has occurred. In short, the doctrine of reasonable force still leaves officers in the position of being sent into the field with little or no understanding of how and when it is appropriate to use any given level of force. Therefore, teaching officers this doctrine would seem to be pointless as a means of providing public safety.

Police officers should be trained in the doctrine of minimum force for coercion by replacing the word "reasonable" with words such as "minimal," "absolutely necessary," and "proportionate" in statutory provisions for police coercion. Terms such as these provide a more demanding requirement than that of "reasonableness" in regard to how officers exercise their coercive powers (Neyroud and Beckley 2001). This gives primacy to low-level uses of force, and the proportionate response rules out any use of high-level force once a citizen has already been subdued. The doctrine of minimum force can provide prescriptive guidelines and rules of engagement that describe the acceptability of specific coercive tactics in any given situation. These prescriptive guidelines can be used to train officers to use force in an ethical manner. Furthermore, prescriptive guidelines can be used to hold officers accountable if they are made accessible to the public (McKenzie 2000).

Training a highly skilled user of force who has the ability to use numerous low- and high-level techniques to perform an arrest, while guided by easy-to-understand rules and regulations may seem unrealistic, but there are many examples that suggest otherwise. Consider a boxer. A boxer is trained in mind and body to use numerous and varied techniques in violent bouts with other similarly trained individuals. During these bouts, the boxer preserves a mental state that controls fear in order to make the appropriate decisions about the strategies used during the bout. Each boxer is ruled by a doctrine of force that stipulates in a clear manner what fighting techniques are legal. For example, it is rare to behold a boxer kicking an opponent because it is against the rules of engagement. Any boxer who breaks these rules is held accountable by the referee and the boxing board of control. When considering this boxing analogy and numerous other martial arts examples, the idea of a police officer being a highly skilled user of force seems a little less naive, or does it?

PROBLEMS WITH TRAINING THE HIGHLY SKILLED USER OF FORCE

Boxers gain their expertise in the use of force from consistent training. This often involves one two-hour training session a week, and in the case of those with aspirations to compete, the time spent training is more akin to twice daily. However, police officers in England and Wales mostly undergo safety training for two days on an annual basis. The time spent by police officers honing their safety skills is considerably less than even the laziest of boxers. This is one of the crucial flaws in the officer safety program, because only a small amount of time can be put aside from normal policing duties in order to produce a skilled user of force. Indeed, it can be argued that, for the most part, the police use force so rarely that an officer safety program could be construed as a waste of police resources.

The safety techniques taught to police officers quickly fade from their memory. This is problematic because the police usually resolve disputes and affect arrests using their powers of persuasion; rarely do officers resort to using physical force (Bailey and Garofalo 1989). By the time they get to use what they have learned in their annual officer safety training sessions, the majority of what they were taught has been forgotten (Buttle 2007). This has led to officers favoring techniques and weapons that are easy to use. So, CS spray is used more than the batons because it is perceived to be easier to use and officers are more comfortable incapacitating someone from a distance (Kock and Rix 1996). Among the batons available is the friction lock baton, which can only be used to deliver offensive strikes; is favored over the expandable side-handled baton that can be used defensively to block. Furthermore, various unarmed offensive strikes (pushes, thigh kicks, and punches) are favored over the more complex defensive techniques (arm and wrist locks). With only limited training, officers favor the use of offensive equipment and techniques that used larger muscle groups over the fine motor skills used for defensive ones (Kaminski and Martin 2000).

This preference for offensive over defensive strategies is compounded by the way in which the officer safety program refines its training based on feedback from officers gained from incident report forms (HMIC 1997). This feedback is used to inform subsequent officer safety training. So with officers favoring the easy-to-learn offensive techniques, their feedback ensured that future officer safety training focused mainly on offensive means of gaining compliance during arrest, much to the detriment of more defensive techniques (Buttle 2007). As time passed, the emphasis on defensive strategies and equipment was eroded by the feedback from officers and replaced with mostly offensive means for gaining compliance (Buttle 2007). The problem with this largely offensive approach to officer safety training is that it favors pre-emptive violence against citizens who are perceived by officers as potentially dangerous when in fact they may not be (Buttle 2007). This is far removed from the ideal of training police officers to become skilled users of force. Rather than teaching a variety of techniques, the feedback process self-selects to reduce the techniques officers are taught to only a few easy-to-learn offensive options.

In order to produce skilled users of force, the officer safety program has to train officers to control their fears of violent situations. However, exposure to techniques that focus on the incapacitation of potentially violent people can exacerbate these fears. This can lead to officers being emotionally over-whelmed to the extent that they cannot defend themselves or protect their col-leagues (Kureczka 1996), leading to the officer being considered a coward who should not be trusted, and is therefore open to ridicule from colleagues (Kroes and Hurrell 1975). Conversely, any exaggeration of the threats to offi-cer safety may encourage officers to overreact in dangerous situations and resort to excessive use of force (Fyfe 1996).

Officer safety trainers should take care to play down the dangers of policing in order to not exacerbate the fears of those they are training. This is important in an occupation where the working culture is one that exaggerates danger and excitement, while ignoring the more pervasive safe and mundane practices that are part of policing (Waddington 1999a). However, police officer safety training often ignores the fact that assaults against the police are rare, and when they do occur, officers are seldom seriously harmed. For example, teaching officers how to defend against the improbable occurrence of a knife attack often only high-lights that there is no reliable means to fend off this type of assault. So, it may be wise to explain that assaults with a knife are not common.

Again, teaching the police to use officer safety techniques may provide officers with the sense of security needed to act in a calm and effective man-ner when undertaking arrests. While this confidence may initially be high, it is likely to fade as time goes by and the memory of the technique fades. It is hard to maintain a belief that your training prepares you for dealing with danger-ous situations when there is little opportunity to put the training into practice.

PROBLEMS WITH THE DOCTRINE OF FORCE

When the officer safety program was started, the legislation regarding the use of force was taken from the Criminal Law Act of 1967, which indicated that use of force must be "reasonable in the circumstances." This is in line with the ambiguous doctrine of reasonable force that provides for rules of engage-ment and regulations that are based on the ability to be able to justify the use of force after it has been used. Later this was superseded by the Human Rights Act of 1998, which states that the level of force to be used be "no more than is absolutely necessary," which is more akin to the doctrine of minimum force because it expresses that the lowest level of force should be used to affect an arrest. This doctrine provides rules of engagement and regu-lations that proscribe what level of force is acceptable in any given situation. It serves as a useful working definition of acceptable and unacceptable force to guide police officers through their working day. Therefore, the officer safety program should have made the transition to the doctrine of minimum force, because the Human Rights Act of 1998 provided statutory provision for this approach to the use of force.

While officers are concerned about their physical safety, they are also concerned about complaints being made against them (Loader and Mulcahy 2003). Therefore, it would not be pessimistic to suggest that the police of England and Wales have often been suspicious of guidelines and rules of engagement. The police have failed to grasp the usefulness of having specific instructions to inform them about how to act in situations where force has been used. Instead, they have favored the maintenance of ambiguity as a means of shielding themselves from public accountability.

According to Brian Rappert (2002a), the first set of guidelines for the use of CS spray in 1996 issued specific instructions that CS spray should be used as a weapon of last resort in line with a doctrine of minimum force. Specifically, "The incapacitant is primarily designed for dealing with violent subjects who cannot otherwise be restrained. . . . It is issued primarily for self defense" (ACPO 1996). However, CS spray was not used as a last resort; it quickly became the preferred means of gaining compliance when compared to the baton, and there were claims that it was deployed early by many officers (Buttle 2003). In response to this violation of the guidelines, a new set of guidelines were introduced in 1999 that were far from explicit in their terminology: ". . . individual officers must be prepared to account for their decisions and to show that they were justified in doing what they did and that they acted reasonably within the scope of the law on the use of force" (ACPO 1999). Rather than provide officers with explicit instructions about how to use force, the new guidelines reasserted the comfortable ambiguity of the doctrine of reasonable force. No longer were CS sprays a last resort, because they could now be used in any situation as long as the officer could provide justification.

In the United States, rules of engagement that generally fall under the term continuum of force have been used since the early 1980s and are now an integral part of American policing (Stetser 2001). These rules of engagement govern all uses of force by regulating the discretion of police officers before and during situations where force is needed to gain compliance. These guidelines act as an operational definition of acceptable force, and while doing so, also make what is unacceptable more apparent (Alpert and Smith 1994). Most continuums of forces can be described as a ladder with the least forceful techniques, such as the mere presence of an officer, followed by conversing with and physically escorting someone during arrest on the lower rung of the ladder. The levels of coercion increase as the ladder is climbed until the most lethal levels of force can be employed, such as the use of firearms. Basically, the continuum of force is a linear hierarchy that guides officers on what techniques are appropriate for use in response to the level of resistance being made during arrest. If the level of resistance to arrest is low, then the officers' choice of force tactic should reflect that, and higher levels of force should only be used if greater resistance is offered. In this context, the use of a continuum is in line with the doctrine of minimum force.

If a continuum of force is taught to police officers as part of their officer safety program, then police officers will be able to use it as a means to justify using force if a complaint is made against them. Furthermore, if the continuum of force is a matter of public record, then it may be used to substantiate claims regarding the misuse of force (McKenzie 2000). However, the police of England and Wales only briefly flirted with the idea of a continuum of force, citing unfounded concerns about the possibility of its use leading to an escalation in levels of force (Neyroud and Beckley 2001). It was this presumption of escalation that led to what became the conflict resolution model that is currently used by the police of England and Wales (Neyroud and Beckley 2001).

THE CONFLICT RESOLUTION MODEL

The conflict resolution model (see below) is not a hierarchy of relatively explicit techniques. Instead, it is based on three platforms, most easily visualized as three interlocking circles that interact depending on the factors present in the situation confronting the officer (Keenan 1997). The first platform (offender behavior) is concerned with the actions of the person being arrested, while the second platform (reasonable officer response) lists the various options available for the officer to make an arrest. On their own, these two platforms are similar to that of a continuum of force, because they appear to form a hierarchy of options in response to the actions of the person being arrested. However, it is the third platform (impact factors) that negates the specificity of the hierarchical approach. Impact factors are the often unique elements of a situation that can exacerbate or nullify the need for any given level of force to be employed by an officer (Keenan 1997). Therefore, any number of officers can decide to undertake the same arrest using different means to do so (Buttle 2007). For example, an officer can decide to use CS spray because he or she feels most comfortable using it when taking into account the size of the person being arrested, whereas a larger officer may decide to use verbal skills to affect the same arrest.

Instead of providing an operational definition of how and when to use force, the conflict resolution model eschews the idea of providing specific guidance as a response to the level of resistance to arrest. The conflict resolution model provides a framework for officers to make decisions based on their own experiences and their favored means of effecting arrests (Buttle 2007). Therefore, rather than acting as guidance in the decision-making process, the conflict resolution model remains ambiguous. It is also used to help officers justify their use of force after the event has occurred and is often used as courtroom tool to defend officers against allegations of the misuse of force (Buttle 2007). There is no promise of public accountability where this set of rules is concerned. When all this is taken into consideration, the conflict

The Conflict Resolution Model

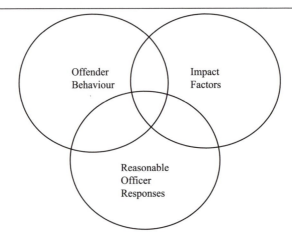

Offender Behavior
– Compliance: The offender offered no resistance and complied with the officers' request.
– Verbal Resistance and Gestures: The offender refused to verbally comply and exhibited body language indicating non-compliance.
– Passive Resistance: Offender stood or sat still and refused to move.
– Active Resistance: The offender pushed or pulled the officer. There was no deliberate attempt to strike or injure the officer.
– Aggressive Resistance: The offender fought with the officer using punches, kicks, wrestling, or biting, etc.
– Serious or Aggravated Resistance: Any assault where there existed the possibility of great bodily harm of death. This included the use of a weapon by the offender.

Reasonable Officer Response
– Officer Presence: This included the method of approach and pronouncement of office. Tactical verbal communications could be used. Sometimes the presence of the uniformed officer was enough to resolve a situation.
– Primary Control Skills: The use of arm locks, wrist-locks, physically escorting the offender, and the use of handcuffs.
– Defensive Tactics: This involved the use of blocks, strikes, and takedowns. Furthermore, the use of batons and CS spray were allowed. Control tactics often followed defensive tactics.
– Deadly Force: This involved any action that may result in serious bodily injury or death from the use of empty hand techniques, batons or firearms.

Impact Factors
– The sex, age and size of the offender relative to the officer.
– The strength of the offender relative to the officer.
– The offender's skill level relative to the officer.

– Any special knowledge that the officer may possess regarding the offender.
– The presence of alcohol and drugs.
– Mental derangement.
– Being in a position of disadvantage.
– Injury and/or exhaustion.
– Imminent danger.
– Numbers.
– Weapons.
– Officers' perception of subject's willingness to resist.
Source: National Police Training.

resolution model used in England and Wales has much in common with the ambiguous doctrine of reasonable force.

DISCUSSION

With just a sideways glance at the boxing ring, it quickly becomes apparent that the ideal of the highly skilled user of force constrained within a set of specific guidelines is an attainable goal, even where law enforcement is concerned. It is also a fair assumption that highly skilled users of force will be better able to protect themselves without misusing force. Furthermore, if a doctrine of minimum force is used to constrain and guide officers in the use of force, then there is a distinct possibility that public safety could be seen as one and the same with police safety. However, that ideal has yet to be realized.

There are two barriers to achieving this goal: infrequent training and an unwillingness to relinquish the doctrine of reasonable force in favor of the doctrine of minimum force. Infrequent training has led to the narrowing down of officer safety techniques through a feedback system that favors the use of offensive techniques and safety equipment, while removing or sidelining the more defensive options from the officer safety program. Rather than training police officers to have a greater range of options at their disposal, officers are being taught the simple offensive means of using force. Therefore the police are likely to be more dangerous to the public. This is exacerbated by a strong reluctance to provide guidelines and rules of engagement that are specific enough to be useful as a working definition of acceptable force. Despite the Human Rights Act of 1998 that leans toward the use of a doctrine of minimum force to protect the public, guidelines and rules of engagement have been clouded in ambiguity and leave little to hope in regard of providing public accountability. Reverting back to the boxing analogy: a boxer with no confidence has been put in the ring after being trained to use only two punches and with little grasp of the rules. This boxer last trained about a year ago. Moreover, there is no referee to clarify and control the fight. This is far removed from the ideal of the highly skilled user of force.

5

Physical and Psychological Force in Criminal and Military Interrogations in the United States

Mark Costanzo and Allison Redlich

ABSTRACT

INTERROGATION IS A process in which the interrogator must induce the person being interrogated to provide statements against his or her own best interest. The goal of a military interrogator is to educe intelligence from enemy combatants; the goal of a police interrogator is to obtain confessions from suspected criminals. Because of these goals, the interrogation process is inherently adversarial and to some, coercive. In this chapter, we will discuss the physical and psychological force used in military and police interrogations. In the United States, physical force has been disallowed from police interrogations for more than 70 years. We will discuss the history and rationale behind the abolition of torture and other harsh methods in police interrogations, and discuss modern-day interrogation techniques involving psychological persuasion. We will also address the use of torture in military interrogations. Finally, we will demonstrate how both physical and psychological coercion can result in false confessions or inaccurate information, thereby impeding the goals and ultimate efficacy of the interrogation process.

In 2008, the city of Chicago agreed to pay nearly $20 million to settle a lawsuit against several police officers who had used torture to secure criminal confessions. Ninety criminal suspects had complained of physical abuse at the hands of a "police torture ring" that forced confessions in a series of cases beginning in the 1970s and extending into the 1990s. The abuse tactics described by the suspects included plastic bags placed over the head for the purpose of suffocation, electric shocks to the face and genitals, severe

Mark Costanzo, Claremont McKenna College
Allison Redlich, University at Albany, State University of New York

beatings, burning with cigarettes and curling irons, and putting the barrel of a gun in the mouth or against the head. The coerced confessions were used to send eleven men to death row. Four of those men were later pardoned, and seven had their sentences commuted to life in prison (Conroy 2003; Washburn 2007). Although it is still possible to find instances of physically abusive police interrogations in the United States, the direct use of physical force in interrogation is now quite rare (and illegal). Over the past 70 years, police have developed a cadre of psychological techniques to replace the physical techniques that were once a prominent feature of interrogations. To some, these tactics constitute a kind of "psychological force" that is used to induce suspects to confess to crimes.

In this chapter, we discuss the physical and psychological force that can be used in criminal and military interrogations. We address the history and rationale behind the abolition of torture and other harsh methods in police interrogations, and discuss modern-day interrogation techniques involving psychological persuasion—techniques that can lead and have led to false confessions and wrongful convictions of innocents. Finally, we provide an overview of police interrogation policies in countries other than the United States.

PHYSICAL FORCE IN INTERROGATIONS

The interrogative techniques of law enforcement in criminal investigations and military personnel in educing intelligence have some shared aspects, particularly in the tactics themselves (Redlich 2007). However, one crucial difference between the two is the permissible use of physical force and even torture as methods of obtaining information. Criminal confessions shown to be obtained via physical force are considered coerced and cannot be used against defendants in court proceedings. In contrast, though highly controversial, torture has been sanctioned by the U.S. government in some military situations.

In 2003, Americans were astonished by photographs of prisoner abuse at Abu Ghraib prison in Iraq. Those photos depicted helpless prisoners subjected to a variety of cruel and humiliating practices by U.S. military personnel. One explanation offered for these abuses was that soldiers had been instructed to "soften up" prisoners for interrogation (Hersh 2004; Scherer and Benjamin 2003). Soon after, allegations of torture surfaced at the U.S. detention facility at Guantanamo Bay, Cuba and at detention facilities in Afghanistan (Amnesty International 2009). By 2005, information had also surfaced about the practice of "extraordinary rendition" whereby prisoners in U.S. custody were transported to "black sites" in countries (e.g., Egypt, Jordan, Morocco, Syria) known to use torture.

In addition to the profound moral and legal issues raised by the use of torture, there is no compelling evidence that abusive interrogations are an effective or reliable method for gaining actionable intelligence. Prisoners may reveal some accurate information in response to the pain of torture, but that information is often conflated with inaccurate or deliberately misleading information (Harbury 2005). For obvious ethical reasons, there is no systematic research on the effectiveness of torture. However, one of the clearest findings from decades of research on the criminal justice system is that the more coercive the interrogation, the greater the risk of a false confession (Drizin and Leo 2004). The very conditions found to raise the risk of false confession in criminal interrogations—long interrogations; physical deprivation (food, sleep, and water); suspect disorientation and extended isolation; physical pain; explicit threats and promises—are the exact conditions torturers seek to create. Other problems include the difficulty of knowing whether the person being tortured actually possesses useful information, the associated problem of torturing many people who have no information, the enduring negative mental health effects of torture on victims and perpetrators, and the complication that those with the most critical information are the least likely to succumb to torture (Costanzo and Gerrity 2009). There are also political consequences. The use of torture by the American military undermines the credibility and authority of the United States when advocating human rights abroad, lends credibility to the claims of terrorists, creates a recruiting tool for organizations that seek to attack U.S. soldiers and citizens, and may endanger the lives of soldiers who take action based on faulty intelligence gained through the use of torture (Costanzo, Gerrity, and Lykes 2006).

Police interrogations have a checkered history in the United States. At least through the early 1930s, police routinely employed what was called the "third degree"—beating, threatening, and abusing criminal suspects in the pursuit of confessions (Hopkins 1931). It was only after the Wickersham Commission Report in 1931 (National Commission on Law Observance and Enforcement 1931) and several Supreme Court decisions (beginning with *Brown v. Mississippi,* 1936) banning harsh interrogation practices that physical abuse of suspects began to decline. By the 1960s, such abuse appeared to be rare in the United States (Leo 1996). In 1940, W. R. Kidd's book, *Police Interrogation,* was published. It became the first police interrogation manual to instruct police in the new, more psychological science of interrogation. By 1942, Fred Inbau had published the first edition of his influential interrogation manual, *Lie Detection and Criminal Interrogation.* That manual (now titled *Criminal Interrogation and Confessions* by Inbau et al. 2001) has been revised and expanded over the course of more than 60 years. The Chicago-based firm Reid and Associates transformed these manuals into a training program and, in 1974, began offering seminars to police and security professionals in several countries. More than a quarter million police officers have now been trained in the "Reid Method" of interrogation. Even interrogators who have not read the manual or taken the training have likely learned components of the Reid Method by observing or working with other interrogators.

Research confirms that the Reid tactics, which rely heavily on psychological manipulation, are widely used by detectives in the United States (Kassin et al. 2007; Leo 1996).

"PSYCHOLOGICAL FORCE" IN INTERROGATIONS

It is an undisputed fact that contemporary interrogation techniques—either police or military—utilize psychological ploys to obtain confessions. Whether standard interrogation techniques constitute "psychological *force*" is debatable, and in the eye of the beholder. We describe interrogation methods used today, highlighting those methods identified as contributors to false confessions. Our focus is on police rather than military interrogations, because criminal interrogations have been studied to a much greater extent.

In criminal settings, police must inform custodial suspect of their *Miranda* rights: the right to remain silent, the right to appointed counsel, and a warning that anything they say can be used against them in court (*Miranda v. Arizona* 384 U.S. 436 [1966]). These warnings, intended to blunt police use of coercion, have much less impact than is commonly assumed. The overwhelming majority of suspects (roughly 80%) waive their *Miranda* rights and submit to interrogation (Leo 2001). Police use a variety of strategies to encourage suspects to waive their rights, including reading the *Miranda* warnings in a rushed, confusing, or perfunctory manner. These strategies minimize the significance of the warnings and disguise the adversarial nature of interrogation (Leo 2008). In this opening phase, police often present the interrogation as an opportunity for the suspect to "tell his side of the story." Military interrogations also often begin with an open-ended, "tell us your side" type of question. Specifically, human intelligence collectors, as they are sometimes called, begin with the Direct Approach, which they claim to be effective in eliciting information 90% to 95% of the time (Redlich 2007).

Skilled interrogators (police or military) are able to reshape a suspect's perception of the nature of his situation, the choices available to him, and the consequences that follow from each choice. To create the preconditions necessary for this perceptual reshaping, police interview suspects alone, in a room where they control all aspects of the immediate situation. This combination of social isolation and control removes the comfort of familiar surroundings, leaves the suspect without an ally in the room, allows police to make claims that are difficult for the suspect to challenge, and creates anxiety and disorientation in the suspect (Costanzo and Leo 2007). In this isolated, tightly controlled surreal situation, interrogators work to convince the suspect that admitting guilt, or providing coveted information, is the best, most beneficial course of action.

Perhaps the most potent tool that police interrogators have at their disposal is the ability to lie to suspects. Law enforcement is permitted to confront suspects with seemingly objective and irrefutable evidence of guilt—whether or not such evidence actually exists. Police may pretend to have eyewitnesses, fingerprints, DNA, or videotapes that establish guilt. They may even falsely inform the suspect that he failed a polygraph test. These interrogation tactics are likely to make the distressed suspect believe that he now bears the burden of proving his innocence. After describing the evidence against him, the interrogators typically argue that any reasonable judge or jury will find him guilty. Military interrogators can also lie, although they have a few specific constraints on what falsehoods are allowed. Although they are allowed to "use the ruses of war" to build rapport, including posing as someone other than him or herself, they cannot pose as 1) medical personnel; 2) a member of the International Committee of the Red Cross or its affiliates; 3) a chaplain or clergyman; 4) a journalist; or 5) a member of the U.S. Congress. These constraints are placed to protect the reputations of the professions listed and not to protect the rights of the source or to guard against obtaining false information (Redlich 2007). Interrogators work hard to create the impression that confessing or disclosing information will actually improve the suspect's otherwise hopeless situation. In criminal cases, interrogators may suggest that they will use their discretionary power to favorably influence the suspect's case. Without making explicit promises, it may be implied that the suspect will be charged with a less serious crime and receive a shorter prison sentence if he accepts responsibility, admits guilt, and expresses remorse (Leo, Costanzo, and Shaked-Schroer 2009). Interrogators often misrepresent themselves as the suspect's allies and suggest that they can help the suspect by writing a sympathetic report, by their testimony at trial, by favorable communications to prosecutors, or through their ability to arrange for social services. The "catch," of course, is that these benefits can only be obtained if the suspect confesses (Ofshe and Leo 1997).

Finally, to further enhance the appeal of a confession, police interrogators suggest honorable or sympathetic reasons why the suspect might have committed the crime. For example, instead of committing a premeditated murder, perhaps the suspect was acting in self-defense, or perhaps he accidentally killed the victim. These "exculpating scenarios" serve to psychologically, morally, or legally justify the crime. Such scenarios are offered to make a suspect more comfortable with admitting guilt and to demonstrate that interrogators can help him control how his admission is framed for prosecutors, judges, juries, and others. Scenarios help to entice an admission by shifting blame to others, by redefining the circumstances that caused the act, or by redefining the act itself (Leo 2008). Suspects are led to believe that they can mitigate their potential punishment by accepting the exculpatory scenario offered by interrogators.

Modern interrogation is designed to break the resistance of a rational person who knows he is guilty by persuading him that the benefits of confessing outweigh the costs. The presumption is that the suspect under interrogation is guilty and will, at least initially, steadfastly deny guilt. This presumption of guilt should be based on solid evidence. Unfortunately, it is sometimes based on little more than a detective's intuition. Interrogators may mistakenly evaluate the suspect's verbal and non-verbal behaviors as indicative of guilt. Once an innocent person has been misclassified as guilty, he is likely to be subjected to psychologically coercive interrogation techniques (Meissner and Kassin 2004). And, because no credible evidence is likely to exist against an innocent suspect, getting a confession may become even more important than usual because police desperately need a confession to build a successful case (Gross 1996).

Most manuals, interrogators, and police trainers claim that their methods only elicit confessions from the guilty (Kassin and Gudjonsson 2004). This is not true. According to the Innocence Project Report (2007), false confessions/admissions are responsible for about one-quarter of wrongful convictions. Also, in recent years, researchers have identified more than 300 proven false confessions that have occurred since the 1970s (Drizin and Leo 2004; Gross et al. 2005). All of these false confession cases involved DNA exonerations or other indisputable evidence of innocence (e.g., the alleged murder victim turns up alive). The central question is not whether police-induced false confessions occur, but why the confessions occur and how they can be prevented.

False confessions usually occur due to a combination of situational and dispositional factors (Costanzo and Leo 2007; Kassin and Gudjonsson 2004). The situational factors are typically the interrogation techniques themselves: bluffing or lying about evidence, implied threats of punishment or implied promises of leniency, and isolating suspects from friends and family for long periods. A large part of the problem is that the same interrogation tactics that are effective on guilty suspects in generating true confessions can be equally effective on innocent suspects in generating false confessions. This problem is exacerbated by the fact that there is no reliable method to distinguish between guilty and innocent suspects, and that the police tend to be overconfident in their ability to discriminate between the two. In addition, lying to suspects and overly long interrogations have been singled out as particularly egregious tactics that have a higher likelihood of leading to false confessions than other interrogation techniques.

The two most oft-cited dispositional factors identified as contributing to false confessions are juvenile status and mental impairment. Both groups are overrepresented among proven false confessors (Drizin and Leo 2004; Gross et al. 2005). For juveniles, the characteristics that typically define childhood and adolescence, such as impulsivity, inability to consider long-term consequences, and immature development, are the same characteristics that can lead to false confessions (Owen-Kostelnik, Reppucci, and Meyer 2006; Redlich and Drizin 2007). Similarly, persons with mental illness and mental retardation may have deficits in legal knowledge and understanding or may be overly compliant and suggestible, all of which increase their risk for false confessions (Perske 2008; Redlich 2004).

Several reforms have been proposed to reduce false confessions with out reducing the number of true confessions. Videotaping of interrogations may be the single most important policy reform available. Videotaping creates an objective, comprehensive, reviewable record of what occurred in the interrogation room, and exposes interrogation practices. Because interrogators know they may be scrutinized, they are less likely to use psychologically coercive or improper interrogation techniques that lead to false confessions (Leo 2008). It is imperative that the entire interrogation should be videotaped; both the suspect and the interrogator should be visible, and the video should carry a time/date stamp (Lassiter and Geers 2004; Leo, Costanzo and Shaked 2009). At present in the United States, only six states have laws requiring police to record interrogations in their entirety in some or all criminal cases (Sullivan 2004).

Another proposed reform is changing from a guilt-presumed interrogative model to one that is more inquisitorial, and information seeking. As described below, England and Wales have adopted such models. Although this chapter focuses on interrogations in the United States, it is useful to summarize the rules governing interrogations in a few other countries to help contextualize American practices.

POLICE INTERROGATION OUTSIDE THE UNITED STATES

In most countries, physical abuse and psychological torture remain standard interrogation techniques (Amnesty International 2009; Conroy 2000). There is, of course, enormous cross-national variation in both interrogation practices and laws governing the conduct of interrogations. Some countries place few restraints on police interrogators while others have established strict procedures for the treatment of criminal suspects. Unfortunately, reliable data on interrogation techniques and criminal confessions are scarce for many countries.

In China, in 1996, it became illegal to use physical coercion to obtain confessions and defendants now have a right to counsel. Research has demonstrated that although confessions are still present in about 66% of criminal cases, the rate of confessions has decreased since the 1996 rulings (Lu and Miethe 2003). In 1997, Chinese courts ruled that voluntary and sincere confessions made before any criminal investigation could serve as a mitigating factor in sentencing decisions. Although torture had already been ruled illegal, it was not until 2005 that courts decided that confessions extracted through the use of torture or coercion should not be admissible as evidence. It was also held that suspects must be questioned by prosecutors to assure they were not ill treated by authorities. Finally in 2006, China ruled that all interrogations for job-related crimes must be videotaped to protect against coercion and corruption. Although coercion persists, these legal changes indicate strong moves toward protecting defendant rights (Russ 2005).

In Japan, torture is rarely reported, with figures decreasing yearly (U.S. Department of State 2005a). Nonetheless, some criminal justice practices exert psychological pressure on suspects that likely elicit false confessions (Johnson 2002; Leo 2002). For example, suspects may be held for up to 23 days before indictment and are unlikely to receive bail if they maintain their innocence or remain silent (Foote 1992). Further, although the law offers suspects the right to counsel, prosecutors can limit access to an attorney before indictment (U.S. Department of State 2005a). If suspects are unable to afford a lawyer, they may not receive one until after their indictment, although the relatively new "duty lawyer" system is increasingly giving suspects access to attorneys. Finally, the right to remain silent carries with it a duty to endure questioning. Concerns have been raised, because approximately 90% of suspects in Japan offer confessions of guilt (compared to around 65% in the United States.) (Ramseyer and Rasmusen 2001). This high rate of confessions probably results from a combination of cultural expectations, police pressure, and/or a tendency to prosecute only cases where there is already strong evidence against the defendant (Johnson 2002).

In Mexico in 1991, amid several scandals involving torture-induced confessions, laws were changed to prohibit the use of torture and to prevent confessions obtained through the use of torture from being admissible in federal court. However, these laws did not appear to curb the use of torture during interrogations, and confessions remained the primary evidence in most cases (U.S. Department of State 2005b). In 1995, the Supreme Court of Mexico held that confessions had to be corroborated by additional evidence to prove guilt. Unfortunately, judges did not always obey this ruling and, in many cases, the corroborating evidence was the testimony of the arresting officer. It was not until 2005 that Mexican law allowed suspects the right to counsel from the time they come into contact with the prosecutor. However, police can still hold people accused of "serious" crimes in jail until trial. Judges do not have the discretion to release suspects prior to trial even if they pose little to no risk. As a result, 40% of prisoners being held in Mexico have yet to be convicted (Human Rights Watch 2006).

In contrast to the countries described above, the interrogations procedures adopted in England and Wales can be seen as models of humane treatment. In 1986, in the wake of several high-profile false confessions, the *Police and Criminal Evidence Act* (*PACE*) became law (Home Office 2005). *PACE* prohibits police from lying to suspects about the existence of incriminating evidence, forbids threats of physical harm, or the use of torture or other forms of cruel, inhuman, or degrading treatment. When vulnerable suspects—for example, juveniles or people with mental disorders—are interrogated, an "appropriate adult" (e.g., independent and responsible) must be present. Finally, all interviews occurring at a police station must be audiotaped and made accessible to lawyers, judges, juries, and experts. Such procedures minimize police coercion, protect suspects from abusive interrogations, and protect police from false accusations of misconduct during interrogations. Encouragingly, research suggests that the number of confessions has not fallen significantly since the introduction of the PACE reforms, and the use of coercive tactics in interrogations has dropped substantially (Gudjonsson 2003). Australia and New Zealand have similar interrogation models in place.

Interrogation will remain an essential investigative tool in military and criminal settings. However, interrogation room behaviors and practices must be carefully monitored if we are to trust the reliability of admissions produced by this psychologically manipulative process. The use of force—both physical and psychological—in the interrogation room is likely to remain controversial. We must be careful to give interrogators the tools they need to help obtain accurate and reliable information while simultaneously putting safeguards in place to help protect the innocent.

Police "Encounters" in Mumbai, India

Jyoti Belur

ABSTRACT

POLICE USE OF deadly force in situations known as *encounters*, where hard-core criminals are killed under somewhat questionable circumstances, are a peculiar police response to the rising organized crime in the city of Mumbai. How the abuse of deadly force can remain largely unquestioned in a vibrant democratic country like India can be partially explained by unraveling the multi-layered nature of the phenomenon and exploring how different individuals understand it. This chapter examines how police officers in Mumbai define the term *encounter*, and reveals a fraction of the complexity in achieving consensus in establishing the acceptability of police actions at individual, organizational, and societal levels.

INTRODUCTION

Police *encounters* are a peculiar feature of Indian policing. The term *encounter*, as it is used in the Indian context, refers to a specific type of police contact—a spontaneous, unplanned shoot-out between the police and alleged criminals, where the criminal is usually killed with few or no police injuries. However, the police "cover story" from official sources and cited in the media is always the same, raising suspicion that it is covering up facts that might not be legally defensible or permissible (Hunt and Manning 1991). The term *encounter* is not just police jargon, but is a part of everyday discourse in India, and is used by police officers, the media, and the public to refer to police use of deadly force.

Police resorting to use of deadly force in the form of *encounters* is not uniform across the whole country of India, as some states that make up the

Jyoti Belur, Department of Security and Crime Science, Jill Dando Institute, University College, London federation have a much better record of the use of deadly force than others.[1] Areas facing serious challenges from Naxalites (communist rebel groups), organized gangs, very high levels of serious crime (e.g., dacoit[2] infested areas), and separatist groups or terrorist operations have a greater tendency to engage in *encounters* than others. Furthermore, the context and circumstances in which *encounters* happen are very different across these varied situations.[3]

Police *encounters* are not only "prized" internally by police organizations and sometimes rewarded by the government (either with one-rank-promotions, bravery medals, and/or other privileges), but also enjoy some societal approval in various parts of the country. There have been several examples when the police have been publicly congratulated for "acts of bravery" that have ridden society of a "menace." Most police officers consider their work to be not just a job, but also a "way of life with a worthwhile mission"—to serve the public and protect society (Reiner 2000; Skolnick and Fyfe 1993). Public adulation is a heady stimulant and, combined with positive press ratings and organizational approval in the form of allowing such actions to continue unquestioned, can serve to demolish any moral compunctions that the police have toward depriving another person of life. Police officers are recruited from among ordinary citizens and are unlikely to have a greater propensity to be inherently evil or natural "killers." The two questions that arise are how and why do ordinary people do evil things (Browning 1993; Cohen 2001)? Phillip Zimbardo (2007) posed a similar question in his Stanford experiment: Do sadistic people pursue jobs as prison guards or do jobs as prison guards make people sadistic? His argument was that situational forces can contribute to such behavior and often override any moral, individual traits (Zimbardo 2007). Contextual and situational factors such as difficult working conditions for the police, an overburdened and corrupt criminal justice system, and the demands of the sociopolitical milieu within which the police operate combined with a spiraling crime problem might explain why "criminals" are perceived to deserve executions. Or, could it be the case that because most police *encounters* are not subject to detailed scrutiny, the decision to invoke deadly force may be undertaken lightly, or without considering the full impact of the moral and legal aspects involved? These were issues that came to the fore in this research as probable explanations for excessive use of deadly force.

MUMBAI POLICE AND ENCOUNTERS

While *encounters* unquestionably exist, how an act, which appears from many accounts to be suspect and arbitrary, has escaped demands for greater scrutiny or accountability in a democratic country like India remains unexplained. This research, focusing on the Mumbai police as a case study,[4] explores these and related issues—such as how officers explain the use of deadly force to themselves and to their various audiences including senior officers, the media, politicians, and the public (Belur 2007). This chapter examines police officers' definition of *encounters* and explores the range of complexities involved in understanding the concept *per se*. The emerging picture of Mumbai was that of a prosperous megapolis with an ever-increasing migrant population, and with a rapidly expanding financial and "infotainment" growth center. The growth of various organized crime syndicates, their inter-rivalry for suprem-acy, as well as their criminal activities, spread panic and insecurity throughout different sections of society. In the 1990s, there was a proliferation of shoot-outs, extortion cases, and kidnappings for ransom cases that were accompa-nied by a rise in the number of *encounters*. The growing menace of organized crime syndicates provided one of the biggest challenges for the police force, which sought to counter alleged hardened criminals with the use or abuse of deadly force in the form of *encounters* as one form of instant justice. The police were under pressure from both the public and politicians to do some-thing about this growing menace. The cumbersome and time-consuming proc-esses of the criminal justice system were perceived to be inadequate to deal with "hardened" criminals. It was in this situation that *encounters* proliferated and came to appear accepted in Mumbai by the public, media, and the politi-cal establishment. Between 1993 and 2003, there were a total of 453 incidents of *encounters* in which 589 alleged criminals were killed, with the numbers killed reaching a peak in 2001 and tapering off thereafter (Crime Branch Sta-tistics, Mumbai Police[5]).

However, the story was just not a simple case of "cops-and-robbers." The injection of the politics of fundamental Hinduism, growing religious dis-cord, terrorism and associated violence, and alleged interference from outside forces into Mumbai's sociopolitical landscape, combined with an already overburdened criminal justice system made the task of policing organized crime groups far more complicated.

METHODOLOGY

This research was primarily a qualitative exploration of officers' perceptions and accounts of *encounters*, ways in which they explained, excused, or justi-fied their conduct, and official and personal discourses through which they reconciled the arbitrary use of deadly force with their moral conscience and professional ethics. A qualitative account could reveal the richness and depth of the police and public discourse and how it contributed to making *encoun-ters* a socially acceptable phenomenon. The emphasis was mainly on under-standing how actors perceived the situation and constructed accounts about the issues surrounding *encounters* and not primarily in ascertaining facts or veracity of the opinions espoused.

The interviews with 38 police officers[6] (33 men and 5 women) were semistructured and open-ended, generally ranging between 45 minutes to

2 hours. The sample of police interviewees consisted of a range of officers of various ranks and was selected using "quota" (various ranks); "purposeful" (those who had some experience of *encounters*); and "snowball" (being referred on to meet other officers who were considered "experts" on some of the issues being researched) sampling (see Lawrence 2000; Patton 2002; Warren 2002). The officers were assured anonymity and confidentiality and their responses were surprisingly open as was their willingness to discuss difficult ethical, moral, and legal issues.

POLICE OFFICERS' DEFINITION OF ENCOUNTERS

In the official reports and media versions, an *encounter* is described as an exchange of fire between the police and alleged criminals where the police shoot to kill in self-defense. While this was the ideal type and widely accepted meaning of the term by all those interviewed and in the media accounts, it was also generally believed that the reality of an *encounter* might be different. As a result of my own experience as an officer and a resident of the city, and during the course of this research, it became evident that the word *encounter* signified a legitimized cover-up for what were essentially police killings of alleged hard-core criminals.

All officers were asked, "What do you understand by the term *encounter*?" Their answers could be broadly classified into four types: standard, incident specific, unusual, and definitions, that elaborated on the distinctions between "genuine" and "fake" *encounters*. A standard definition is the classic, textbook definition described by one officer:

> Police *encounter* means—when the criminal has come in order to commit a crime and at that time police get definite information—and on this definite information, police lay a trap and then we try as far as possible to arrest him. But while arresting, the criminal fires in the direction of the police, to avoid his arrest, and with the intention of killing the police. At that time for our own defense, even after giving him a warning the criminal does not heed it, then there is cross firing and he gets injured and dies in the hospital, or even before that. (T 20: Inspector)

This definition includes all the requirements of a legitimate *encounter* in both the legal and moral senses, covering all aspects that could be questioned or examined in an inquiry or by a court of law. When broken down, its elements include:

1. The "criminal" had every intention of committing a crime at the point of contact.
2. The police had authentic and reliable information about the activities of the "criminal" to counteract any accusations of mistaken identity.

3. The main intention of the police in laying a trap was to arrest the "criminal."
4. The attack was initiated by the "criminal" with the twin intentions of escaping and killing the police (thus laying the grounds for self-defense on the part of the police).
5. In spite of this provocation, the police gave due warning to the "criminal," which was not heeded and the police were forced to fire back in self-defense. (The police are thus protected under section 100 of the Indian Penal Code, which refers to "when the right of private defense of the body extends to causing death.")
6. The fact that the person died in the resulting cross fire allays suspicions that there was any preplanning or targeting of the "criminal" in order to lethally shoot him.
7. The "criminal" was injured and died, either on the spot or on the way to the hospital, despite the police having made every effort to provide immediate medical assistance.

On being asked what they understood by the term *encounter*, a majority of officers (28) responded by giving different versions of this basic plot. The stories given out to the press, and the First Information Reports (FIR) lodged at the police station, largely followed this standard format of police firing in self-defense. In Mumbai, it appeared as if the repetitive *encounter* story had become part of police lore, to be accepted uncritically by all the officers. Holdaway (1983) described "folk narratives" and "keeping the tradition alive" through storytelling as part of police culture, and added that although the stories are frequently "exaggerated, highly dramatic and probably inaccurate, their power is considerable" (138–39).

The second type, an "incident specific" definition, sought to explain what an *encounter* was by describing a particular incident or experience. One officer vividly described one of the first *encounters* that he was involved in and then went on to say, "We had no idea how to conduct the case. Now *encounters* have become very regular—there is a standard procedure to be followed. That time, I did not know much, no experience, not many had any experience, but we somehow got through it. The Commissioner was very pleased. He said put this up for a medal . . . that is how I got my first Gallantry medal" (T 7: Lower Middle Management). The officer's story went on to hint that with increased experience, the police from the latter half of the 1980s onward arranged events and appearances so that they could be represented as completely justified *encounters*. The minority of officers who used stories to explain their understanding of an *encounter* lends strength to Shearing and Ericson's (1991) contention that "police references to 'experience' as the source of their knowledge, and their persistent story-telling, appear as glosses that arise from their inability to identify and articulate the rules that generate their actions" (321). Perhaps this indicates that either there are no fixed rules,

that the rules are very crude, that the officers do not think the rules and principles that actually guide police actions in *encounters* are legally or morally
acceptable, or that the rules are such that they are either unable or unwilling
to articulate them.[7] It could also be the case that these officers could not think
homothetically in terms of patterns but only ideographically in terms of individual cases. On the other hand, these officers might have used stories from
personal experience as illustrations to explain what *encounters* were to them.

Alternatively, officers may have described their own experience in
response to questions about *encounters* as a safe way out of answering what
they might have perceived as being a tricky question. Their stories almost
always involved a "genuine" *encounter* that occurred in the pursuance of
self-defense by the officer. By telling a thrilling story of their chase and hunt
of a "wanted" criminal, they relived an exciting moment in their career; and
also, by restricting their answers to personal experience, they sought to avoid
speaking about *encounters* in general terms and commenting on their perception of *encounter* experiences of others.

Yet there were some officers who deviated from this general pattern and
defined *encounters* in the third, and more "unusual" way. This indicates that
there was not total connivance on the part of all officers to cite the standard
story, but officers did improvise and, in some cases, openly discussed what
actually happened in *encounters*. These officers gave creative answers to the
question and in doing so diverged from the two categories of responses discussed above. One example of an unusual definition was "Aborted Arrest"
(T 28: Inspector), indicating that it occurred as a result of a failed arrest operation. Another example that was reminiscent of the "Dirty Harry" (Klockars
1991) talk was: "That criminal, who has been committing as many crimes as
possible by using the loopholes in the law, if he is not stopped now or jailed now,
then he will become a great burden on society. To act against him, whatever steps
we take are known as *encounters*" (T 14: Lower Middle Management).

Only 6 of the 38 officers talked about *encounters* without invoking self-
defense. These officers also directly admitted that *encounters* involved some
degree of illegality in police actions (wrongdoing in the legal but not the
moral sense).

Finally, the fourth type of definition was by way of distinguishing
between "genuine" and "fake" or "false" *encounters*. As one senior officer
explained:

> This word *encounter* has taken a big, devious meaning. *Encounter* is—it is an
> *encounter* between you and me today, ok? One-to-one . . . the way it is printed in
> the newspapers and the way the public also think is—*encounter* is where a person
> is lifted, brought and shot, and put somewhere. I call that a fake *encounter*. An
> *encounter* is one where we go for a search or a raid on a place or premises—they
> attack us, they fire at us, and we fire back at them. In the process, the chances are
> we can get injured, they can get injured. (T 24: Senior Management)

Although the meaning of the term *encounter* is somewhat negatively loaded, the addition of the label "genuine" or "fake" in routine use could only imply that the person suggesting such a distinction is actually making a value judgment about whether a particular *encounter* is considered justified or not. Thus, it is the label that demands a positive or negative response to the act—a "genuine" *encounter* is to be lauded and a "fake" one is to be criticized. As with deviance generally, "genuineness" is not a quality that lies in the act itself, but in the interaction between those who commit the act and those who respond to it (Becker 1963, 14). Perception of *encounters* differs subtly when described with the terms "justified" or "legitimate." While these terms are generally used interchangeably, here they are used to convey slightly different meanings. A "justified" *encounter* is one that is acceptable to the person making the judgment and involves subjective interpretation of the situation, which may have legal and or moral referents. On the other hand, "legitimate" means that the *encounter* is acceptable on objective criteria, which include both legal and moral elements in it.

The distinction between "fake" and "genuine" *encounters* existed in most of the interviews; officers were equally certain that their perception of what constituted a "genuine" (and by corollary, "fake") *encounter* was different from what they thought was the general public's perception of a "genuine" *encounter.*

According to officers' viewpoints, a "genuine" *encounter* had the following features:

- It involved "hard-core" criminals who had notorious criminal records. The police description of someone as a hard-core criminal was deemed to be accepted as uncontroversial and no officer even exhibited awareness that the use of such a term was problematic.
- It occurred in the presence of the public or in locations with high visibility, with no reference to the extent and seriousness of the threat posed to the lives of officers or others or the proportionality of force used by the police.
- It occurred while chasing a dangerous criminal, or while responding to an actual crime in progress.
- A significant proportion of officers expressed the view that if an *encounter* was "well managed" (e.g., if the legal requirements were fulfilled, the paperwork was in order, and no messy incriminating evidence was left unaccounted for), then the *encounter* was to be counted as "genuine" (even if they knew it wasn't). Thus, a "good story" (Chatterton 1979), even if the person offering an account may not himself regard it as true, will be accepted by colleagues and supervisors because it is what "everyone knows" and has accepted (Scott and Lyman 1968).
- The majority of officers felt that an act committed in good faith, with good intentions, in the interests of society, and that involved controlling

criminals was legitimate. Delattre (2002) echoes a similar sentiment when he claimed that even if officers have employed illegal methods in "hard" or "Dirty Harry" situations, they are neither morally tainted nor necessarily to be condemned in any subsequent legal proceedings (201).

Officers were almost unanimous in what constituted "fake" encounters, and acknowledged encounters occurred that possessed one or many of the following characteristics:

- involved a person with no criminal history;
- resulted from a mistaken identification of the person killed;
- employed blatantly excessive use of force;
- emerged from a "catch-and-kill" policy—this involved the suggestion that the police actually place a target (the criminal on whom they have chosen to focus) under surveillance, follow him for a few weeks or months, build up a case against him, he is then picked up by a unit of plain-clothed officers, kept in a safe place overnight or for a few days, and after questioning is taken to a lonely spot, late at night, and executed;
- resulted from bad faith or malice on the part of the officer concerned. There were suggestions of corruption—of certain officers being hired hands for particular gangs, taking money from one gang to eliminate members of its rivals. It was alleged that some "encounter specialists" specialized in eliminating members of certain gangs.[8] It was also suggested that under the guise of encounters some officers eliminated people against whom they had a personal grudge, or for revenge.[9]
- involved personal gain for the officer involved in the encounter (for example, ego gratification, anticipation of gallantry medals, promotions,[10] or enhanced status within the department and in society, of the kind the "encounter specialists" enjoy).

Despite their personal feelings and moral compunctions about illegalities and wrongdoings, officers generally agreed that if an encounter was well managed and/or committed in good faith for noble ends, then even if it did not fulfill any of the other conditions, it would be treated as a "genuine" encounter.

Officers tended to obfuscate the borders between what they personally considered "genuine" incidents and what as an organization, or in their official capacity, they would accept as "genuine" incidents. For example, one officer gave the standard definition of what an encounter was, and then added "That is what is said in the FIR (First Information Report) in these cases. And experts in this area will tell you that this is the only way you can justify an encounter" (T 33: Upper Middle Management). When asked if that is what actually happened in an encounter, he replied, "As I said, that is what the FIR says happened and that is what is relevant. However, in real life, many times even the basic procedures are not followed." Because the First

Information Report is legally a very important document, and the information contained in it is treated as sacrosanct by the courts in India, the police tend to be very careful while drafting it. This comment of the officer suggests that while he personally did not think that most cases were "genuine" *encounters,* good paperwork would satisfy the criteria for being "genuine" for the organization. Good paperwork here included among other things the fact that the official police story, its timing and other details are corroborated by all the relevant police documents and wireless messages. It also ensures that there are no discrepancies in the various versions of the officers and "independent witnesses" (if any) involved. A good paper trail would ensure that all the relevant procedures and follow-up reports were filed on time and without flaws or unexplained gaps. After all, any departmental inquiry, commission of inquiry, or the courts could examine the documentary evidence and paperwork submitted by the police.

It was clear that these officers were more interested in the "recipe rules" that would guide a police officer on "how to get the job done in ways that will appear acceptable to the organization" (Ericson 1982, 224).

DISCUSSION

It is important to acknowledge that there are incidents where the police have actually fired in self-defense and this has resulted in the death of an alleged criminal. I term this a *"bona fide"* encounter, to distinguish it from the terms "genuine" or "real" that are in common usage. Thus, a *"bona fide"* encounter is an "ideal type" where police use of deadly force is, in some abstract and impersonal sense, legitimate. It embodies all the elements of a classic textbook definition mentioned above (e.g., is a police response in actual self-defense after all due care and precaution has been taken and legal procedures followed). However, even *"bona fide"* encounters are deeply problematic because they are always viewed through a filter of perception. Thus, even those incidents, which in an abstract, pure sense (what accords with law, ethics, and human rights) are *"bona fide,"* may not be universally regarded as such.

There are three main interpretive frameworks through which the different meanings of the term "genuine" *encounter* can be understood. The first is the Human Rights interpretation, where an *encounter* could be considered "genuine" if it is enacted in self-defense, as a last resort, and without impinging arbitrarily on the Right to Life of the "criminal." This is an essentialist viewpoint that considers the actual circumstances of an *encounter* situation and comes closest to the *"bona fide"* encounter. In India, the National Human Rights Commission oversees matters pertaining to human rights violations by state agencies, including the police. However, this quasi-judicial body bases its findings primarily on legalistic grounds.

From a legalistic interpretation, an *encounter* would be "genuine" when it is presented as having fulfilled all the legal requirements that justify the use of deadly force by the police; and/or met the exacting standards of required paperwork; and/or which had been adjudicated as being genuine in a court of law. However, because this study is not based on observation of actual *encounters* but on perceptions of these events, it adopts a formalistic legal perspective, whereby the interpretative framework limits itself to an examination of whether the formal records show that all actions and procedures in an *encounter* are in accordance with the law.

The final interpretive framework adopts a more subjective, individualistic value judgment of whether the *encounter* is justifiable, and therefore "genuine." This framework suggests that it is for individuals to perceive a particular incident as a "genuine" *encounter,* based on subjective criteria that are relevant to the individual making the evaluation. For example, "necessary evil" may be a rational justification for some to consider an *encounter* to be "genuine," but may not appeal to others.

The three approaches outlined above use different criteria for establishing whether an *encounter* is evaluated as being "genuine." For example, what may be a "genuine" *encounter* in Human Rights framework (e.g., actually done in self-defense, after all due care and consideration has been taken by the police) may not be considered to be legally "genuine" if there are shortcomings in the paperwork or procedural formalities. Even more acutely, the research revealed that police and others often see as "genuine" *encounters* that are not *"bona fide"* in the pure and abstract sense of the term.

It could be possible that an incident which is *"bona fide"* (in every sense) may be perceived as being "genuine" by both public and police; or it may be perceived as being "genuine" by the police but "fake" by the public; or vice versa; or both the public and the police might perceive it to be "fake." An individual might perceive an *encounter* as either "genuine" or "fake" and even interchangeably depending on the interpretive framework influencing his or her decision at that particular moment. The boundaries between perceptions of the different types are fluid and permeable, diagrammatically represented as follows:

Because there is so much secrecy, lack of credible information, and even misinformation surrounding *encounters,* it becomes difficult to ascertain how particular incidents would be perceived by different audiences. This makes the task of controlling the police abuse of deadly force that much more difficult.

CONCLUSION

This chapter describes the complicated network of terms associated with the core term *encounters,* and the interrelationships that exist between these terms. The research shows that police officers' perception that their own

Figure 6-1 Perception of Encounters

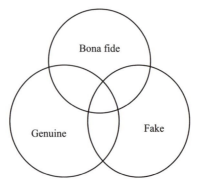

understanding of the difference between "genuine" and "fake" *encounters* is different from their understanding of the public perception of same. The confusion in the way in which particular incidents are viewed as "genuine" or not by different social actors merely serves to indicate that despite the awareness that *encounters* are questionable police conduct, there is a lot of effort put into trying to put forward reasons and scenarios for justifying police use of deadly force against alleged criminals.

This complex nature of defining the term *encounter* itself is indicative of how problematic the issue is, but when other variables are added into the perception matrix, such as the different roles of officers in *encounters* (either as participants, supervisors, or bystanders) or their diverse perceptions on the legality, morality, effectiveness, and justifications for *encounters,* the whole phenomenon becomes increasingly multi-layered and multi-faceted. Simply controlling or condemning police of use of deadly force becomes that much more difficult when there is an underlying current of apathy, acceptance, or approval, both by the public and the police, for such use.

The myriad understandings of what should be a straightforward concept implies that addressing police (ab)use or excess use of deadly force is not uncontroversial. Police officers' definitions of *encounters* do not portray a black-and-white picture, in which either a shooting incident is an illegal and unwarranted execution, or necessary and legitimate. Instead, what we have is a range of shades of grey and perception of the exact shade is subjective. The lack of social, legal, and moral consensus about acceptable levels of (ab)use of deadly force implies that ensuring police adherence to agreed-on standards of use of force is more complicated than previously envisaged.

Mano Dura: Fighting Crime, Violence, and Insecurity with an Iron Fist in Central America

Marie-Louise Glebbeek

ABSTRACT

ONE OF THE main concerns in many Central American countries is insecurity, caused by violence and criminality. Instead of a transition toward a more peaceful and secure period, many post-war Central American countries saw a rise in criminality and violence. Most citizens feel less safe than during the conflict. Whether these security concerns are real or moral panics, citizens increasingly ask their security forces for thorough policing, zero tolerance or *mano dura* strategies. However, demands for more repressive policing have put police forces in Central America in an uncomfortable position. Their doctrines, and in some cases reform strategies, postulate that they should focus on citizen security and prevention rather than on repression, while the effectiveness of repressive policing strategies can also be questioned. This chapter examines the social and political context of *mano dura* public security policies in Central America, focusing in particular on the contradictory consequences for police forces, policing, and police reform initiatives in the region.

INTRODUCTION

For the last decade, processes of reconstruction, democratization, and social and institutional reforms have been initiated in Central America. The bitter civil wars and authoritarian rule that marked many Central American countries in the 1970s and 1980s have ended and have been followed by peace agreements and democratic governments. One would expect that a new phase of

Marie-Louise Glebbeek, Utrecht University

peace, tranquility, and order would enable the countries to build solid, trust-worthy, professional governments that in their turn would restore democratic governance by providing social stability and protecting citizens' rights and the rule of law. Unfortunately, in most Central American countries this was not the case. In spite of efforts to reform their security forces, the majority of the new democratic governments saw their efforts to restore democratic gover-nance thwarted by serious security problems of rising crime and violence. The ever-increasing levels of violence and crime have become the main concern of citizens in Central America. Many citizens feel less safe now than during the brutal civil wars in which hundreds of thousands of lives were lost and many citizens disappeared. In Guatemala, community members reported that although political violence had declined, in the post-conflict context "they suf-fered more violence than during the worst years of the war" (Moser and McIl-waine 2001, 41).

This chapter will provide an overview of this thwarted process to restore order and the rule of law in Central America. There are many differences in this process between the Central American countries discussed here, but the fact that they are all equally challenged by the same phenomenon—insecurity—make the similarities telling and interesting. As will be revealed, the security forces or police forces of the Central American countries dis-cussed here—El Salvador, Guatemala, Honduras, Nicaragua, and Costa Rica—traveled different routes toward their current state of development. Four of the five countries display similarities with respect to the repressive and vio-lent involvement in the civil conflicts and authoritarian governments (that characterized Central America and most of Latin America for decades). With the return to democracy, similar efforts were also made in all four countries to demilitarize, democratize, depoliticize, and professionalize. The exception, the Costa Rican police force, also saw some reforms and suffered similar problems of distrust from its citizens.

Attention will now turn to how the rising crime, violence, and insecurity weakened the reformed institutions, such as the police, in their efforts to enforce the law and restore order (FLASCO 2007; WOLA 2006a). In most countries, citizens considered the police force incapable of providing security, they did not trust the police and the justice sector and, as will be shown, they took their own measures to protect themselves (FLASCO 2007; WOLA 2006a; WOLA 2006b). Furthermore, three consequences of this rising vio-lence and strong feelings of insecurity among the population will be dis-cussed. The reaction of several governments was to introduce the so-called *mano dura* strategies, which were tough policing policies by which it became, *inter alia*, easier to arrest suspects because their civil rights were limited or taken less seriously. The different governments relied heavily on the armed forces in order to implement such tough security policies (Schneider and Amar 2003). The other two responses are the measures citizens took to protect themselves either by relying more on private security, gated communities, and arms possessions or by relying on vigilantism and forms of popular justice (WOLA 2006b).

Assessing the consequences, this chapter concludes that none of the efforts—tough policing and the measurements citizens took—have actually resulted in a safer society and less violence. The consequences are serious. By tolerating and justifying all kinds of illegal or semi-illegal and repressive methods of fighting crime, it has led to more violence, more distrust among citizens, and even weaker and distrusted police forces. In some countries it has led to even less support for democracy.

THE HISTORY OF LAW AND ORDER IN CENTRAL AMERICA

Most of the Central American police forces recently underwent reform. In El Salvador, Guatemala, and Nicaragua this was a result of the termination of civil conflict and the signing of peace agreements in which police reforms were a central element. With the exception of Costa Rica, all four countries went through processes of demilitarization and democratization as a consequence of their authoritarian and repressive past. Police forces underwent comparable processes of demilitarization, democratization, and professionalization in order to provide substance to a new way of policing in tune with the building of democratic governance and effective law enforcement.

The Central American police forces that were created at the end of the 19th century were not created to protect the population, but rather to control them in order to carry out extensive liberal and economic reforms during that period. In Guatemala, new laws were drafted in order to satisfy the ever-increasing demand for labor, by which the indigenous population was forced to work for private land corporations. The police and the military, in particular, were assigned the task of enforcing these new labor laws and maintaining order when resistance arose. In the years that followed, the Central American countries were often ruled by despotic leaders, oligarchic families, or military leaders who all used the police as an instrument to intimidate and oppress their political rivals and the population in order to protect their own reign (Glebbeek 2003).

From the 1930s until the end of the 1970s and 1980s, almost all Central American countries were headed by military *juntas* or presidents supported by the army, with Costa Rica (where an army does not exist) as the exception. In Guatemala, El Salvador, and Nicaragua these military regimes were fiercely opposed by the guerrilla movements which came into existence in the 1960s and 1970s. Several small guerrilla movements jointed forces in a larger movement in the 1970s; in Nicaragua, the FSLN (Sandinista National Liberation Front) was created in 1979; in El Salvadore, the FMLN (Farabundo Martí Liberation Front) was created in 1980; and in Guatemala, the URNG (National Revolutionary Union of Guatemala) was established in 1982 (Kruijt 2008). Although the actual strength of these guerrilla forces differed from country to

country, they were a serious threat to the military governments and as a consequence, tough counter-insurgency strategies were initiated in each of the countries. Over the years a system of repression developed toward civil society in
which the use of terror and the dominance of fear became "normal" (Koonings
and Kruijt 1999). The police forces in these countries played a key role in those
counter-insurgency campaigns; in their repression, all strategies and tactics
were permitted: illegal detention, kidnapping, torture, rape, extra-judicial killings, disappearances, etc.

POLICE REFORM IN CENTRAL AMERICA

The police forces that emerged from the Central American civil wars had a
reputation of being among the most repressive, violent, feared, and corrupt
institutions within their societies, and in El Salvador and Guatemala reforming
these institutions was an essential part of the peace accords that were signed.[1]
In Nicaragua, where police reform was not part of a negotiated settlement,
reforms were initiated as a result of the Sandinista Victory over the Somoza
dictatorship in 1979. With the following defeat of the Sandinistas in the 1990
elections, the incoming government of the United Nicaraguan Opposition
(UNO) made further reforms possible in an effort to "de-Sandinize" the Nicaraguan police (WOLA 1995).

   In El Salvador, the peace accords called for the abolition of the three
existing security forces and the creation of a new National Civilian Police
force (PNC). Postulated by the accord, 20% of the PNC was to be formed by
members of the former militarized National Police, 20% from the demobilized
guerrilla movement (FMLN), and 60% were new recruits. In this way a more-
or-less "new body," with a new organizational structure, a new doctrine, new
officers, and new training mechanisms was created. It operated under the aus-
pices of the Ministry of Interior and Public Security which would be more in
tune with democratic governance and democratic policing.[2]

   In neighboring Guatemala, a "new" force, with the same name, National
Civilian Police (PNC), was created as a result of the September and December
1996 signed peace agreements. In accordance to the agreements, the new
PNC would fall under authority of the Minister of Interior and would be the
only competent armed police force at the national level; they would serve to
protect and guarantee the rights and freedom of individuals; they would prevent, investigate, and combat crime, and would maintain order and internal security. One of the main objectives of the reform and consequent constitutional
reform was to remove responsibility for internal security from the military
and to hand it over to the PNC in order to build a professional, trustworthy
police force (Glebbeek 2003). Unfortunately, contrary to El Salvador, Guatemala did not place restraints on the entrance of PNC members, resulting in
over 90% of members from the old force moving into the new force,

including the entire police leadership. This negatively affected the quality and also the credibility of the PNC.

Guatemala and El Salvador initiated intensive police reforms, as did Nicaragua, Honduras, and Costa Rica, although in the latter group of countries the reforms were less comprehensive. When the Sandinistas seized power in 1979 in Nicaragua, one of their first actions was to dissolve the National Guard and to create a new state security force out of the ranks of their combatants and supporters. The police and military functions were clearly separated and the new Sandinista Police Force operated under the Ministry of Interior. While human rights abuses fell in the first years of the new force, complaints were heard that the police were overtly politicized and were still being used as an instrument to stifle internal political dissent (WOLA 1995). After the 1990 elections, the government of Violeta Chamorro initiated a second phase of reforms by changing the name of the police force to *Policia Nacional* and initiating the enforcement of a new law in 1992, followed by a constitutional reform in 1995 which defined the National Police as an armed civil institution, apolitical, impartial, and deliberative (Gómez 2005). From the 1990s until 2004 the police leadership changed several times. These were important years to recuperate the National Police, restoring trust in a police institution capable of adjusting to a new national reality (Lara 2006).

Changes to the National Police force in Honduras were stressed in order to diminish illegal detentions and human rights violations (UNDP 2006). In 1993, the police were formally separated from the military; however, as shown in the case of Guatemala, most police officers were "simply transferred to the new civilian force, without any serious review of their record, without a substantial influx of new members, and without substantial re-training" (WOLA 2006a, 9).

Costa Rica's police force has not experienced problems on a similar scale. Its police force, compared to the other forces in Central America, is one of the most professional and the country is considered the safest.[3] The UNDP (2005), however, has identified in its Human Development Report on Costa Rica, some organizational problems, which prevent the police from fulfilling its obligations. These challenges include deficient coordination of the entire police community, lack of national policy on citizen security, disparities in police corps training, lack of institutional support from some police corps, and deficient budgets (UNDP 2005). More seriously, Costa Rican citizens feel that state security mechanisms do not provide adequate protection. A National Survey on Citizen Security in 2005 revealed that almost 87% of the interviewees held the police partially responsible for the insecurity in the country, and almost half (49%) believed they were highly responsible (UNDP 2005).

VIOLENCE, CRIME, AND INSECURITY IN CENTRAL AMERICA

Most Central American countries have experienced an extremely violent past. In the civil conflicts of Guatemala, El Salvador, and Nicaragua, hundreds of thousands of people were killed. Many of the citizens of these countries believe, however, that current violence levels, crime and insecurity are worse than during the violent civil wars. Statistics on violence and crime seem to confirm this perception. The rise in criminality and violence can be attributed to a number of factors, such as certain economic policies that increased unemployment, economic hardship, inequality, urbanization, legacies of conflict, the loosening of authoritarian controls, the proliferation of arms and demobilized members of armed groups, and demographic factors (Glebbeek 2003; Perez 2003).

Homicide rates have risen in Guatemala, Honduras, and El Salvador and are around 45 murders for every 100,000 inhabitants, the highest within Latin America (Alas and Argueta 2007). Similarly, rates of robbery and assaults have risen (WOLA 2006b). The Inter-American Development Bank stated in May 2006 that in Guatemala the annual homicide rate, as measured by the number of homicides for every 100,000 inhabitants per year, rose by one-third between 1996 and 2005 to a level of 36.6. In metropolitan Guatemala City, which is home to 15% of the country's population, the rate stood at 103 in 2005. The Honduran General Direction of Criminal Investigation (DGIC) reported a 2007 homicide rate of 49.9 for every 100,000 inhabitants (UNAH 2008). According to estimates of the National Civil Police, El Salvador's 2005 crime statistics showed 55 murders for every 100,000 inhabitants (Macías and Alas 2007).[4]

Even in Central American countries with comparatively low incidents of violent crime, such as Costa Rica, citizens feel very unsafe. In all Central American countries, large majorities (over 85 out of 100) believe that crime is a threat to the country's well-being (Cullell and Bixby 2006). Regardless of whether the perceptions are realistic, they do influence the whereabouts of people, levels of freedom, stigmatization of certain groups in society, as well as substantially lowering interpersonal trust, including trust in state institutions such as the police, the government, and ultimately the democratic political system.

In most Central American countries the credibility and trust in the police is very low. As has already been seen, a majority of citizens in Costa Rica hold the police responsible for the insecurity in the country. However, they do not feel threatened by their presence. In Honduras, people do feel threatened by the institution that should protect them which is considered corrupt and repressive (UNDP 2006). Consequently, trust in the police fell from 57% in 2004 to 50% in 2006 among the respondents participating in a survey carried out by the Latin American Public Security Opinion Project (LAPOP) (Alas and Argueta 2007). In El Salvador, in a similar survey carried out by LAPOP, a majority of the respondents (54.9%) were of the opinion that the police are participating in criminal activities against a minority that believed the police did their job by protecting citizens (Macías and Alas 2007). In Guatemala, where trust in the police fell dramatically in 2006 after a scandal which involved the PNC in the murder of three El Salvadorian congressmen, similar trends are also visible.

Low levels of trust and credibility in state institutions and widespread perceptions of insecurity have created a vacuum that in most countries has been filled with alternative forms of protection. In many cases this has led to social instability, more violence, and the weakening of state institutions to maintain order. Moreover, it has increased the demand for authorities to take stronger actions against criminals, even if this means that they should act outside the law.

GOVERNMENT AND CITIZEN RESPONSES TO RISING CRIME

At least three reactions can be observed in Central America as a consequence of the increasing violence. First, tougher or repressive security policies (*mano dura* policies) have been introduced in all countries and penalties have increased. Many politicians have used a discourse of *mano dura* in their election campaigns. Second, citizens are increasingly relying on private security, the purchasing of firearms, and spending more money on security measures such as alarms, fences, and guards (Chinchilla 2003). Third, citizens who cannot afford to hire private security or to spend money on security measures tend to rely on certain forms of popular justice, creating their own vigilante groups by taking the law into their own hands, as we will later see for example through the lynchings in Guatemala.

In 2002, President Maduro of Honduras pioneered the *mano dura* or zero tolerance policy, which promised to make the country safe through repressive force. Soon the presidents of El Salvador and Guatemala followed and introduced similar iron-fist policies to fight crime in their respective countries. Most of these *mano dura*, or as they were called in El Salvador *super mano dura*, were directed toward youth gangs that were held responsible for the majority of the crime in Central America. As a result, the Penal Procedural code in Honduras (in particular Article 332) was reformed, after which "illicit association" with gangs was prohibited. Gangs or other groups "that associate with the permanent goal of executing any act constituting a crime" could be fined or arrested (NACLA 2007, 28). In reality, the appearance of youths with tattoos, baggy pants, and T-shirts was enough to consider them gang members and they were consequently arrested without any evidence that a crime had been committed.

While such zero tolerance strategies have been carefully designed and might have been arguably successful in certain countries, such as the United States, Latin American police forces often lack adequate funding and resources to implement comprehensive zero tolerance strategies (Dammert and Malone 2006). As a result, *mano dura* policies in Latin America can and have deteriorated into a repressive and militarized style of fighting crime, often associated with illegal detentions, severe punishment for minor offences, military style occupations, and collective punishment of entire neighborhoods. The *mano dura* strategies go far beyond what is considered "tough on crime" or "tough policing" in the United States, mainly because the Latin American police forces lack the police reforms and the infrastructure that accompanied the implementation of these policies in that country (Dammert and Malone 2006).

There are at least three areas in which these *mano dura* policies have undermined the previously initiated police reforms in Central America (WOLA 2006a). First, they removed the boundaries between the police and the military. In Honduras, El Salvador, and Guatemala, the *mano dura* policies allowed for combined military and police patrols, justifying the role of the army in civil security as a matter of "temporary emergency" (NACLA 2007; WOLA 2006a). However, despite the temporary character, the military, which has a long-term involvement in citizens' security (dating back to 1996 in El Salvador and Guatemala; Glebbeek 2003), has not returned to the barracks and seldom does. With this involvement of the military in citizens' security in all three countries, important steps intended to separate the police and the military functions that had been made were annulled, such as the creation of the Ministry of Security in Honduras in 1998 and the separation of powers in the peace accords of Guatemala and El Salvador.

Second, the *mano dura* policies increased the arbitrary authority of the police by allowing them to carry out arrests based on vague criteria, as described earlier. Personal judgment and prejudice can lead to arrests, not based on clear evidentiary standards (WOLA 2006a).

Finally, the "war on gangs" and the new powers given to police have led to a climate in which extrajudicial killings, or so-called "social cleansings" of suspected criminals (especially gang members), are tolerated by the State and supported by the population. In Honduras, about 2,000 youths have died since *mano dura* was adopted. In 2002, the UN Special Rapporteur on Extrajudicial, Arbitrary, and Summary Executions issued a report which stated that not only extrajudicial executions were taking place, but that the government security forces were involved in covering up their involvement in some of the summary killings of youth and children, and that some of the killings involved police (WOLA 2006b).

Another consequence of the increased crime, violence, and insecurity in Central America is that citizens increasingly try to protect themselves. More and more gated communities have arisen in Central America. Middle- and upper- class neighborhoods are now separated from the "common" population with high walls and security guards. Private security firms are mushrooming and outnumber the personnel of police forces. In Honduras, there are some 10,000 national police members and it is estimated that there are 30,000 private security guards. This ratio is similar in Guatemala and El Salvador (WOLA 2006b). These private security companies operate virtually without any control; many of their members have been part of notorious security forces during the civil wars and were fired due to serious human rights violations and crimes committed (Glebbeek 2003).

In most Central American countries, where large parts of their population live in poverty and the distribution of wealth and land are extremely unequal, the majority of its citizens can not afford such measures. It becomes clear from Central American opinion polls that the majority of the population experience a high sense of insecurity and a considerable lack of institutional response after repressive measures are proposed, supported, and even carried out that confront public insecurity (Chinchilla 2003).

RESULTS AND CONSEQUENCES OF *MANO DURA*

With respect to the results of the iron-fist or *mano dura* policies one can be very brief. None of the Central American countries have reported that these policies have led to a decrease in crime. On the contrary, when compared to the year that *mano dura* approaches were systematically implemented in Honduras, El Salvador, and Guatemala in 2003, overall crime levels increased (WOLA 2006a). The feelings of insecurity in many other Central American countries have also not decreased following the implementation of *mano dura*. Citizens do not believe that police forces and the justice system are capable of solving problems and many consider those institutions to be a threat to security (Arriagada and Godoy 1999). In Honduras, the policy's only visible effect is "the saturation of the country's jail to the point of collapse" (NACLA 2007; UNDP 2006). It has also been argued that youth gangs in Central America have not been weakened by *mano dura*, but have become more clandestine and more organized (WOLA 2006a).

The consequences, however, are clear. *Mano dura* approaches have led to an acceptance and tolerance toward illegal and repressive violence, such as extrajudicial killings and lynchings, which undermines the rule of law and the authority of the state. In Guatemala alone there were 240 people killed and 723 injured by lynchings between 1996 and 2002 (MINUGUA 2003). *Mano dura* feeds the culture of violence that has existed in many Central American countries since the end of the civil wars. High levels of violence and insecurity affect democracies, especially emerging ones. The support of illegal and repressive alternatives has put the exercise of civil liberties and rights of democracy at risk (Macías and Alas 2007). In Honduras, a failing *mano dura* effort has led to a drop in support of democracy between 2003 and 2004 and a large majority of people interviewed (70%) in a citizens poll stated that they do not care if a government is undemocratic as long as it solves the economic problems (UNDP 2006). In Guatemala and El Salvador similar sentiments have been echoed. A slight majority in those countries would approve a government overthrow by the military under conditions of high crime (Macías and Alas 2007).

High levels of insecurity and repressive measures to restore security undermine the ability of police forces to maintain order and stability and it furthermore sets the police reform processes in Central America back a step. *Mano dura,* or iron-fist strategies and policies, are not the solution to end the current rising crime and violence that brings instability to Central America. Obviously, any reactionary response to insecurity will never be able to resolve it, if there are no efforts made to respond to the underlying causes of this insecurity. In Central America, these causes are diverse, complex, and very challenging for the new and young democratic governments. Being tough on crime or implementing *mano dura* policies should therefore be supplemented with policies that focus on prevention and most importantly attempt to ameliorate the often harsh and sometimes hopeless conditions in which the majority of the Central American citizens, especially the youth, live (e.g., poverty, inequality, and unemployment).

There have been some initiatives to combine *mano dura* strategies with more proactive strategies in Guatemala and Nicaragua. In Guatemala's Villa Nueva, a neighborhood with a lot of gang violence, soccer games between the police and members of youth gangs were organized in an effort to build trust between them (Glebbeek 2009). In a similar neighborhood in Nicaragua, the police made an effort to become familiar with every individual gang member in the neighborhood, and a special program was started to help the gang members leave the gang and integrate back into society. Unfortunately, these activities were often the initiatives of individual police officers or a certain group of officers and were not supported across the institution. In Nicaragua, gang members were safe in one particular neighborhood, but were not at all safe in another (ERIC et al. 2004). In Guatemala, the police played soccer during the day with the same gang members they forcefully hunted down during the night. *Mano dura* strategies have not been effective and, as the examples of Guatemala and Nicaragua show, a combination of enforcement and prevention strategies has also been difficult to establish.

Systemic Police Violence in Brazil

Martha K. Huggins

ABSTRACT

FOCUSING ON POLICE violence in its most lethal form of homicide, a combination of official and unofficial statistics indicate that on-duty Brazilian police are responsible for up to 70% of all civilian murders in Brazil. Such figures may even underestimate the extent of lethal violence by off-duty Brazilian police. This chapter explores four sources of lethal violence by Brazilian police: extreme societal inequality that encourages and excuses it; pervasive societal violence that justifies and hides it; organizational institutionalization that enables and legitimizes it; and, a public-private social control fusion that fosters and conceals lethal police violence. Without assigning particular weight to any of these four factors, this chapter uses original and secondary research on police violence in Brazil to illustrate the difficulties with separating police claims about lethal shootings from emerging data to assess such claims. The conclusion explores how the four conditions of promoting, hiding, legitimizing, and justifying lethal police violence intersect to foster such violence systemically.

This chapter is complicated by a methodological reporting issue that leads to a terminological problem: police killings of civilians in Brazil are not recorded by police organizations as a "homicide,"[1] based on the *a priori* assumption that they are not homicides. Rather, lethal shootings by police are registered as having used "legitimate force" against a "criminal's threatening actions," a designation that is almost never investigated. For reasons discussed shortly, this chapter will therefore refer to lethal violence by Brazilian police as "killings," except when evidenced by an empirical case, which is the subject of this chapter's section on "Assessing Evidence," that investigates even the possibility of criminal homicide.

Martha K. Huggins, Tulane University

SOCIETAL INEQUALITY

Extreme societal inequality encourages and excuses police violence. Brazil, a formally democratic country of 196 million, has the world's fourth highest level of inequality.[2] The richest 10% of the population is 85 times wealthier than the poorest 10%. Among Brazil's poor, a sizeable proportion make substandard wages in their formal-sector employment, and supplement this by working in Brazil's immense "informal"[3] sector. Now housing 40% of Brazil's money earners, those who are exclusively informal-sector workers live the most fragile economic lives of all. Among Brazil's poor, rank-and-file police often supplement their own extraordinarily low regular salaries[4] by moonlighting illegally as private rent-a-cops, with their superiors' knowledge and acceptance. Police officers that work undercover with gangs and in drug interventions far too frequently end up in this illegal informal-sector as gang enforcers, militia "soldiers," or in death squads. Such "off-duty" police work—representing what some might call a "privatization" of Brazilian policing (Huggins 2000b; Huggins and MacTurk 2000)—is in fact a countrywide phenomenon, rather than an exception. Labeling this as a "multi-lateralization" of policing, Bayley and Shearing (2001) argue that with such an interface, "the very concept of government, technically the state . . . [becomes] problematic [with the transfer] of security to nongovernmental groups" (39). Yet, as this chapter will continue to show, police connections with various levels of government remain even as police become more privatized.

However this process may be labeled, citizen killings by Brazilian on-duty police are *de facto* legitimized by where a Brazilian lives, how much security and safety are violated, and where within a city they "should" and "should not" be. Dwelling space and type of security services ipso facto designate a person's "honesty" or "criminality." In urban Brazil, where gated upper-class white communities sit side-by-side with poor, dark-skinned slum communities, richer Brazilians hire private rent-a-cops to keep the unwanted out; the poor are "kept in their places" by public police invasions of their dwelling spaces[5] (Caldeira 2000; Hinton 2006; Husain 2007; Korda 2006; Torres et al. 2002; Weiss-Laxer 2006). Being visibly and negatively associated with public police and informal social control agents, such as militia, gang enforcers, and death squads, contributes to defining the poor and where they live as "criminal." In other words, the place of residence and level of security as consumption commodities shape a group's image as "friend" or "foe" (Loader 1999, 381; see also Allston 2008; Caldeira 2000; Huggins and Mesquita 1999).

It follows that the "right" to be in some social spaces and to be excluded from others is also assigned *ipso facto* according to a person's wealth or poverty and age and color. Police, both public and private, manage urban social spaces on the assumption that some Brazilians—especially poor dark males—are "matter out of place," and are therefore "criminals" (see especially

Scheper-Hughes and Hoffman 1994; Huggins 2008; Korda 2006; Weiss-Laxer 2006). Thus, whether due to a person's dwelling location, the kind of social control associated with it, or where they "should" or "should not" be, some Brazilians are labeled as "criminal" and are treated as such by police.

PERVASIVE SOCIETAL VIOLENCE

Pervasive societal violence justifies and hides police lethal violence. One of the most compelling outcomes of Brazil's profound social class and color inequalities is homicide. In the words of Jayme Benvenuto, coordinator of the Recife/Olinda human rights group GAJOP (Colitt), "Violence is the price Brazil pays for social injustice." In practical terms, one more homicide inside poor urban spaces and of certain kinds of people, particularly poor, male youth of color, does not usually attract much negative attention.

Dubbed one of the world's most violent countries, Brazil continues to live up to this designation. With 50,000 homicides annually and a country-wide homicide rate of 28.5 per 100,000[6] (Ramos), Brazil's homicide rate is more than four times that of the United States; it is second highest in Latin America (after Colombia), and fifth highest in the world (after Guatemala, El Salvador, Colombia, and Jamaica) (Buvinic, Morrison and Shifter; U.S. Department of State 2008). Brazil's homicide rate is on a par with nations undergoing civil war (Dantas Mota 2004).

Sixty percent of all *recorded* homicides[7] in Brazil are urban (Soares Filho et al. 2007), but inside Brazil's largest cities[8] homicide rates are highest in slums (*favelas*) and lowest in more affluent areas. For example, Rio de Janeiro's more affluent neighborhoods of Copacabana, Ipanema, and Leblon each had a 2004 homicide rate of five per 100,000, while Rio de Janeiro's poorest neighborhoods of Vigário Geral, Parada de Lucas, and the Zone Oueste, had homicide rates exceeding 80 per 100,000 (Ramos 2005). This pattern is repeated in São Paulo City, where in 2004, Jardim Ângela (a poor neighborhood in the city's south zone) had a homicide rate of 123 per 100,000, in contrast to São Paulo City's middle-class Moema district (only a few kilometers from Jardim Angela) where the homicide rate was three per 100,000 (Amnesty International 2005). Those in São Paulo City's poverty-stricken Morumbi district were 18 times more likely to be murdered than their fellow impoverished citizens in the city's less sharply stratified Jardim Paulista district (*Estado* 1997).[9]

According to UNESCO (Amnesty International 2005), males constitute 93% of all homicide victims in Brazil. Why not females? Huggins and Mesquita (1999) point out that poor females are much less likely to be killed by strangers—police on and off duty, for example—and more likely to be victims of domestic violence. Poor females are less likely to live and work on the street and more likely to live and work inside a house or establishment as cleaners, caregivers, and sex workers, which makes them more vulnerable than males to sexual victimization and to other forms of domestic violence, including murder by fellow family members and acquaintances (see also Moser and van Bronkhorst 1999).

It is especially risky to be an adolescent or young adult male in Brazil (Barradas, de Almeida and de Moraes 1999). In some Brazilian cities, youths (ages 15 to 24) have homicide rates that exceed 150 per 100,000 (Ramos). For example, in 1997 in northeastern Recife City, youth murder rates were 207.7 per 100,000 compared to the city's rate of 90. In Rio de Janeiro, youth homicide rates were 190 per 100,000, and in São Paulo City, the rates were 155. Rio's and São Paulo's youth homicide rates were 200% above each city's gross homicide rate at the time (*Folha* 1998). All of these youth murder rates were more than 500% higher than for the Brazilian population as a whole (*Folha* 1998).

Researchers maintain that a black Brazilian's ("*negros*") chance of death by homicide is ten times that of a white Brazilian. According to Amnesty International (2005), in 2002 among all known homicides in Brazil, young black Brazilians constituted 63% of recorded homicides (11,308 of 17,900 overall).[10] In 2001, across Brazil the homicide rate for (largely poor) white men was of 102.3 per 100,000, itself very high, but for young black men, the rate doubles to 218.5 murder victims for every 100,000, a risk comparable to living in a country in civil war. Most of these latter homicide victims lived in shantytowns on the urban periphery or impoverished sections of big cities (Dreamscanbe Foundation; see also Ramos 2005; Gawryszewsk and Costa 2005; *Principios*). Color in Brazil is very closely associated with income and probability of living in a *favela,* where the darkest Brazilians predominate and where homicides are most prevalent.[11] In Rio de Janeiro, homicides are six times higher in slums than in non-slum areas. The heavy-assault policing carried out in slums by Militarized Police against Brazilians profiled as dangerous goes a long way toward explaining police-perpetrated deaths and injuries in the slums of Brazil.

Profiled as criminal, poor urban blacks are frequently the subjects of shoot-first-ask-later police repression, an outcome for which there is seldom citizen outrage. Not surprisingly, a 1997 survey showed that Brazilian blacks were the only color group to assert that they were more afraid of the police than criminals. Nearly half (47%) of all blacks in that survey had been searched by the police, compared to one-third of whites (34%). A 1997 São Paulo poll (Cano), found that only 6% of whites, compared to 14% of blacks, claimed to have been physically assaulted by a policeman.

POLICE VIOLENCE NORMALIZED AND INSTITUTIONALIZED

The third premise of this chapter, that police organizational institutionalization enables and legitimizes police use of lethal force, develops from the finding that in Brazil, a high proportion of all citizen homicides are carried out by on-duty police. In 1996, Paul Chevigny (1996) described Brazil as having one of the worst records of urban police violence in the Americas (see also Reuters 1997). Yet, then as well as now, not all Brazilian police organizations are equally complicit in citizen deaths. Between Brazil's two main state-level police forces, the *Policia Militar* (Militarized Police) (78% of all state police forces [McCaulay 2002]) and the *Policia Civil* (civil police), the uniformed Militarized Police (PM) commit the majority of citizen killings, as Huggins and colleagues (2002) and Ahnan (2007) have illustrated. Looking at the differences between on-duty citizen killings by Civil and Militarized Police across Brazil at the millennium, of the 1,442 known police murders of civilians, 1,365 (95%) were committed by Militarized Police and 77 (5%) by Brazil's *Policia Civil* (Cano 2003).[12] Huggins, Haritos-Fatouros, and Zimbardo (2002) found that Brazil's Civil Police are more likely to torture than murder, given their role as investigative "judicial police" assigned to post-crime interrogations.

The ordinary and normal nature of police murders of civilians (the fact that they continue to occur, without public outcry and without regular investigation and punishment)[13] helps to normalize them. Six other factors internal to police organizational operations also foster an acceptance of police killings, beginning with *violence equals "success."* The Brazilian NGO Global Justice (2004) reported in its 2003 *Human Rights in Brazil Annual Report* that, "Often police violence is encouraged by state governments as a sign of effective policing" (42). In the words of São Paulo State's Secretary of Public Security, "Confrontations with criminals [are] related to an increase in the [police] effectiveness in the streets" (Global Justice 2003, 42).[14] Second, *invisible murders* occur when the police reduce public knowledge about police killings of civilians by failing to include them in homicide statistics. This renders such murders something other than "criminal homicide." *Legitimate murder,* on the other hand, includes the Militarized Police institution's de facto policy of defining civilian murders as the result of a guilty person's "resistance to police authority." This transforms "victims" into "perpetrators" through a procedure adopted "by [Brazilian] police during the 1990s and [while] not mandated by law, [has] now [become] standard [police] practice across Brazil" (Alston 2008, 11). "Resistance followed by death" homicides are neither recorded nor investigated by police.

In the unlikely event that such murders are investigated, Civil Police control each state's forensic "morgues" (Instituto de Medicina Legal, or IML) making it possible for cooperating Civil Police officers to hide information that could transform a police shooting into a homicide. This defines *intra-police cooperation.* Further, if the lethal actions of Militarized Police are investigated in the end, a military tribunal adjudges their actions, providing a type of "in-house" secrecy and possible insider support for lethal actions. Finally, *war-like conditions* means that the militarized style of policing—SWAT raids on slums by heavily armed Militarized Police, often in tank-like assault vehicles—frames multiple citizen injuries and deaths as "casualties of war." The consideration that "in war, those who die are not innocent,"[15] apparently resonates with the military officials judging the lethal outcomes of Militarized Police slum raids[16] (see McCaulay 2002).

Assessing Evidence

Academic researchers and human rights organizations continue to explore police claims that their civilian killings: 1) are not homicides and thus should not be included in homicide statistics; 2) occurred because of a guilty person's resistance to authority; and 3) resulted from shoot-outs associated with a state of war. Finding that the dead speak better than secondary police statistics, Brazilian and other researchers count the number of bullets in bodies, note the physical locations of bullets, record the age and color of victims, and the location of the killing (e.g., as inside or outside a slum).

Pointing to the failure of Brazilian police organizations to include police murders of civilians in their homicide statistics, Alston (2008) cites São Paulo City, where in May 2006 a city-wide police crackdown on gang threats and violence resulted in police killing 124 suspected gang members and alleged criminals. By labeling such deaths "resistance followed by death," these homicides were neither recorded nor investigated by police. Academic research for São Paulo City has illustrated that police killings of civilians from 2005 to 2008 increased as São Paulo City's official homicide rate was declining. By 2007 in São Paulo City, on-duty police (largely Militarized Police) were killing on average one person a day (Alston 2008), a fact obscured by official police statistics.

Alston (2008) cites a Rio de Janeiro police raid that resulted in 19 civilian murders. Fourteen of these victims had twenty-five gunshot wounds from the rear, six more had additional head and face gunshot wounds, and five had been shot at point-blank range after having been subdued. Research by the Rio de Janeiro NGO Institute for Religious Studies (ISER) has discovered that up to a quarter of citizen killings by Rio de Janeiro police are execution-style, meaning after the victim is immobilized, police shot the individual at point-blank range (U.S. Department of State 1999). Police usually claim that these shootings resulted from resistance followed by death.

Turning the tables on police assertions that civilian deaths result from resistance to police during a citizen-initiated "shoot-out," academics have developed a formula for exploring this claim. A police shooting takes the form of an execution, rather than necessitated by civilian aggression against police, when: 1) after immobilizing an alleged criminal, police continue to shoot ("immobilization/'over-kill' ratio"); 2) police kill more people than they injure ("lethality ratio"); 3) more civilians are killed than police ("citizen-police death ratio"); 4) those civilians killed are largely despised "others"—a recognizable "underclass"—using a "representational lethality index" (deaths to injuries of "outsiders" in relation to majority actors). These

indexes can be used to suggest "homicidal profiling."[17] All primary data findings from these "execution formulas" can then be compared to official statistics to derive yet another finding—the differences between officially reported
homicides and those committed by police and not reported ("gray-area police
homicides").

Pointing to the "immobilization/over-kill ratio," Cano (1997) has demonstrated that in at least half of Rio de Janeiro slum neighborhood killings, the
victim had four or more bullet wounds—the majority of these in the shoul-
ders, chest, and head, where death would very likely follow.[18] In fact, according to Cano's (1997) Rio de Janeiro data, 65% of the victims of police deadly
force in Rio during 1996 were hit from behind, suggesting that they had been
fired at while fleeing police rather than confronting them. Allston (2008)
reports for São Paulo indicate that, among 124 deaths in one confrontation
between police and gangs, "multiple shots [had been] fired from a close distance, [with] a high proportion of shots to the [alleged perpetrator's] head and
vital organs . . . indicating that the victim was kneeling or lying [down] when
shot.' In this particular 'shoot-out,' "no police were killed . . ." (12). The vast
majority of citizen murders by Brazilian police exceeded even the "shoot-to-
kill" violence of the 1999 Amadou Diallo killing by four New York City
policemen.

Using the "lethality ratio," Chevigny (1996) argues that if police kill
more than they injure, or if the precision of shots increases suddenly, then lethal shots may have been fired deliberately. Employing a "lethality ratio" of
citizen deaths to injuries, Cano (1997) has shown that, of those hit by Rio de
Janeiro police gunfire, approximately 70% died—a "lethality index" of 2.3 to
1 (942 killed and 410 injured), contrasting with a U.S. urban lethality rate of
less than one. Such measures of "one-sided victimization" call into question
that citizen shootings by police resulted from a "shoot-out."

During alleged "shoot-outs" when few or no police are wounded or
killed ("one-sided victimization"), questions arise about police claims about a
shoot-out. As Cano (1997) has shown, Rio de Janeiro police are eight times
more likely to kill alleged perpetrators than to be killed themselves. Employing these data to explore the possibility of "homicidal profiling," Cano discovered in Rio de Janeiro that police deaths are less common in non-slum
areas (the whiter neighborhoods of more privileged social classes) than in
slum areas (where poorer and darker populations live) (*Folha* 1999a). One
Rio police officer is killed for every 35 deadly-force shootings in non-slum
areas compared to one officer for every 75 police shootings in Rio slums
(Cano 1997; see also Cano and Santos 2001).

Comparing citizen killings by Brazilian police to rates from large U.S.
cities reveals the true extent of the problem. New York City's annual average
for that period was 23 (*New York Times* 2000; Kacieniewski 1998). Between
1989 and 1992 in Washington, DC, police killings of citizens ranged between
four (1989) and seven annually (1990 and 1992), increasing to sixteen in

1995, and then decreasing abruptly to six in 1996[19] (Leen et al. 1998). At the average annual rate that Washington, DC and New York City police kill citizens,[20] it would take approximately 50 years for Washington and 25 years for New York to have as many citizens killed as São Paulo police murdered just in 1999. As for Rio de Janeiro, police there kill almost as many citizens annually as all police forces in the United States combined, although Rio's population is five-and-a-half million and the U.S. population is over 250 million (Cano 1997).

PUBLIC AND PRIVATE CONTROL: A FUSION

This chapter's fourth premise begins with the assertion that the boundaries between formal and informal policing in Brazil are highly porous. In the first place, Brazil's on-duty police live and work in a lucrative opportunity structure of drug and gun sales. In 1996, Brazil was the second largest international market for firearms in the world, after the United States (Walsh 1999). In the process of work, whether in drug interdiction or in quashing gun tracking, some police devolve into extorting gang members, along the way becoming full-time gang affiliates with access to money from drugs and guns. Likewise, through on-duty surveillance of community militia, opportunities present themselves to extort and then join these groups or become part of a death squad, in both cases illustrating how killing turns lucrative.

A defining feature of privatized social control across Brazil is its emergence from formal police work and its ongoing attachment to the formal police system (see Huggins 1991; Huggins 1997; Huggins 2000a; Huggins, Haritos-Fatouros, and Zimbardo 2002). Such a working interface is very likely one factor in creating what Bayley and Shearing (2001) labeled as police "multi-lateralization." Philip Allston (2008), pointing to the ebb and flow between on- and off-duty police and gangs, reported that, in one [Rio de Janeiro] *favela*, every weekend police would come to the community to collect money from the traffickers (23). The leader of each gang generally has a number of "directors" in charge of the different types of trafficked drugs. The police would come to negotiate with "directors" (who in turn negotiate with their leader) on payments (to police). Refusals to pay the police are met with death threats and murder. The weapons and drugs confiscated by police are regularly fed back into the trafficking system. Police "arrest" traffickers for the purposes of making money—demanding a bribe in return for the criminal's freedom. When the gangs do not have sufficient funds to pay for one of their members, the gangs collect small sums from each resident to pay the police fee.

This public-private social control fusion conceals the systemic nature of police corruption and the lethal police violence frequently associated with it. At most, those police exposed for their illegalities can be passed off as atypically "bad apples." On a systemic level, as we have seen, such police illegalities, including citizen killings, are not reported and recorded as police-related, even though on-duty police are indirectly involved, quite often with police officials' knowledge and permission. Using data from interviews with Brazilian justice and police officials, Allston (2008) connected Brazilian police to militia, defined as "groups composed of police, ex-police, fire fighters, prison guards, and private citizens, who attempt to take over specific geographical areas, and engage in extra-state policing" (23). Murders perpetrated by militia and the police who make them up, of course, almost never make it into statistics on police homicides.

Death squads, according to Allston (2008), "are . . . formed by police and others whose purpose is to kill, primarily for profit" (25). Huggins also documented the connections between death squads, Brazilian justice officials, and police (1991; 1997; 2000a), including disclosing some of the fees derived from murders. Allston's (2008) newer data demonstrate that at the millennium in Pernambuco state, "hired killers earn 1,000 to 5,000 *Reais* per killing"—between 500 USD and 2,500 USD for each contract murder (42). Given officers' low pay and a work schedule of 24 hours on duty and three days off, there are financial pressures and ample opportunities for moonlighting off-duty. Police officials often know that such illegal work is going on and even encourage it as a way to increase rank-and-file incomes without asking the state to raise their poverty-level wages.

Such on- and off-duty porosity begs an important question for researchers: When a Militarized Policeman, with the encouragement and acceptance of his superior, works off duty illegally in private policing, is he fully detached from the police organization? This question is relevant because the lethal violence of such police is far from exceptional. In 1999, São Paulo State Militarized Police, mostly off duty in private security work, experienced an 82% increase in citizen killings over the previous year. As for São Paulo Civil Police, they killed 24 citizens in the last quarter of 1999, one-half by off-duty officers—a 140% increase of off-duty Civil Police killings over the same period in 1998 (*Folha* 1999b).

This chapter argues that understanding lethal violence by Brazilian police requires explicitly recognizing the porous boundaries between on- and off-duty policing in Brazil. Such inclusion will highlight the range of powerful actors involved in police violence and suggest the dynamics of a policeman's movement into quasi- and fully off-duty lethal violence, including how one police role feeds the other in nurturing violence.

CONCEPTUALIZING POLICE VIOLENCE: SYSTEMIC

This chapter has identified four factors related to lethal violence by Brazilian police. *Extreme societal inequality* encourages and excuses lethal violence; *pervasive societal violence* obscures it; *organizational institutionalization* facilitates and legitimizes it; and a *public-private social control fusion* fosters and hides much police violence. Recognizing that police violence occurs within larger sociopolitical and police organizational systems, this chapter further proposes that police violence be seen as situated within both normal and systemically deviant organizational arrangements. As Huggins and colleagues (2002) argued elsewhere, understanding and reducing systemic police violence requires focusing on more than the putatively atypically deviant "direct perpetrators"—in Brazil, Militarized Police rank and file, for example. The range of "enabler/facilitators" of lethal police violence include international actors (Huggins 1998); national and municipal politicians and legislators, judges, and other justice system actors (Cannon 2000; Global Justice 2003; Huggins 1998); as well as police organizational systems (Cao 2002; Huggins 1998; Huggins, Haritos-Fatouros, and Zimbardo 2002; Lifton 2000; Lundman 1980; Skolnick and Fyfe 1993); police technologies, and work group dynamics (Henry 2004; Huggins, Haritos-Fatouros, and Zimbardo 2002; Toch 1995). By examining these enabler/facilitators and including them within a "lethal violence system," researchers will capture more fully the systemic nature of police violence.

Within the wider sociopolitical and police organizational system that fosters, hides, and excuses lethal police violence, rank-and-file police are subordinate minorities. The enabler/facilitators are powerful dominant majorities, even though numerically in the minority. Using combined macro and micro approaches to explore torture in Brazil, Huggins and colleagues argued that torture would continue unless or until the (usually) behind-the-scenes work of enabler/facilitators and the functioning of police-organizational systems (also relatively invisible in their normative banality), are recognized as part of a torture system (Huggins, Haritos-Fatouros, and Zimbardo 2002; Huggins 2005). In any case, police violence in Brazil will not be reduced until the violence facilitating and excusing actions of powerful enabler/facilitators become as transparent as the post-facto condemnations of "bad apple" rank-and-file perpetrators. Murderous police can always be found, shaped, and hung out to dry by political actors and police organizations. The system that relatively invisibly fosters, hides, and excuses their violence will continue unabated until deep changes in policing are instituted, including for Brazil, and the poor cease to be seen as *a priori* criminals to be managed as enemies in an ongoing civil war.

PART II

Police Use of Firearms

Introduction

Johannes Knutsson

POLICE HAVE BEEN granted the mandate to use the ultimate means of deadly force—firearms. Use of firearms should generally be perceived along a use-of-force continuum. The mere knowledge that police have access to firearms may therefore be one factor that affects suspects' behavior, even if the firearms are not actively used. In situations where police officers draw weapons but only threaten to shoot, such actions may or may not be considered and recorded as use of firearms, depending on the country and the departmental policy. Police want to achieve an immediate effect by the threat of the use of firearms, and even when shots are fired, in some countries those shots may be intended to serve as a warning only. The purpose of first relying on verbal threats, reinforced by a display of guns or warning shots, is to make adversaries obey officers' commands but not resort to lethal force. If verbal commands are not followed, the next step in a process of force escalation might be effective fire. At the endpoint of the continuum are shots fired with the intent to kill.

When it comes to departmental policies for firearms use, there are significant differences among police forces across countries. In their contribution, P. A. J. Waddington and Martin Wright discuss policy changes in the United Kingdom, where the vast majority of officers are unarmed. Norway also has an unarmed police force, as described by Tor-Geir Myhrer and Jon Strype. While somewhat different from the United Kingdom, all Norwegian police officers are trained in the use of firearms. Guns, albeit sealed and unloaded, are normally stored in police cars and can be used only following authorization by a Chief of Police. The consequence is somewhat higher accessibility of firearms for the Norwegian police compared to those in the United Kingdom. This accessibility could be part of the explanation for a higher estimated Norwegian rate of incidents where police open fire (on average .44 per million inhabitants per year) compared to the rate for England and Wales (.13). Perhaps not surprisingly, the rates of suspects injured or killed by police are considerably lower compared with countries that have regularly armed forces, as documented by Johannes Knutsson and Annika Norée in their review of the Nordic countries of Denmark, Finland, Norway, and Sweden. Sweden has a regularly armed force but, as explained in the chapter by Johannes Knutsson, it also has a restrictive firearms policy. Warning shots should, if possible, be fired before effective fire is commenced and shots should, if feasible, in order to minimize injuries, be aimed at the legs of the adversary. Sweden, like Norway, has high rates of firearm ownership because both countries are societies of hunters, but both are also very restrictive regarding handguns, something that cannot be claimed for the United States. The situations are therefore radically different for the police as evidenced by comparisons of suspects shot to death. Further, warning shots are not encouraged or allowed in the United States where officers are trained to shoot at body center mass. In their Nordic comparison Johannes Knutsson and Annika Norée also argue that in Finland, despite a lack of an explicit rule stating that warning shots ought to be fired, many shots discharged by Finnish police are actually warning shots.

In closed societies like China, information on police use of force is difficult to come by. In the account of firearms use by the Chinese police, Kam Wong restricts his discussion to the regulatory framework and discusses different issues connected to the rules. Problems for the police that have been created by the regulations are also highlighted.

As pointed out by Gregory Morrison in his chapter about U.S. police firearms use, incidents where police shoot and injure or kill suspects are very rare events in that country. However, it is estimated that in the United States on average 1.22 citizens per million inhabitants are shot to death by police annually, compared to 0.16 in Sweden. The rate is thus about 8 times higher in the United States, which incidentally is about the same as for homicide in general.

Among the states in Australia, Victoria emerges with the highest rates of fatal police shootings. David Baker analyzes the Australian situation and addresses different measures taken to restrict firearms use. He points out the critical need for a policy that is able to handle particularly difficult encounters that involve mentally ill persons and argues for the importance of non-lethal alternatives to firearms. In the final contribution of this section, David Klinger, using data from his interviews with 80 officers who have been directly involved in the use of deadly force in the line of duty, reports that shortly after the incident many officers experience multiple negative reactions. However, for the majority the negative consequences wane away with time. This chapter serves as an important reminder of the potential impact of deadly force on police officers and on their departments.

9

Police Use of Guns in Unarmed Countries: The United Kingdom

P.A.J. Waddington

Martin Wright

ABSTRACT

BRITAIN HAS LONG epitomized the unarmed policing tradition. Since their inception in 1829 the British police have not routinely carried firearms. Even today, most police officers throughout Britain do not have either training in the use of firearms or ready access to them. However, this is in stark contrast to one part of the "United Kingdom"—Ireland before the partition of Northern Ireland from the Republic in the south, and Northern Ireland thereafter, has always hosted an armed police. This is instructive, for Ireland was never heir to the police traditions of Britain; indeed it was the model for a quite different style of policing—colonial (Ellison and Smyth 2000; Ryder 1989; Sinclair 2006; Townshend 1992). This is enlightening, because the status of those who are policed plays a crucial role in the development of policing, not least in its use of force (Waddington 1999a). In Britain, police officers deal with citizens and are institutionally wary of anything that suggests oppression, whereas in Ireland the task of repressing a restive peasantry provided plentiful incentive to the creation of an armed gendarmerie. Since the second half of the last century, the use of firearms by British police officers has become much more common, suggesting that the relationship between police and citizen has undergone significant shifts. This chapter will explore the tradition and the changes that it has recently undergone.

"UNITED KINGDOM"---HISTORY AND TRADITION

The United Kingdom (UK) is not a single jurisdiction, but consists principally of England and Wales, Scotland (which has always enjoyed a distinct criminal

P.A.J. Waddington, University of Wolverhampton
Martin Wright, University of Wolverhampton

justice system), and Northern Ireland. In addition, the Republic of Ireland won its independence from the UK after the partition of Ireland in 1922.

These boundaries are directly relevant to the police use of guns throughout Britain and Ireland. In 1829 Sir Robert Peel installed professional policing in London along lines that were soon disseminated throughout the Anglo-Saxon world, but this was not his first expedition into policing. Previously, as Chief Secretary for Ireland, he created the "Peace Preservation Police" (Palmer 1988, Ch 6) that was destined to evolve rapidly into an armed paramilitary gendarmerie, eventually becoming the Royal Irish Constabulary (RIC), which after partition became the Royal Ulster Constabulary (RUC). It was this latter style of policing that became the model for policing throughout the British Empire (Anderson and Killingray 1991; 1992). Thus, the same coterie of officials under the leadership of the same politician, with much the same vision and facing much the same political opposition, gave birth to two diametrically opposed models of policing. On the mainland of Britain policing aspired to the "liberal" ideal and remained lightly armed, whereas in Ireland (and throughout the Empire) policing was the armed, authoritarian repression of native populations (Ellison and Smyth 2000). The reasons for policing taking such dramatically divergent paths either side of the Irish Sea, lay in *who* was being policed: on the mainland, the civil population was composed of *"freeborn* Englishmen" for whom full citizenship beckoned; whereas the majority of the population of the colony of Ireland was composed of a rebellious peasantry to be repressed (Waddington 1999a).

The struggle for Irish independence continued after the Partition in the guise of the Irish Republican Army (IRA) terrorism, which reached its crescendo in the campaign that consumed the last quarter of the 20th century. Throughout this period, the RUC (like other colonial police forces) became dominated by the demands of counter-insurgency reminiscent of "dirty wars" fought elsewhere (Anderson and Killingray 1992; Sinclair 2006), with allegations that the force operated a *de facto* policy of "shoot-to-kill," or more accurately "summary execution" (Amnesty International 1988; Asmal 1985; Jennings 1988). Despite the end of the terrorist campaign, incorporation of Republicans into the devolved government of Northern Ireland and the transformation of policing into the "Police Service of Northern Ireland," its officers remain routinely armed.

The Garda Siochana of the newly created Republic of Ireland, on the other hand, was created deliberately as an unarmed civil force. This explicitly political decision reprised Peel's insistence a century before, namely that the police of London should not have the "manners and customs of the military" (Critchley 1978). Peel's "New Police" were attired in a style of clothing that was deliberately civilian; blue was adopted as the color of their uniform in order to distinguish them from red-coated soldiers; they carried a short wooden staff or "truncheon," but they did not carry firearms.

The infant Metropolitan Police of London (the Met) did not forsake firearms because it was heir to an unarmed policing tradition, or because the streets of London were quiescent. On the contrary, those police forces that preceded the Met's introduction were invariably equipped with firearms: the famous Bow Street Runners carried pistols; the Horse Patrol that policed the main routes in and out of the capital to deter highwaymen carried horse pistols; the River Police that patrolled the docks and wharfs were equipped with blunderbusses; and even the often-decrepit watchmen employed by towns to keep watch at night were typically armed with all manner of weaponry including firearms (Gould and Waldren 1986). Peel's "New Police" broke with that armed tradition, but also as these pre-existing forces were assimilated into the Metropolitan Police, they too were in turn disarmed.

Significantly, this policy of disarmed policing was implemented against the background of enormous social and political turmoil (Critchley 1970; Gould and Waldren 1986). Unarmed policing was a deliberate political strategy of winning the reluctant acceptance of the "respectable classes" by emphasizing the vulnerability of the police, in stark contrast to the despised French model of policing that aimed to convey a formidable appearance (Emsley 1983). Strangely, there was no popular appetite for such vulnerability; egregious episodes of violence toward police officers periodically prompted demands in the popular press for them to be armed. During the 1880s in the wake of a spate of armed burglaries the Metropolitan Police succumbed to pressure from its officers and allowed those on the outer and more sparsely populated divisions to carry a pistol on night duty if they wished. Yet this policy was kept strictly out of the public view as were the pistols themselves (Gould and Waldren 1986). This official secrecy surrounding the use of weaponry extended to training and maintaining competence in the use of firearms and persisted until the 1960s. Since World War Two, successive generations of senior officers and policymakers displayed the utmost reluctance even in acknowledging that the police had access to firearms and knew how to use them (Waldren 2007).

INCIDENT-DRIVEN ARMED POLICING

In the 1960s, events conspired to produce a fundamental rift with this past. In 1965, in the teeth of fierce opposition from the police service as a whole, Parliament repealed the death penalty for the murder of police officers—a special exemption from the general abolition of capital punishment enacted in 1957. In the summer of 1966 three unarmed detectives were brutally and callously shot dead when they tried to question the occupants of a suspicious car. Not only was this seen as a harbinger of things to come, but the prolonged search for the principal murderer, Harry Roberts, by armed officers exposed laxity in how officers used their firearms (Waddington 1991). Hitherto, the police had relied on ex-military personnel to use firearms on the rare occasions when it was necessary. With the abolition of military conscription in 1960, the supply of firearms-trained officers began to evaporate and it became imperative that the police should now commence training their own personnel in the use of firearms and maintaining standards of competence. In London (which played host to approximately three-quarters of armed incidents and led developments in armed policing), the Firearms Branch of the Metropolitan Police was created—successively designated as D11, PT17, SO19, and currently CO19 (Waldren 2007).

The system that was established in the wake of these events was much the same throughout the country, and remained for almost 25 years. Officers who continued normally to fulfill their duties unarmed, volunteered to be trained and periodically to re-qualify as "Authorized Firearms Officers" (AFOs). In the event of an armed incident, they would be dispatched to the nearest armory, where they would be equipped with a revolver and ammunition, before attending the incident. Occasionally, officers would be armed to carry out specific operations (such as the planned arrest of a wanted person thought to be in possession of firearms). There were also a few highly specialized officers (such as Special Branch responsible for national security, anti-terrorist operations, and royalty protection) who were routinely armed. London differed from most of the remainder of the country in equipping members of its tactical reserve, the Special Patrol Group, with firearms kept in a locked armory box on board the personnel carriers in which they were transported.

Not only did the installation of D11 break with a past of refusing to acknowledge the necessity for the police to have an armed capability, it also initiated a pattern of what a later Commissioner of the Metropolitan Police (Sir Paul Condon) accurately described as 'incident-driven' policy on firearms. The killing of the three detectives was the first such incident. In 1973, three apparently armed Pakistani youths invaded the Indian High Commission, which led to a confrontation with armed officers that resulted in the deaths of two of the youths. Occurring against the backdrop of a rise in international terrorism, this exposed the threat to embassies in London, and the following year a specialist permanently armed Diplomatic Protection Group (DPG) was established with the sole purpose of providing protection for such locations. D11 was originally conceived as a training unit, but it gradually acquired an operational role comparable to Special Weapons and Tactics squads that were emerging throughout the developed world. This operational role came to light in 1975 when a criminal gang was disturbed during a robbery at the Spaghetti House restaurant and took hostages as they retreated into a basement room. The police laid siege to the "stronghold" for days before the hostages were released and the robbers arrested (including one who had shot and injured himself). A similar siege was staged in the full glare of news media attention very shortly afterward when Provisional IRA terrorists were pursued by unarmed officers and took a middle-aged couple hostage in their apartment on

Balcombe Street. Eventually, the terrorists surrendered and the hostages were released to widespread acclaim for the police policy of patient negotiation.

What remained in the background at Balcombe Street came to the fore at the Iranian Embassy siege in 1980, where the policy of patient negotiation was peremptorily terminated after the hostage-takers executed one of the hostages. The siege was forcefully ended by soldiers from the Special Air Service (SAS) who abseiled into position in the full glare of the television cameras before assaulting the building and shooting dead all but one of the terrorists. The SAS instantly acquired celebrity status and the use of such methods for terminating sieges achieved public acceptance, but the SAS were a military unit and the government was uneasy about using soldiers against criminals. So, D11 began to acquire the same skills and equipment lest it became necessary to use them against criminals.

Events of a quite different kind were to prompt the next major shift in armed policing in Britain. These were a succession of mistaken shootings by armed officers of innocent people, in some cases fatally. Police hunting for a dangerous escaped criminal—David Martin—opened fire on a car in which they believed Martin was a passenger; the police were wrong, the passenger was Stephen Waldorf, a film editor. When traffic came to a halt in a West London street, an officer was dispatched on foot to confirm the identity of the wanted man. Waldorf's innocent action of reaching for his briefcase on the rear seat was erroneously interpreted by the armed officer standing on the footpath as that of reaching for a gun. The passenger was shot repeatedly not only by the officer standing alongside the car, but two others who believed that a gunfight was in progress. When Waldorf lay sprawled in the roadway, one of the officers struck Waldorf's head with the butt of his revolver. Stephen Waldorf was fortunate to survive. The three officers involved in the shooting were all prosecuted for attempted murder. Their acquittal did not save the Met from public opprobrium at a time when, for reasons unconnected to armed policing, public attitudes toward the police had taken a negative turn.

Three years later officers searching for another armed fugitive burst into the fugitive's mother's home in the early hours of the morning and mistakenly shot her; leaving her permanently disabled. Again, the officer was acquitted of attempted murder, but the reputation of the Met was even more severely damaged. Meanwhile, officers in the West Midlands of England had twice opened fire in controversial circumstances: first, when an armed man used a pregnant young woman as a "human shield." Unable to see the woman in the dark, officers returned fire and killed her. The second occasion was when an officer searching the home of a suspected armed robber mistakenly shot dead his five-year-old son, John Shorthouse. This catalogue of error and mistakes resulted in a national review and a fundamental shift in policy away from authorizing approximately one in ten officers to carry firearms if needed, to concentrating armed policing in the hands of a smaller number of selected specialists.

Meanwhile, during the 1970s, airplane hijacking became a common tactic of international terrorists that prompted the escalation of security at many airports worldwide. Consistent with the traditional secrecy surrounding armed policing, officers at London's Heathrow airport routinely began to carry firearms covertly. In 1986, Palestinian terrorists launched murderous attacks on El Al check-in areas at airports in Rome and Vienna, with considerable loss of life. This incident drove the escalation of armed policing to a new level with the routine deployment of police patrols in the airport terminals *overtly* armed with Heckler and Koch MP5 carbines.

Also in 1986 another very high-profile event occurred that was to lead to a further transformation of policing. In the small rural town of Hungerford in southern England a man went on an armed rampage, killing 16 people (including an unarmed police officer) before committing suicide. The inability of the police to mobilize an effective armed response caused controversy and Her Majesty's Chief Inspector of Constabulary wrote a confidential report, which *inter alia* proposed that these circumstances represented a "window of opportunity" for the police to achieve their long-held wish of routinely deploying vehicles with firearms on board. The adoption of this policy was hesitant and uneven throughout the country, but currently Armed Response Vehicles (ARVs) are commonplace, if not universal. A succession of murders of unarmed police officers in London in the early 1990s, prompted demands for the routine arming of all police officers by the police union—the Police Federation. Although rejected by a 70 to 30 percent majority, the pressure of this ballot prompted the Met to amend its policy and allow the crews of ARVs to permanently carry pistols, instead of requiring them to await the authorization of a senior officer on each occasion that they requested to be armed. Again, this policy was followed unevenly by other police forces.

The final step in this narrative occurred in the immediate aftermath of the London terrorist bombings of July 7, 2005 and the failed attempted bombings two weeks later. Police hunting for Hussain Osman, whose bomb on a London underground train failed to detonate, were led to an address in an apartment block. Surveillance officers monitoring those leaving the building saw a young man who resembled the grainy photographs of the wanted man recovered from a CCTV camera on board a bus and on a membership card found in the rucksack in which he had secreted the bomb. They followed the man for some considerable time as he traveled by bus to an Underground train station, but were unsure whether he was the wanted suspect or not. Eventually, and fearing that the man was indeed Osman and might be trying to carry out another attack, the officer commanding the operation at New Scotland Yard ordered armed officers to stop this man before he was able to board an Underground train. When those officers arrived minutes later, the suspect was sitting on board a train still under the watchful gaze of two surveillance officers. Alerted by the commotion as armed officers descended to, and ran along, the platform, the man rose from his seat, as did other passengers. One of the surveillance officers grabbed him in a "bear hug" and the two men toppled over. The armed officers who boarded the train saw the two men struggling and shot the suspect repeatedly in the head (IPCC 2007a; 2007b). After some initial confusion, during which the Metropolitan Police Commissioner, Sir Ian Blair, released a statement that suggested that the man was indeed the wanted terrorist, it was belatedly disclosed that he was actually a wholly innocent Brazilian immigrant, Jean Charles de Menezes (IPPC 2007a; 2007b). The success in arresting the four terrorist suspects did not stem the tide of public outrage at this tragic loss of innocent life. The Independent Police Complaints Commission (IPCC) began an investigation and although no individual officers were prosecuted in connection with killing, the Met was corporately convicted of offenses under health and safety at work legislation.

Two issues emerged from this episode: first was that the competence of the police in conducting armed operations was once again called into question. The prosecution and IPCC report painted a picture of chaos and confusion, especially regarding the deployment of specialist firearms officers to support the surveillance operation outside the apartment building (IPCC 2007a; 2007b). The central allegation in that report was that had those firearms officers been available earlier then Jean Charles could have been stopped under more controlled conditions before entering the Underground station. This is not very credible. Yes, the deployment of these officers was inexplicably delayed, but this was not the major problem that the operation faced. The fundamental problem lay with the inability of surveillance officers to confirm that the man (de Menezes) was actually the wanted suspect, Osman. When the officer commanding the operation ordered that the suspect should be stopped from entering the Underground train station, the armed officers were as readily on hand as they would have been in almost any conceivable circumstance. There was more justice in accusations of confusion and noise in the control room, but there is no evidence that this in any way contributed to the death of Jean Charles. However, what was undoubtedly damaging to the reputation of the Met was evidence that subordinate officers knew or suspected that the dead man was *not* Osman before the Commissioner made his announcement to the press. Certainly, the whole episode was far from being the most glorious moment in the history of British policing.

The second issue was the brutality of Jean Charles' death—shot repeatedly in the head at close range. This brought into the public domain a tactic hitherto obscured in secrecy, known as "Operation Kratos" to defeat suicide bombers. This envisages inflicting sufficient damage to the brain as to sever the brainstem and thus preventing detonation of a bomb as a dying act. There is nothing peculiarly British about this tactic, indeed it is shared by many police forces worldwide (Bunker 2005a; 2005b). However, its brutality sits uneasily in a culture that has for so long valorized its unarmed police.

WITHER UNARMED POLICING?

Currently, the situation throughout the mainland of Britain is that in most large urban areas and many others, routinely patrolling police officers do not carry firearms, nor are they trained in their use. However, ARVs patrol as dedicated first responders to armed incidents that might arise, specialist officers conduct SWAT-like operations when necessary, and there is a plethora of permanently armed squads with specific responsibilities for diplomatic and royalty protection, security at airports, anti-terrorism, bodyguards for VIPs, and much else besides. The weapons carried, the tactics employed, and the appearance of armed officers in Britain is indistinguishable from their counterparts in many other parts of the world.

This transformation has been driven by events: the growth of armed crime and terrorism exposed the need for the police to acknowledge and increase its armed capability, while errors in the use of firearms and controversies surrounding armed policing have led to increasing specialization. However, this has been an incremental process that with each step had to overcome an entrenched reluctance to abandon the traditional notion of the unarmed British "bobby."

10

Police Use of Guns in a Routinely Unarmed Police Force: Regulations and Practice in Norway

Tor-Geir Myhrer and Jon Strype

ABSTRACT

The Norwegian police may not be armed during ordinary duty unless specially authorized by the Chief of Police. The first part of this chapter gives an overview of the relevant legislation. The right of the police to use force of all kinds and the general principles for the use of force is regulated by the Norwegian Police Act of August 4th, 1995, Section 6. More detailed regulation on when the police may be armed with firearms and under which conditions and situations the police are entitled to use their firearms, is given by the Ministry of Justice in an instruction from August 1, 1990. The main criteria for when the police can be armed, and in which situations the Ministry instruction allows the police to use firearms, will be presented. A brief overview of the regulation on how use of firearms shall be reported, controlled, and investigated will also be given. In the second part of the chapter, statistical data regarding police use of firearms in Norway (1985–2007) is presented. This includes the number of times armed police have threatened to use firearms, how often weapons have been fired, and the outcome in terms of injury or death. Furthermore, these figures will be compared with the number of Chief of Police authorizations in order to present how often authorizations to be armed are followed by actual use of firearms.

INTRODUCTION: REGULATIONS

The right for the police to use force is established in the Police Act (August 4, 1995 no. 53) Section 6, Subsections 2 and 4. The act does not regulate

Tor-Geir Myhrer, Norwegian Police University
Jon Strype, Norwegian Police University

which instruments of force the police are allowed to use. This follows from different administrative regulations given by the Ministry of Justice or the Police Directorate. The situations in which the Norwegian police are authorized to carry firearms and under which situations and circumstances they may be used, are laid down by the Ministry of Justice.

Authorization to Be Armed

The Norwegian police are unarmed and do not carry firearms on duty—at least formally. In most patrol cars, however, firearms will be stored in locked and sealed containers; mostly pistols or revolvers, but some cars also carry automatic weapons. Breaking the seal equates to being armed, and the police officer must have prior authorization by a superior officer, usually the Chief of Police. The officers may arm themselves only if there is no time or they are unable to get prior authorization from a superior officer (e.g., no communication or already under fire). Authorization can be given if specific information provides a reason to believe that an armed person will confront the officers or if the assignment is believed to be particularly dangerous for the officers involved. Authorization can also be given if it is considered necessary to be armed for others reasons.

The Chief of Police may also give permanent orders that authorize the police to be armed when certain "standard" situations or incidents occur (e.g., when an armed bank or money transport robbery is being reported). The Chief of Police can also issue standing orders to authorize the police officers to be armed when securing embassies or court buildings for longer or shorter periods, depending on the risk assessment.

Use of Firearms

Use of force shall be conducted in accordance with the principle of *"continuum of force"* and whatever instrument of force is used must be suitable (effective), necessary, and proportionate. To ensure that the principle of necessity is adhered to, it is normally a requirement that more lenient methods should be attempted before more force is considered, and firearms must only be used as a last resort. The methods of less lethal force that have to be tried before firearms may be employed will depend on the situation. But, as the Norwegian police are routinely unarmed, some time will normally pass before authorization is given and armed officers arrive on the scene. This period of time is often used to "freeze" the situation and to control the surroundings, thus creating a better basis for negotiations or use of non-lethal force. The requirement of using less force first is not unconditional. If it is *obvious* that more lenient measures will not be effective in preventing the danger, firearms may be used immediately. This will be the situation where there is *no time* to try other measures (e.g., the offender has already fired one shot at the victim, but missed) or it may be obvious that other measures *will have no effect* regardless of time (for instance when the police are facing a severely disturbed person or a determined suicide bomber).

The requirement of proportionality is also described more closely in the Regulations Section 19, Specifically. firearms may be used:

1. To prevent an imminent danger of grievous bodily harm;
2. To arrest very dangerous persons;
3. To prevent substantial damage on foreign property (e.g., embassies and residences); or
4. To prevent objects or institutions of public interest to be seriously harmed.

Prevent an Imminent Danger from Grievous Harm

Firearms can be used when the police officers or others are threatened with weapons or threats of grievous bodily harm. Weapons can include firearms, knives, axes, and other such devices. But firearms can also be used even if the offender does not make use of any weapon (e.g., if he tries to strangle a person or in any other way presents a life-threatening danger to someone, and there is no other possibility to stop the offender). It is not required that the act of inflicting harm or danger has actually started, but there must be perceived an imminent danger that grievous bodily harm will be the result if the police do not make use of their firearms. For evidentiary reasons, that section of the Regulation is called "The Provision of Self Defense."

Arresting Very Dangerous Persons

The situation regulated in Section 19, Letter B, describes a person who is regarded as very dangerous, but not an imminent danger. Two groups of persons are considered to be very unsafe. The first group includes individuals who are under suspicion, charged with, or convicted of murder or other severe and violent crimes (e.g., armed robbery or causing grievous bodily harm). If the police only suspect an offender, the suspicion must be strongly supported by evidence before it will be considered proportionate force to use firearms during an arrest.

Firearms can also be used when arresting a person that "for other reasons is considered to be a grave danger for the national security or for other persons' health." This category includes arsonists, hijackers, spies, and terrorists. Persons having committed serious drug offenses are probably not included in this category. Although trafficking in drugs ultimately represents a danger to others, the danger is too distant from the smuggling or dealing itself. Psychologically unstable individuals, who with reason are believed to have made their minds up to commit serious crimes, are also included in this category and can be subjected to deadly force as a last resort.

Substantial Damage on Foreign Property

Although the wording in the regulations refers to foreign property in general, it is clear that the use of firearms is only allowed when protecting foreign properties that are entitled to special protection according to the Vienna Convention on Diplomatic Relations. According to Articles 22 and 30 in the Convention (1961), the receiving state is under a particular obligation to take all appropriate steps to protect the premises of the foreign mission and the residence against any intrusion or damage, and to prevent any disturbance of the peace of the mission or impairment of its dignity. For the police to be able to employ firearms, it is required that the damage on the mission or residence is substantial. "Substantial" is not a reference to how much it will cost to repair the damage, but whether the attack is likely to have resulted in such damage that the building can no longer give persons, documents, and archives sufficient protection. An agitated crowd throwing paint on the embassy cannot be stopped with firearms. Police could, however, use firearms if someone tried to make a forced entry into the embassy to set a fire. The authorization to use firearms, given in Section 19C, is most relevant if there are no persons present in the building. Otherwise, the "self-defense provision" will often be applicable as well.

To Prevent Objects Or Institutions of Public Interest from Serious Harm

Theoretically, firearms can be used as a last resort to stop an agitated crowd from occupying the Parliament, government offices, etc. In such a situation, it is believed that the police may not shoot to hit, but may only fire warning shots. The regulations also allow the police to use firearms to stop, for example, sabotage of an important power plant that supplies a large part of the country with electricity. Such an act will, supposedly, most often be considered a terrorist attack or an attack on the national security, and firearms can then be used. However, the perpetrator(s) might also be a person or group wanting to increase their power or influence in different matters by exposing the vulnerabilities of the society.

To use firearms in these situations, it is required that the object or institution is at risk to be "seriously harmed." This generally means that the object or institution must be harmed or hampered to such a degree that for a period of time it is unable to function or serve its primary purpose.

Proper and Proportionate Use

When authorized use-of-force situations occur and shots are fired, an officer must use his or her gun in a proper and proportionate way. According to the regulations, the gun should be fired in such a way that the damage caused is as little as possible. This means that aiming must be different when shots are fired to carry out an arrest compared with shots fired in self-defense. Normally, it is also required that the officer assesses the effect of the first shot before the second shot (or subsequent shots) is fired. Officers must also consider the possibility that others in the surrounding area may be hit. If persons in the surroundings are not threatened by the same situation which authorizes the officer to use his or her gun, it follows that shots cannot be fired if there is a foreseeable risk that these third persons can be hit.

PRACTICE

In the following section, firearms use in the Norwegian police will be explored from a statistical point of view. This section will examine how often (1) authorizations to be armed are given to officers; (2) guns are used as a threat; and (3) guns are fired during police service in Norway. The final section will consider whether the frequency of firearms use in the Norwegian police has increased over time.

Beginning with the first issue, exploring the number of armed situations in a police service is obviously only possible if the police are regularly unarmed, as is the case in Norway. In the Norwegian context, the number of armed situations may indicate how often firearms are chosen as a means of resolving problems when the normal (unarmed) toolbox of police options is perceived as inadequate. In addition to exploring the frequency of shooting in a normally unarmed police service, our data may also shed light on the proportion of armed situations that are solved merely by the threat of a police gun. In countries where only shooting situations are reported to the police authorities, information about police gun threats may be lacking. By knowing the number of situations in which police guns were fired, it was also possible to see how often being armed led to actual shootings in the Norwegian police service. Finally, with data from 1990 to the end of 2007, we were able to investigate how the above-mentioned aspects of police use of guns have developed over a relatively long time period.

DATA

All firearms use (i.e., threatening with or firing police firearms) is reported to the Norwegian Police Directorate. Until 2000, reports were submitted to the Ministry of Justice. Cases in which police officers have received authorization to be armed, but no subsequent firearms use (i.e., threatening or shooting) occurred, are not centrally reported, but are recorded for statistical purposes in the respective 27 police districts.

Data were collected in three waves. First, data from archival reports of police firearms use between 1990 and 1999 were coded as numerical data by one of the authors. In addition, data concerning authorizations to be armed from this period were collected by means of a postal questionnaire to the Norwegian police districts. The results were published in a study of police use of guns in Norway and Sweden (Knutsson and Strype 2002; 2003; Strype and Knutsson 2002). In the second wave, the Norwegian Police Directorate supplied official statistics of police use of guns (threats and shootings) from 2000 to 2002 (Strype 2005). For the purpose of the present chapter, the corresponding figures for 2003–2007 were supplied by the Norwegian Police Directorate. Finally, the local police districts supplied yearly arming authorization figures for the period 2000–2007.

RESULTS

Authorizations to Carry Guns

Data from the earliest years were of poor quality due to a very large proportion of missing data. Thus, the analysis of authorizations is restricted to the years 1995 to 2007. A few police districts also failed to provide data in the first wave. The missing police districts represented 8.8% of the population outside Oslo. In order to estimate the national authorization figures, the numbers were adjusted according to the population size in missing districts. From the years 2000–2002, data were only available from Oslo police district.

The most prominent feature of Figure 10-1 is probably that the number of situations in which the police carry guns is rather modest. In the observed period, Norwegian police have on the average been armed in 4.6 situations per day (ranging from 2.8 in 1995 to 7.0 in 2004) while policing a population of approximately five million inhabitants. Oslo police district, the police authority of Norway's capital and largest city (approximately 500,000 inhabitants), reported a relatively large proportion of the authorizations to carry guns. With roughly one-tenth of the population, Oslo reported between one-fourth and one-third of the authorizations.

As can be seen in Figure 10-1, the annual number of authorizations has increased during the observed time period. The increase was statistically significant ($p < 0.01$) both for Norway as a whole and for Oslo. There are two particular leaps in the curves, occurring in 1998 and 2004. Obviously, a number of factors may have contributed to these leaps. However, one factor should be mentioned in particular: there were only two situations in which police officers were shot and killed during the observed period that occurred in March 1998 and April 2004. In the 1998 incident, two officers were killed in a police operation against an armed psychiatric patient. During the robbery of the NOKAS teller central in 2004, the largest robbery by value in Norwegian history, a police officer was

Figure 10-1 Authorizations to Be Armed in the Norwegian Police, 1995–2007

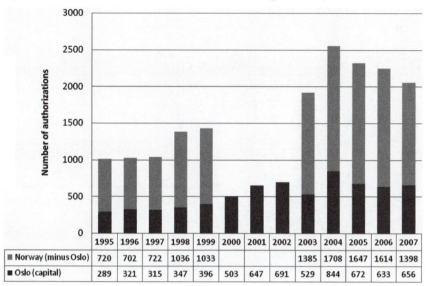

	1995	1996	1997	1998	1999	2000	2001	2002	2003	2004	2005	2006	2007
■ Norway (minus Oslo)	720	702	722	1036	1033				1385	1708	1647	1614	1398
■ Oslo (capital)	289	321	315	347	396	503	647	691	529	844	672	633	656

shot and killed (while sitting in a police car). In our view, it appears reasonable to hypothesize that these incidents may have called for a heightened perceived need for guns for protective reasons.

Use of Guns (Threats and Shooting Incidents)

The number of arming authorizations constitutes the upper limit for how often the Norwegian police are in a position to solve situations through the use of firearms. Annual data on actual use of armed force (i.e., threatening to use or firing a gun) is presented in Figure 10-2.

As Figure 10-2 shows, there has been a (statistically significant) increase in reported gun threat situations during the observed period. In the early 1990s, the annual number of threat incidents fluctuated around 20, and then rose to around 30 incidents per year in the mid-1990s, with a leap to around 50 in the late 1990s. Since 2000, the annual number of threat incidents has fluctuated around 70.

The largest increases in incidents appeared in 1998 and 2000. Although our data do not allow for certain explanations for these increases, a few potential factors should be mentioned. As previously shown, the increase in police use of gun threats in 1998 may have been related to the killing of two police officers in March 1998. To our knowledge, there was no similar incident to account for the sudden increase in the gun threat figures in 2000. However, a shift in the reporting practices in 2000 deserves mentioning. In 2000, the Norwegian Police Directorate started to receive the incident reports previously

Figure 10-2 Annual Number of Gun Threats and Shooting Incidents in the Norwegian Police, 1990–2007

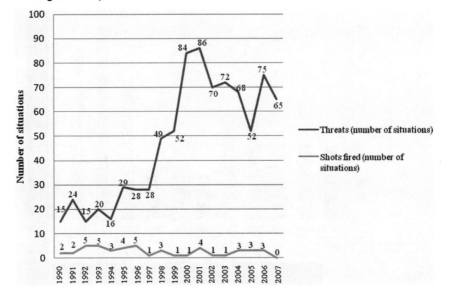

sent to the Ministry of Justice. Although the same conditions for reporting incidents applied, one could speculate that this organizational change may have contributed to some of the observed increase (e.g., by a change in the categorization of cases).

As can be seen, police shootings are very rare in Norway. In 2007, not one single shot was fired during police service. During the observed period, a total of 47 incidents were registered (2.6 incidents per year on average). Further, unlike the gun threatening situations, no increases in police shooting situations has been observed in the period 1990–2007 (see Figure 10-2).

Armed Situations Leading to Shooting or Gun Threats

A visual inspection of Figures 10-1 and 10-2 reveals that although the scales are different, the curves for arming authorizations and gun threats have similar shapes, suggesting that a relatively stable proportion of armed situations lead to the use of guns in terms of threatening the opponent. Table 10-1 shows the relationship between number of authorizations and use of guns in the Norwegian police.

Column D in Table 10-1 shows the proportion of armed situations leading to some sort of firearms use (e.g., threatening with or firing a gun during police service). This proportion has been stable during the observed period. In approximately 3% of armed situations, police guns are used to resolve the situation. In other words, in 97% of armed situations, other means are sufficient

Table 10-1 Proportions of Arming Authorizations Followed by Police Use of Guns in Norway, 1995–2007

Year	A # of Armed Authoriza-tions	B Reported Use of Firearms	C # of Situations with Police Shootings	D Use of Firearms per # of Author-izations	E # of Situations with Police Shootings per Authorizations
1995	1009	29	4	0.03	0.004
1996	1023	28	5	0.03	0.005
1997	1037	28	1	0.03	0.001
1998	1383	49	3	0.04	0.002
1999	1429	52	1	0.04	0.001
2000	*	*	1	*	*
2001	*	*	4	*	*
2002	*	*	1	*	*
2003	1914	73	1	0.04	0.001
2004	2552	71	3	0.03	0.001
2005	2319	55	3	0.02	0.001
2006	2247	78	3	0.03	0.001
2007	2054	65	0	0.03	0.000

* National authorization data unavailable.
Note: Arming authorization figures for 1995–1999 are estimates, see text.

in order to solve the problem at hand. However, it could be argued that the unusual sight of armed officers (in Norway) may be effective in itself.

The proportion of arming authorizations leading to police shooting (column E) is strikingly small. For most of the observed years, one to two per 1,000 armed situations actually led to police shooting. It appears that more armed situations led to police shootings early in the observed period, but with missing arming authorization data for the first years, conclusions regarding a decline in the number of authorizations leading to shooting remains speculative. However, the absence of police shooting episodes in 2007 is noteworthy, although it is too early to label this development as a trend in the Norwegian police service.

Isolating Oslo as the capital and largest city in Norway, we find that a larger proportion of the arming authorizations are followed by police guns being used as a threat. During the years 1995–2002, an average of 7.9% of authorizations in Oslo led to reports of police weapon use. The annual proportion ranged from 4% to 13%, but with no clear trend over time. On the other hand, only one police shot was fired in Oslo during this time period (and the target of this shot was a car tire).

CONCLUSIONS

Norwegian police are routinely unarmed. We have shown that the exception from this practice (i.e., armed police) is an infrequent sight in the Norwegian society. In addition, the police use their guns as a means of threatening the opponent in only a small proportion of the armed situations, and police shootings are extremely rare.

The annual numbers of authorizations to be armed and police gun threats have, however, increased since 1990. Various factors may explain this increase. As we have seen, there seems to be a temporal relationship between incidents in which police have been shot and killed and heightened levels of police arming and gun use. Although speculative, it seems reasonable to hypothesize that when the threat against the police is perceived as more severe, the perceived need for guns in police service will consequently be stronger. This hypothesis is also supported by the fact that there is an over-representation of arming authorizations and police gun threats in Oslo, the capital city area with a higher crime and violence level than in the rest of Norway. In 2004, 11.54 per 1,000 inhabitants were charged for crimes in Oslo, compared to 8.05 per 1,000 in the entire country (Statistics Norway). Looking at reported violence crime (per 1,000 inhabitants), the total proportion for Norway and the proportion for Oslo were 5.5 and 8.4 respectively (Statistics Norway).

On the other hand, we have seen that the number of shooting incidents is on a low and stable level, contrary to what should be expected from the rise in the number of arming authorizations and gun threat situations. In other words, almost no situations escalate to the point at which the police need to fire guns. It is our view that the strict regulation of police weapon use contributes to heightening the threshold for police shootings in at least two ways. First, in a normally unarmed police service, the use of guns could be said to represent a deviation from the normal police conduct. Further, in many situations, the time delay inherent in asking for and receiving arming authorization calls for alternative police tactics, such as freezing the dangerous situation. It also seems reasonable to assume that the time delay also provides more optimal conditions for making informed and rational decisions about how to solve critical situations.

Police Use of Firearms in Sweden

Johannes Knutsson

ABSTRACT

SINCE 1965 SWEDEN has had a regularly armed police force. Using data from incidents where police have opened fire, various aspects of these shootings are described and analyzed. Furthermore, recent trends in the use and consequences of these incidents are discussed. In most of the incidents where police open fire, an ordinary two-man patrol of uniformed officers, during a routine assignment, has ended up in a situation where they are assaulted and are shooting in self-defense. The distance between the firing officer and the target is typically short. The assailant was injured in about 25% of the cases and killed in 4% of the incidents. In 10% of the incidents, an officer was injured. The numbers of incidents, as well as incidents involving injured and mortally wounded suspects, have been fairly stable during the last two decades.

INTRODUCTION

> Staircase in multi-apartment house. A man with two knives threatened police officers. Call and two warning shots without effect. Was shot in the thigh and arrested. Chief of police: Self-defense. Correct to shoot two warning shots in this case. Prosecutor: Preliminary investigation will not be opened.

The above incident describes briefly some typical features of situations when Swedish police officers use their service guns, but also identifies some characteristics that are specific to this particular incident. The description has been formulated by former superintendent Sven Silverudd. He has collected data for all 430 incidents between 1985 and 1998 in which Swedish police officers have opened fire in line of duty. This information was used to create a database for the study of police use of firearms.[1] Besides a short description of the situation, the data includes information about the firing officers, the counterparts and the shots

Johannes Knutsson, Norwegian Police University College

fired. Information from that database is used in this chapter that reviews different aspects of police shooting incidents in Sweden and describes the recent trends in police use of firearms in that country. As to the trends, information from the 583 incidents for the years 1985 to 2004 is used. In the concluding remarks some suggestions for improvement of Swedish police firearms use will be put forward.

ARMAMENT

Swedish officers carry service guns as part of their standard equipment. When a patrol car, like in the described incident, responds to a call for service the officers have firearms immediately available. This has not always been the case. As a part of a huge reform of the Swedish police force in 1965, with a shift from a communal to a unified state police system, the police were armed on a regular basis with guns. Since then officers undertaking outdoor service activities have been equipped with firearms; initially 7.65mm Walther PPs (Polizei Pistol) that were later exchanged for 9mm Sig Sauer during the late 1980s. The change to a regular armed force might best be described as a gradual process. When the police organization in its modern form came into existence during the latter part of the 19th century, the standard weapon for the police was sabers, a practice that lasted until 1965. An odd and interesting fact is that female officers, when they were allowed to carry out uniformed police services in the mid-1950s, were prohibited from carrying sabers. Police officers could be armed with firearms on a need-to-use basis. When police cars with radios were introduced in the late 1930s, pistols were stored in the cars. During World War II, in which Sweden did not take part, the police were included in the military preparedness and were equipped with firearms. After the war ended, police officers working night shifts (after 6 pm) were routinely armed with firearms. The change in firearms policies and practices in 1965 was not debated or questioned, but was perceived as a natural and necessary step in an organizational modernization process.

THE PROLOGUE OF SHOOTING INCIDENTS

The prologue for situations where police officers discharge their firearms is often vague, as in the case described above. It is difficult to meaningfully describe, categorize, and analyze the precise events that result in officer shootings. In some circumstances, it may be rather trivial crimes or incidents that end with officers firing their service guns. Reports that include suspects with histories of psychiatric problems and drug abuse are relatively common. There are, of course, also cases involving armed robberies and other serious crimes but these are, like the one described below, comparatively rare.

> Suspected robber with shotgun tried to pass a police checkpoint. The car was shot at by two officers and ended up in a ditch. The robber was arrested.

It is more fruitful to understand and analyze the immediate circumstances surrounding these events. In about 90% of the cases officers have fired their arms to avert acute threats or attacks directed against them. In many cases, like the example described in the introduction, an ordinary uniformed two-officer patrol was unexpectedly attacked by an assailant during a routine assignment.

JUSTIFICATION FOR POLICE USE OF FIREARMS

There are three types of situations where Swedish police officers have the right to use firearms while on duty: *in lawful authority*, *in self-defense*, and in an *emergency*.[2] As it is defined in the government's Decree on Use of Firearms in the Police Service from 1969, the police may, according to lawful authority, for some specified very serious crimes and if an intervention is immediately necessary, shoot in order to arrest suspects, to stop them from escaping, or to apprehend escaped criminals who have committed such crimes. Furthermore, the police may use firearms to arrest persons who present an apparent danger to the lives and health of others. The police, just like everybody else, also have the right to protect their own and another person's life, with force including deadly force through use of firearms. There is also justification for the police, in some extraordinary emergency situations, to use firearms. An example would include an officer that has to shoot in order to protect himself from an attacking dog.

It is much easier for an officer in a rapidly occurring event to determine if a situation warrants self-defense than to establish whether there are the necessary preconditions to shoot according to lawful authority as it is defined in the decree. Especially problematic is the requirement that deadly force must be immediately necessary and to ascertain that the crime in question is included in the rules. The list of potential crimes, however, is outdated and does not, for instance, include acts of terrorism (Norée 2004; 2005). Therefore, to make this judgment in an acute situation is extremely difficult. In the shooting incidents reviewed here, the most common justification for the police to fire their guns was self-defense, which was the explanation in 81% of the cases. Lawful authority accounted for 19% of the incidents and emergency responses accounted for just 2%.

ACCIDENTAL SHOTS

Accidental shots fired by officers in service are unfortunately not uncommon, with accidental discharges occurring in 10% of the reported cases examined here. These situations can be divided into two sub-groups: (1) incidents where officers have been handling their firearms incorrectly, as is described in the first case below; or (2) situations where officers have lost control of their arms during hand-to-hand fighting. Situations that involve an officer losing control of their firearm are fortunately very rare. An example of each situation is described as follows:

> Burglary in a tobacco shop. When making his arm ready, an accidental shot was discharged, whereby the officer superficially injured his right knee and perforated his uniform trousers.
>
> Car chase. Suspect wanted. Wrestling. The suspect grabs the officer's gun. Colleague loses his grip. Thereafter the suspect fires four shots against the first officer, who gets badly injured. The suspect gives up after a shot in his right shoulder.

NUMBER OF OFFICERS FIRING AND NUMBER OF SHOTS FIRED

In most shooting incidents only one officer fired a gun (86%), even if in the majority of the situations two or more police officers were actually present. Even when teams of officers were present, it was usually the case that just one actually discharged his or her weapon. Two officers discharging their guns occurred only 12% of the time. Most of the situations involved only one shot being discharged (72%) followed by two shots (20%), three (3%), and four or more (5%). In this sense, the situation described in the beginning, where three shots were fired is rather atypical.

WARNING SHOTS

According to the shooting decree, warning shots should, if possible, be fired before effective fire. Warning shots were fired in 37% of the cases and the combination of warning shots and effective fire occurred in 12% of the events. Situations with only effective fire accounted for 40% of the incidents. In incidents where the firearms were used *against a person*, warning shots were discharged in 54% of the events, a combination of warning and effective fire in 15% of the cases, and effective fire in 31%. Where vehicles were targeted, effective fire was shot in 90% of the cases. The majority of the bullets were aimed at the front wheels with the intent to stop the vehicle. However, officers are taught to not shoot at vehicles at all. In the words of one of the instructors: "How can you stop a car with an eight-gram bullet?"

In general, warning shots were often fired from a greater distance—thirteen meters between firing officer and suspect—than effective fire with an average of six meters. The skewed distribution with more shots fired from a short distance, makes the median a better measure than the arithmetical average. The median was six meters for warning shots and three meters for effective fire.

SUSPECT AND OFFICER INJURIES AND DEATHS ASSOCIATED WITH POLICE USE OF FIREARMS

In the incident described in the introduction, the suspect was injured, which also happened in 24% of use of firearms incidents. Death was the outcome in just 4% of the cases. This means that of suspects hit by bullets, 14% died. It is extremely rare that shots were fired with the intent to kill—of all the examined incidents there is only one possible case. To get the desired effect with the least amount of force, Swedish officers are taught and trained to initially aim at the suspect's legs. However, in pressing situations of self-defense, officers may of course aim and shoot at the chest.

Officers were injured in 10% of the instances and killed in only one of the 583 shooting incidents that occurred between 1985 and 2004. Compared to the suspects in this sample, who in all cases were hurt by *bullets*, types of inflicted wounds varied for the officers. Some have been injured by their own firearms or from shots fired from assailants; other officers have been cut, and some have received crush wounds. Injury severity varies from minor injuries to the two deaths that happened in an incident where two officers were shot and killed. The so called "Malexander incident" occurred in 1999, with three bank robbers who executed the officers with their own handguns.

REPORTING AND INVESTIGATION OF SHOOTING INCIDENTS

In Sweden, formal reports are only needed when shots have been discharged. According to the rules each incident must immediately be reported to the closest commanding officer, generally the shift leader. If there is a question about a shot against a person, the chief of police must also be informed and a report must be submitted. All incidents must also be reported to the National Police Board, which has the central administrative and supervisory responsibility of the Swedish police service.[3]

All shooting incidents are examined both by a prosecutor, who determines if there are reasons to start a preliminary investigation, and by the chief of police who checks on whether all rules have been followed. There may thus be situations where rules have been transgressed but the violations do not constitute a crime.

Almost 4% of the cases of self-defense ended in some kind of formal reaction (e.g., decision to prosecute, incident reported to board for personnel matters, or action by chief of police), compared to 20% of lawful authority situations and 60% of accidental shots. The rather high proportion for lawful authority underlines the difficulty required to make judgments in accordance with the shooting decree. As per accidental shots, the reason is often that the officers have not handled their arms according to correct procedures (e.g., not checking that the chamber was empty and then accidentally discharging a bullet).

CATEGORIZING SITUATIONS WHERE FIREARMS HAVE BEEN DISCHARGED

So far the description of use of firearms in Sweden has centered on different aspects of the incidents. The majority consist of cases where police officers have tried to avert an immediate danger, in most cases a direct threat toward them. These incidents may be further divided into six categories according to type of threat (see Table below for illustrations). In cases that are categorized as *Feared armed,* the officer is uncertain whether the counterpart carries a weapon or not. Usually the suspects have not obeyed commands from the officer to show their hands. The category *Firearms* includes all events where guns have been present, irrespective of whether they were fired or whether they were real firearms. The important aspect is what the officer perceived in the situation. *Threats with knife or other sharp object,* and *Assault with knife or sharp object* differ with respect to the actions by the suspects, specifically whether or not they are close and moving toward the officers. In *Assault with vehicle* cases, the assailants have tried to run down officers, most often with a car. A final category, *Other,* occurs less frequently (nine incidents) and consists of diverse cases.

Examples of Categories of Threats Where Swedish Police Officers Have Opened Fire

Category	Example
Feared armed	In connection with an arrest of a man, suspected for an attempted robbery, an officer felt threatened when the request to take the hands out of the pockets was not obeyed. After a warning shot, the man took out his hands and let go of a knife.
Firearms	A man reported that he would go out and shoot people, and then himself. Alarm about shooting. Shot against police officers when calling to the perpetrator. Two officers answered the fire.
Threats with knife or other sharp object	Conflict with knifing between neighbors. The perpetrator returned carrying a baseball bat and threatens to kill the police officers who both fire warning shots and then persuade the doer to give up.
Assault with knife or sharp object	Apartment. A man refuses to be transported by an ambulance. He threatened a police officer with a big and sharp fork and when he tried to stab a police officer cornered in a bedroom, he was shot in the leg and fell down.
Assault with vehicle	Car theft and leaving petrol station without paying. Drove against an officer, in spite of warning shot. The officer then fired against the tire of the car.

The annual average number of incidents and additional summary information is shown in Table 11-1. On a yearly basis the numbers of shootings are fairly small, with "feared armed" incidents somewhat more common than the other types of threats. The average distance between the firing officer and the target is shown in the second column. For the "feared armed" threats the distance was typically about 12 meters. This figure provides information about the minimum distance the officers tend to keep between themselves and the counterpart. The police can control the situation and will be able to follow up with effective fire if the opponent, in fact, has a weapon and attacks. For incidents involving firearms, the distance was greater with an average of 20 meters. A reasonable explanation is that guns present a danger at greater distances and officers want to maintain a safe distance between themselves and the assailant. For the other categories of incidents the average distance was shorter, particularly for attacks with a knife or other sharp object, in which officers fired from only about three meters. This seems to be a self-evident finding because assaults with these kinds of objects occur in close proximity.

One factor affecting the short distance associated with knife attacks is the rather high proportion of these incidents occurring indoors. It might be the case of police officers that are suddenly attacked inside an apartment or other

Table 11-1 Average Yearly Number of Incidents, Average Distance between Officer and Suspect in Meters, Proportion (%) of Incidents Taking Place Indoors, Proportion (%) of Incidents with Effective Fire, Proportion (%) of Incidents with Injured Officers, and Proportion (%) of Incidents with Injured (Including Killed) Assailants, by Type of Threat Situation

	Average # of incidents per year	Average distance (meters)	Indoors (%)	Effective fire (%)	Injuries to police (%)	Injuries to assailant (%)
Feared armed N = 82	5.6	11.6	7.7	20.9	0	16.0
Firearm N = 67	4.7	19.3	13.8	63.1	6.1	36.1
Threat with knife or other sharp object N = 56	4.0	6.1	23.2	43.6	0	34.5
Assault with knife or other sharp object N = 59	4.1	3.3	39.7	73.6	15.3	71.4
Assault with vehicle N = 68	4.4	5.1	3.3	91.7	3	8.9

confined space. The seemingly odd result for assaults with vehicles that have taken place indoors (3%) is explained by incidents in garages.

"Feared armed" threats have the lowest proportion of effective fire (including combinations with warning shots), only about 21%. This finding indicates that officers gained control with warning shots in the majority of the incidents. Besides shots fired against vehicles, effective fire was most common in those cases with knife assaults, followed by firearms incidents.

For police officers the most dangerous situation is often an attack with a knife or other sharp object. In about 15% of these incidents the officer was injured. The corresponding value for incidents with firearms was 6%. From the point of view of the counterpart, the most risky situation was to assault an officer by means of knife or other sharp object. When the officers decided to use their firearm in defense, most of the assailants were shot and injured. The picture that emerges for both officers and assailants is clear. Attacks from shorter distances, with knives or other sharp objects, are the most dangerous situations for both parties.

USE OF FIREARM TRENDS OVER TIME

The trend for the 20-year period 1985 to 2004 is shown in Figure 11-1. On average there have been 29 incidents per year. There is some variation across time, with a low 19 incidents in 2001 and a high of 35 that occurred in 1988, 1995, and 2004. The long-term trend over the period suggests that the number of incidents has been slightly decreasing.

The number of incidents where suspects have been injured has been fairly stable with an average of seven per year. As to incidents resulting in a fatal

Figure 11-1 Number of Incidents Where Police Officers in Service Have Opened Fire: Sweden, 1985–2004

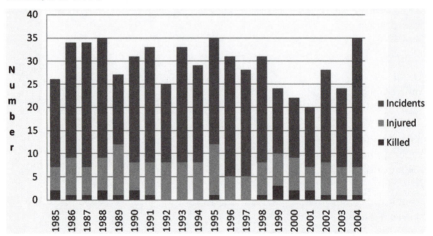

outcome, the value is more or less constant with about one civilian death per year. In about three incidents per year police officers were injured or killed, including incidents of police accidental fire, and this number has been stable during the 19-year observed period. These figures include the Malexander incident in 1999, which was the only incident resulting in a fatal outcome for police during the study time frame.

CONCLUDING REMARKS

In a commentary to the Police Act, it is stated the most lethal means of force available to police—firearms—should be used with "extraordinary restrictive-ness" (Berggren and Munck 1998, 74). There are good reasons for this posi-tion, given that violence, irrespective whether it is legitimate or illegitimate, in a civilized society should be as restrained as possible. Shootings resulting in serious injuries or death are dreadful events, not only for those who have been shot, but also for their kin and for the officers who discharged their weapons. Even to end up in a situation where a police officer contemplates using a gun might be deeply traumatizing (Karlsson and Christianson 2003).

There are some possibilities for improvements in policies and training that might help decrease the police use of firearms in Sweden. Some of those improvements might come from reviews of policies in neighboring countries (Knutsson 2005). There are three areas that are of particular interest and that might provide some insights into potential changes. First, in Denmark, Fin-land, and Norway police officers must also report incidents to a central agency whenever guns have been used only for the purpose of threats, (i.e., where guns have been displayed but not discharged). Second is the Norwegian policy regarding unarmed police force and third the Finnish policy, which is the most recent and well thought through.

How often Swedish police officers use their weapons for the purpose of threat without discharging bullets is unknown. Taking the Danish-Swedish ra-tio of roughly 1:2 for incidents involving discharges, and applying that ratio to "threat without discharge" incidents for Denmark, would result in about 500 threat incidents on a yearly basis. However, there are good reasons to believe this rough estimate is too low. Absence of active follow-up of threats with firearms may encourage extensive use that is not founded on the rules in the shooting decree. It has been shown that clear rules and strict follow-up routines have restraining effects on police officers in their use of firearms (Geller and Scott 1992; White 2001; 2003). One way of both getting an opin-ion of the level of threat use, and also restricting use, would be to introduce the same rules in Sweden as those in the other Nordic countries.

In Norway, the police are unarmed. For the officers to get armed requires an order from the chief of police. The Norwegian tactics for the police are characterized by this fact. To a large extent the incidents in Sweden consist of situations that began as a routine assignment on ordinary patrol and ended up in a rapidly occurring situation of self-defense that officers try to resolve through use of a firearm. These situations differ fundamentally from the incidents in Norway where officers discharge their firearms. More officers are present in Norway—the median value is five officers compared with two for Sweden—and the shots are fired from greater distances. The median value between the firing officer and the target is eight meters in Norway compared to three meters for Sweden (Knutsson and Strype 2003).

The explanation for this difference can be brought back to the Norwegian policy.[4] If Norwegian police officers end up in an emergency situation, they typically retreat, take stock of the situation, and ask for an order of armament. A tactical group is then organized to take care of the situation. The time delay means that many situations will be resolved without shots needing to be fired. For incidents in which an order of armament has been given, about 4% result in the use of threats and only two per thousand in guns discharged (Strype 2005; see also the chapter by Myhrer and Strype in this volume). Because the Norwegian police do not have access to firearms to start with, and must look for other solutions, it stands to reason that the Swedish police can learn from improved training and tactics in the field, both for use of force in general and for conduct in dangerous situations.

According to the Finnish policy, the threshold for taking the gun out of its holster is generally higher; only in situations where the officer is fully prepared to use it. There is no escalation in the rules with respect to the need for warning shots before effective fire may be commenced, as is stated in the other countries' rules (Åminne and Lounaskorpi 2005). This does not mean that shots necessarily will be aimed at the suspect because the desired effect can also be achieved by shots not fired directly at the opponent. The absence of warning shots in the written rules probably also makes it easier for the officers to apply those rules in the stressful and rapidly occurring situations in which shots are fired. Judgments can be made faster and shots may be fired earlier on with greater control. There are important lessons to learn from Finland when the Swedish shooting decree—especially regarding lawful authority—is rewritten, something that really should have happened many years ago.

Police Use of Firearms in the Nordic Countries: A Comparison

Johannes Knutsson and Annika Norée

ABSTRACT

IN THE NORDIC countries, the right of the police to use force is based on "lawful authority." That authority, in the most severe cases, includes the use of firearms. The Penal Codes in all the Nordic countries states that anyone, including police officers in service, can use force—including firearms—in self-defense. However, the specific rules for police use of firearms differ. In the Danish, Norwegian, and Swedish rules, it is explicitly stated that warning shots should be fired before effective fire is commenced. The concept of using warning shots does not, however, exist in the Finnish regulations. An important dividing line between the Nordic countries also exists for armaments, where historical practices and traditions vary. The Finnish, Danish, and Swedish police are routinely armed, but not the Norwegian. As a result, the Norwegian police fire their arms to a much lesser extent, both in absolute and relative terms, compared to officers in the other countries. The rates of officers firing their arms (thereby considering population differences) are the same for Danish, Swedish, and Finnish police forces. When the consequences in number of injured and killed persons are compared, the Danish and Swedish rates are similar, but higher than the Norwegian and Finnish which are comparable. Because the Finnish firearms policy for the police recently has been changed with the aim to restrict use, this result points in the direction of a successful reform.

Johannes Knutsson, Norwegian Police University College
Annika Norée, Stockholm University

INTRODUCTION

In the Nordic countries, the right of the police to use force is based on what is known as *lawful authority*,[1] which in the most severe cases includes the use of firearms. A police officer who shoots in such cases does not commit a crime, as lawful authority comprises a so-called general ground for exemption from criminal liability.[2]

There are considerable similarities among the Nordic countries concerning the use of legitimate force. However, when it comes to the use of firearms, there are differences that can be observed in rules, armament, training, and follow-up routines. This in turn affects the actual use, the number of injured and killed, and, importantly, the number of traumatized officers. Police officers ending up in situations where they have discharged their arms and caused injuries or death, have deep and hard experiences to handle (see the chapter by Klinger in this volume; also see Klinger 2004; Gersons 1989). Even those situations where officers have contemplated shooting may have a severe psychological impact (Karlsson and Christianson 2003).

In this chapter we will compare the Nordic policies concerning police use of firearms and try to understand the consequences of actual use. With respect to firearms policy we refer to rules, armament, training, and follow-up procedures. The American experience shows that the choice of policy has a significant impact on police use of firearms and, ultimately, the number of persons that will be shot to death by police officers (Alvarez 1992; Geller and Scott 1992; Milton et al. 1977).

RULES

The starting point within the Nordic countries is that police use of force must have statutory support. Lawful authority, as it is defined in the Police Act in each country, is intended to satisfy the requirement of legality (*statutory support*).[3] In all of the Nordic countries, the police authority to use force is also restricted by a set of other common principles, including the two basic principles of necessity and proportionality.

The rules that guide *the authority of the police to use force* are generally fully comparable in the Nordic countries, where Finland currently has the most modern regulation after a comprehensive penal law reform in 2004. Aside from the lawful authority to use force, a police officer has the same legal right as all other citizens to use force in self-defense.

The similar regulations within the Nordic countries are also fairly consistent when it comes to the issue of *the authority of the police to shoot*. In this regard, Denmark stands alone as the only Nordic country where the authority of the police to shoot is regulated by law (specifically in the Police Act).

More rules are found on a lower constitutional level, like in the other countries.[4] There are also some guiding cases concerning the matter.

Within the Danish regulations, the limits for the authority of the police to shoot are most clearly expressed. It is a weakness in both Norway and Sweden that the police have to act according to rules on the use of arms that were actually written decades ago. In Sweden, the police officers have to act according to rules established in 1969, which are both complex and outdated (Norée 2004; Norée 2005). The Finnish regulation is the most recent and is a result of a comprehensive effort to restrict officer's use of firearms when in service.

REPORTING AND DOCUMENTATION

Finland differs in that reports about use of firearms should be made to the Police Academy and not to the central administrative bodies like in the other countries. The reason is that the reports may contain useful information with possible consequences for training. The *use of firearms* does not only include shootings; threatening to shoot is also considered use.[5] In Denmark, Finland, and Norway, all firearms use must be reported including threats with firearms. Exceptions are made in cases where police officers only make their arms ready to fire. Sweden differs in this area because the police are required only to report incidents where shots have actually been fired. The Swedish definition of use of force is therefore more narrowly defined than the Danish, Finnish, and Norwegian.

In the Danish, Norwegian, and Swedish rules it is explicitly stated that *warning shots* should be fired before effective fire is commenced. The concept of warning shots does, however, not exist in the Finnish regulation. It is thereby not stated that Finnish police officers necessarily shoot to hit the counterpart. The desired effect can also be achieved by shots not aimed at the suspects (e.g., what in practice are warning shots). In Finland, it is therefore particularly important that the police make clear what the weapon was aimed at when shots were fired. Denmark differs in comparison with Finland, Norway, and Sweden where there are explicit rules stating that all use of firearms must be carefully documented and be reported to superior officers by the officers who used the weapons. The Swedish rules regarding reporting are more comprehensive than the Finnish and Norwegian.

INVESTIGATIVE ROUTINES

If an on-duty police officer has committed a contested act, neither the culpability nor the grounds for the criminal proceedings is affected. Accordingly, it is on the public court to try the act and, in the event of a conviction, to determine the sanction. This holds true for all the Nordic countries. On the other hand, police officers in Denmark, Finland, and Sweden occupy a special position in relation to the majority of other criminal suspects inasmuch as the investigation takes place under the aegis of their own office, although with *immediate entrance of the prosecutor*. The police in Denmark, Finland, and Sweden have special units that handle these investigations. Norway has another model altogether, relying on an independent body from the police and prosecutors.

ARMAMENT

An important dividing line between the Nordic countries exists for armament, where history and traditions vary.[6] The Finnish police were first to issue a routine armament in 1918 following the civil war. After a tragic episode in which four officers were killed in one incident, the Danish police were routinely armed with firearms in 1965. The same year the Swedish police transformed from a communal to a unified state police system, and as part of the reform became a routinely armed force. Norway, with its longstanding peaceful history, including policing (Næshagen 2000), has the only police force where the police still normally serve unarmed. Armament may only occur following an order by a chief of police.[7]

In Denmark, Finland, and Sweden, the service guns are automatic pistols. Norway is gradually changing from revolvers to pistols (Table 12-1).

Except for Norway, police officers in these countries have immediate access to firearms. In foreseeable situations where police may end up using firearms, there are generally no principal differences in the basic situations in which firearms might be used among the Nordic countries. Once equipped with firearms, police officers will be prepared to intervene. A fundamental

Table 12-1 Armament of Police in Denmark, Finland, Norway and Sweden

	Denmark	Finland	Norway	Sweden
Armament	Armed 1965	Armed 1918	Unarmed	Armed 1965
Service guns	Heckler & Koch 9mm	Glock 9mm	Smith & Wesson cal .38; Heckler & Koch 9mm	Sig Sauer 9mm
Arms for support	Heckler & Koch MP5	Heckler & Koch MP5; Shotgun ga.12	Heckler & Koch MP5	Heckler & Koch MP5
Ammunition	Hollow point Non-expandable	Expandable	Jacketed	Expandable

difference does exist for rapidly occurring incidents. The Norwegian tactic is basically to freeze the situation, get an order of armament, and organize an armed team to solve the problem. This often allows the situation to be resolved without the use of firearms.

All Nordic countries use the MP5 automatic gun as a reinforcement gun, or guns for support as it is called in some of the countries, which has a limited range of fire. In Finland, the police also use shotguns as special weapons.[8] In all Nordic countries, a decision must first be made by a chief of police for weapons of support to be used.

The choice of ammunition is a sensitive and controversial issue. Finland and Sweden use expandable ammunition, while Norway still uses jacketed bullets (a request by the Norwegian Police Directorate to change to expandable ammunition was turned down by the Department of Justice). Arguments supporting the introduction of expandable bullets include minimizing the risk for bystanders (resulting from ricochets or bullets that go through the target), and expanding the impact on the actual target. But the concern is that the greater effect has been assumed to increase risk for more civilians getting severely injured or killed. Denmark uses non-expandable hollow point cartridges. This type of bullet has a greater effect on the target compared to jacketed ammunition, but unintentional injuries are less likely than with expandable bullets.

In all the Nordic countries, the policemen are trained in the use of service guns during basic education. Denmark and Norway also instruct officers in the use of weapons for support during basic training, while in Sweden this training occurs when the officers enter their positions in the police districts. Finland has another training system, whereby only especially selected officers are trained in and authorized for the use of support and special weapons.

FIREARMS USE

Annual average number of reported incidents where police have used firearms, and the consequences of the incidents where fire has been opened, is shown in Table 12-2 (because Swedish police officers do not have to report incidents where they have only threatened to use their firearms, it is not possible to give this information). The time periods chosen did not include any considerable changes in the respective firearms policies for the police.

The number of incidents where firearms have been used varies considerably across Nordic countries.[9] One explanation is the great differences in incidents where firearms have been used for the purpose of threat only. However, to make this comparison fruitful, the values must be presented in rates relative to respective country populations (see Figure 12-1). The reader must bear in mind that caution is needed when interpreting these results. It might not be the case that findings may represent only differences in firearms policies. There could be some other factors as well. But considering the general

Table 12-2 Annual Average Number of Incidents Where Police Officers in Service Have Used Firearms for Threats, Opened Fire, Injured or Killed Suspects: Norway, Denmark (1996–2006), Sweden (1996–2004), and Finland (1997–2006)

	Denmark	Sweden	Norway	Finland
Threat	242	n.a.	60.4	23,4
Fire	14.5	26.4	2.4	13.1
Injured	3.5	6.7	0.7	1.6
Killed	1	1.2	0.3	0.2

similarities of the countries and some evident differences in policies, the most likely explanation is that a fair number of the divergences are likely due to differences in the national shooting policies for the police.

The results from two countries are particularly noteworthy. Denmark has both the highest absolute and relative rate of weapons use, which is also much higher than Norway—an expected result because of the differences in firearms availability. The most intriguing results were from Finland with a lower reported frequency than Norway. In both Denmark and Norway firearms use consists, in more than 90% of the incidents, of threats only, in contrast to Finland where the only 64% of the incidents were threats only. To define threats

Figure 12-1 Annual Average Number of Incidents Where Police Officers in Service Have Used Firearms for Threats or Opened Fire, per 1,000,000 Inhabitants, Norway, Denmark (1996–2006), Sweden (1996–2004), and Finland (1997–2006)

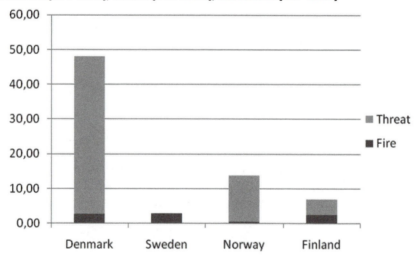

is admittedly not an easy task, and some of the variation may possibly be explained by differences in definitions and routines of reporting, but it is unlikely that the great dissimilarities are not due to real differences in police behavior. In Finland, the threshold to use the firearm is high, and when the officers have drawn their arms, they tend to fire. Finnish officers may resort to other forcible means (baton and pepper spray) to a higher degree, which is in line with their policy for use of various tools of force.

When it comes to incidents where firearms have been discharged, the frequencies are much lower than those for threats; ranging from Norway with slightly more than 2 incidents annually during the observed period, to Sweden with about 26. Norway has, as expected, both in absolute and relative terms, the lowest levels of use in the sense of police opening fire. The most probable explanation, of course, is the policy with a routinely unarmed police. It is reasonable to assume that comparable situations, which in the other countries would have ended up with officers firing their arms, are resolved in other ways in Norway. Finally, when rates are compared, Denmark, Sweden, and Finland have about the same levels of incidents where police officers have actually discharged bullets (Figure 12-2).[10]

When considering the consequences of firearms, on an annual basis about seven civilians are injured in Sweden and about one is killed. Corresponding values for Norway are slightly less than one injured and one shot to death

Figure 12-2 Annual Average Number of Incidents Where Police Officers in Service Have Opened Fire with no Injured Suspects, with Injured Suspects or Cases of Death Per 1,000,000 Inhabitants: Norway, Denmark (1996–2006), Sweden (1996–2004), and Finland (1997–2006)

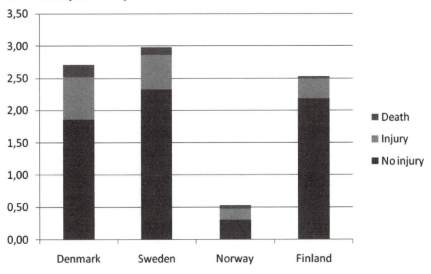

about every three years. The comparison of rates suggests that even if incidents with deadly outcomes are somewhat more common in Denmark, both level and structure as to consequences are strikingly similar to that of Sweden.

The most intriguing result is the outcome for Finland. Finnish officers fire their weapons to the same relative extent as Swedish and Danish officers, but the rate of injured and killed civilians are as low as that for Norway with its unarmed force.[11] A closer examination shows that Finland has the highest proportion of incidents with shots that have not injured or killed someone (about 86% for Finland and about 70% for Sweden and Denmark; Norway has the lowest at 58%). These data indicate that, in spite of the fact that the concept of warning shots does not exist in the Finnish regulation, actually a large portion of the Finnish shots are warning shots. A possible explanation is that their rules makes it easier for Finnish officers to make quick decisions, enabling them to shoot earlier in incidents where they may achieve the effects of what, in practice, are warning shots.

LAWFUL AUTHORITY OR SELF-DEFENSE?

Firearms are ultimately tools for the police to use to enable them to perform their mission. Given that task, they are also at risk for ending up in emergency situations where they have to resort to firearms for self-defense. The situations where firearms may be used are often dynamic and rapidly occurring events, where in one moment grounds for lawful authority exist and, in the next, self-defense may be justified. It is reasonable to assume that when shootings occur in such emergency situations—as self-defense situations often are—the police have less control than when the justification is based on lawful authority. This highlights the importance of clear rules that can guide the police. Unfortunately, the information about justification for use is not directly comparable between the countries. It is, however, possible to establish points of comparison.

When Danish police officers open fire, the motive is considered self-defense in about two-thirds of the cases (Holmberg 2004). In Finland, the most common reason is lawful authority (65%), followed by self-defense (23%), and a combination (12%). The Finnish data includes incidents with threats. But even if all self-defense situations had resulted in firearms being discharged—something that is most unlikely—shots supported by lawful authority would still constitute about 40% of the cases. There is no comparable information from Norway. The Norwegian policy implies that when shots are fired, as a rule, it is under more controlled situations (Knutsson and Strype 2002, 84–85; 2003, 437). However, when it comes to Sweden, cases of self-defense strongly dominate (81%) and there are few incidents that rely on lawful authority as the justification for firing (19%). These results emphasize

Norée's conclusion that the Swedish rules on lawful authority are inadequate (Norée 2004; 2005). It is extremely hard for a Swedish police officer to determine whether the conditions for lawful authority exist, ending up with what ought to be the exception (self-defense) as the major reason for police officers discharging their arms.[12]

CONCLUDING REMARKS

Among the Nordic countries, three protrude.[13] Finland has the most recently established rules on police use of forcible means, enacted in 2004—a result of a major reform of its policy. The effort started in the late 1980s because of uneasiness with unrestrictive use of firearms by the police. The results clearly indicate that the endeavor has been successful. Firearms use has decreased (Åminne and Lounaskorpi 2005) and, compared with their Nordic counterparts, the Finnish police injure at the same level as the normally unarmed Norwegian police. Given the reactive nature of police firearms use, and the stable levels of employment of firearms by the police in Norway as well as in the other Nordic countries (Knutsson 2006), it is hard to find reasons for Norway to change its policy of a routinely unarmed police force. As for Sweden, an overhaul of the rules is in dire need. Especially the rules regarding lawful authority needs to be rewritten enabling the police to use them. A positive sign is that the National Police Board recently has asked the Swedish Department of Justice to take a look at the rules.

13

Police Use of Firearms in China: An Overview of a Regulatory Framework

Kam C. Wong

ABSTRACT

THIS CHAPTER PROVIDES an overview of the legal framework regulating police use of firearms in China. After a brief review on recent debates over police firearms abuse, the chapter details the legal doctrine, regulatory framework, and administrative remedies over police use of firearms. The chapter ends with a discussion of the impact of such a firearm control scheme on policing in China.

INTRODUCTION

Police or public security (*Gongan*) in the People's Republic of China (herein-after P.R.C. or China) are given extensive power to execute their duties, the most formidable of which is the right to bear arms (P.R.C. 1981, Ch. 3) and use deadly force (P.R.C. 1980, Article 3). To date, other than occasional reports of egregious cases of police illegal use of firearms (or "guns" or "deadly force") in the news, there is little accessible data and few published research studies on police use of deadly force in China. Kam C. Wong (2009) observed that "Until very recently (1990s), research into China is handicapped by unavailability of sources, inaccessibility to places/people, scarcity of bi-lingual researchers, and incompatible scholarship style" (1). This chapter is a first attempt to provide an overview of the legal framework regulating the police use of firearms in China.

This chapter is organized as follows. Section I contextualizes this research with an overview of the police use of firearms debate. The next section details the legal framework governing police use of deadly force in China. Finally,

Kam C. Wong, Xavier University

the conclusion section begins with lessons learned from this study and closes with some suggestions for how legal control over police use of deadly force can be improved in China.

POLICE USE OF FIREARMS DEBATE

Police use of firearms in China against the "masses" (people) was unheard of before the Deng's reform in 1979 that opened China to the world. According to Mao, contradictions among the people are best resolved through education and with reason, not by force and coercion (1968). During Deng's reform the use of deadly force to effectuate arrests (Zheng 2004), suppress disturbances (*Asian Political News* 2005), and maintain self-defense (*People's Daily* 2007) are becoming more prevalent, and in some cases, deemed a necessity based on Deng's doctrine of security and stability above all (Scobell 2003).

Since 2000, the right to use deadly force has been a subject matter of heated debate in China, being brought to the forefront by high-profile cases of on- and off-duty police causing the wrongful killings of civilians, and repeated citizens' assaults of the police in the line of duty. In response, the Ministry of Public Security has taken resolute action to deal with the problem, including publishing "bright line rules" (e.g., Ministry of Public Security 2003), adopting zero tolerance polices (e.g., strict liability; Yi 2008), and mounting national gun control campaigns (Bao You Municipality).

POLICE AND PEOPLE'S PERSPECTIVE

Increasingly, police officers have been feeling vulnerable, impotent, and frustrated in the face of belligerent challenges and violent attacks in the line of duty. For example, according to the Ministry of Public Security (MPS) data (see Table 13-1), from 2001 to 2006 (January–May), there were 313 deaths and 23,970 injuries to police officers in the line of duty due to obstruction and resistance to police authority (Ministry of Public Security 2006).

A case in point: On February 13, 2006, a Tianjin traffic officer tried to stop a vehicle for making an illegal U-turn. The driver knocked the officer over and the officer hung on to the hood while the vehicle sped away. The officer was finally thrown off the vehicle and was seriously injured (*Enorth* 2006).

In a field study conducted between August and September of 2006 on why police officers did not defend themselves in the face of attacks, it was found that the police were afraid of offending the people (She 2003). Particularly, the police were instructed by their superiors to be "hit without reacting and yelled at without responding" ("da bu huan shou, ma bu hua kou"). Otherwise, police were subject to strict and uncompromising rules against the use of force. The

Table 13-1 Nationwide: Police Deaths and Injuries Due to Assaults in the Line of Duty

Year	Injuries	Deaths
2001	3,429	68
2002	3,663	75
2003	4,000	84
2004	3,786	48
2005	1,932	27
2006 (Jan. May)	160	11
Total	23,970	313

Source: Enorth 2006.

prospect of administrative discipline, criminal sanctions, and civil compensation creates significant anxiety on the police every time the gun is drawn.

Police officers want more liberal authority surrounding the use of deadly force to enforce the laws and protect personal safety. For example, Zhang Guifang, deputy Party secretary of Guangzhou (capital of South China's Guangdong Province) became a folk hero when he advocated the use of force to stop crime on April 4, 2006, by urging that police officers "not . . . be afraid of shooting criminals when their lives or the lives of common people are seriously threatened. Otherwise, it would be deplorable for the Chinese police force" (Mo 2006, 1). A substantial majority of the public is also supportive of giving the police more authority. A self-selected Web survey in China found that as of April 1, 2006, with a total of 21,700 votes, 86.4% support police shooting offenders to deter crime, while only 9.2% are concerned with police abuse of firearms (http://www.sjskw.com).

In 2008, mounting public concern and officers' frustration with strict gun policies resulted in an internal police study that openly admitted to a police gun control problem. Over the last three years, there were instances of public officials having guns lost and stolen and violations of gun control rules that resulted in injuries and killings. Some staff did not return their guns after retiring, leaving their post, transferring, or being terminated. Some of these staff members were under investigation, suspended from duties or in custody, suffered from Party discipline and administrative sanctions, dealing with family conflicts, economic disputes, or work pressure, and other violations of regulations deserving of removal of the right to bear arms (Bao You Municipality). A typical case serves to highlight the nature of the problem:

> On April 26, 2007, Wang Hongwu, a 32-year-old unlicensed "black taxi" was soliciting business at Xiongyuecheng train station. Wang got into an argument with police officer Su Kai for stepping into the prohibited zone. Su chased Wang away. Wang fell into convulsions after 100 yards. Wang's 62-year-old father

Wang Changyuan and 29-year-old wife Wang Jing later went to see Officer Su over the incident and had an argument. Wang, Sr. fainted and had to be hospitalized. At around 3 pm, Wang Changyuan, Wang Hongwu and Wang Wang Jing went to the duty room of the public security bureau in Xiongyuecheng town, Dalian to seek compensation from Officer Su. Su shot the three with five rounds. The crime scene was closed and a complete media blackout was maintained. The incident was briefly reported by local papers—Yunnan's Chuncheng *Evening News* and Fujian's Haixia *Metropolis Daily*—on April 28. National reporting was prohibited. It was not until April 29 that a deputy director of the Dalian Railroad Public Security Bureau met with the family of the victims at the Bohai Hotel to settle the case. (Guo 2007)

This example, and other similar cases nationwide, called for more oversight over the police use of firearms (*Fazhi Ribao* 2007). In the past, police use of firearms has generated deep-seated dissatisfaction and resulted in concerns with police abuse of powers during the reform era (O'Neill 2007).

REGULATORY FRAMEWORK

In China, there is no constitutional or common law right to bear and use arms. The manufacturing, distribution, transport, possession, and use of firearms are comprehensively regulated and strictly controlled (P.R.C. 1996, Ch. 2–6). Nevertheless China remains one of the more heavily armed nations in the world (Graduate Institute of International Studies 2003), in spite of repeated attempts by the police to purge the private holding of guns.

THE POLICE RIGHT TO BEAR ARMS

As a practice, police in China rarely carry guns on duty, due to ideological (Mao), moral (Confucianism), legal, bureaucratic, and resource considerations. As a P.R.C. citizen observed: "I grew up in a small town and then lived and worked in a mid-size city in China. I'd never seen police carry guns, even never seen police patrol the streets except traffic cops" (Fools Mountain Blog 2008). In China, the police right to bear arms is specifically provided by the "Law of the People's Republic of China on Control of Guns" (P.R.C. 1996), Article 5: "People's policemen of the public security organs . . . when performing their functions pursuant to law and when it is definitely necessary for them to use guns, be armed with guns for the discharge of official duties." A close examination of Article 5 reveals that the police right to bear and use arms is informed by the following principles:

1. There is no general right to bear arms, but by special empowerment based on functions (e.g., security organs and contingent on needs, e.g., discharge of duties).

2. The right to bear arms does not presuppose the right to use arms. Gun should only be used "when performing their functions . . . and . . . definitely necessary."
3. The right to bear arms and use force is subjected to strict State Council and Ministry of Public Security administrative rules.

CONTROL OF POLICE USE OF DEADLY FORCE

Police use of deadly force is subjected to three kinds of legal control: (1) accessibility to arms control; (2) gun use control; and (3) administrative sanctions for neglect or abuse. Gun use control provides rules and regulations governing permissible use of firearms. Administrative sanctions details penalties for violation of firearm control rules and regulations.

Legal Doctrine

In China, police right to use deadly force is based on the legal doctrine of "legitimate self-defense' ("zheng dang fang wei"). Police not only have the right but the duty to protect the rights of people and property of state (Supreme People's Court 1983). The basic principles of legitimate self-defense are spelled out in P.R.C, Criminal Law (1997): "Criminal responsibility is not to be borne for an act of legitimate defense that is undertaken to stop present unlawful infringement of the state's and public interest or the rights of the person, property or other rights of the actor or of other people and that causes harm to the unlawful infringer."

Police Law

After 1995, all aspects of police authority were governed by People's Police Law of the People's Republic of China (1995), and Article 10 governed the use of deadly force: "The people's policemen of public security organs may, in accordance with the relevant regulations of the state, use weapons in case of emergencies such as resisting arrest, rebellion, escaping from prison, grabbing firearms or other acts of violence." As a general rule, police can use arms to stop criminal activities and reduce harm to people and property. In doing so, as a first principle, the police should seek to avoid harm and damages to people and property as much as possible. The law further specified situations where use of firearms is generally allowed, including: preventing serious harm to public safety (such as arson); during the hijacking of planes or the robbing of guns and explosives; during crimes perpetrated with guns and explosives (such as armed robbery); preventing the destruction of strategic and infrastructural assets (such as telecommunication networks); protecting personal safety and public order from violent attacks; and dispersing unruly crowds or uncontrollable riots as a last resort. Such force is also acceptable when utilized for the purpose of protecting police officers in the line of duty (including during attacks on police); preventing the escape of prisoners; assisting in arresting felons and dangerous criminals; confronting criminals equipped with guns and other dangerous weapons; and any other circumstances allowed by law.

ADMINISTRATIVE REGULATIONS

In 2003, the MPS adopted a zero tolerance policy toward abuse use of guns on and off duty with the issuance of "Ministry of Public Security Five Prohibitions" (Ministry of Public Security 2003). This law included strict prohibitions against:

1. Violating gun control regulations;
2. Carrying arms while drinking;
3. Driving after drinking;
4. Drinking on duty;
5. Participating in gambling.

The "Five Prohibitions" provides administrative sanctions for the violator and immediate supervisory and senior leadership, which can include a mandatory transfer, resignation, or termination. For instance, when a violation of law by an officer leads to death or a gun-related crime, the immediate supervisor would be removed from office. In all cases with serious circumstances and consequences, the immediate supervisor and senior leadership would be asked to resign or be removed from office. Finally, if there are cover-ups, supervisors and leaders responsible will be held strictly accountable.

REMEDIES

Under the Constitution of the P.R.C. (1982), Chinese citizens harmed by government officials are entitled to restitution or compensation for harm done. As a foundational principle, the P.R.C. Constitution provides that: "the freedom of person of citizens of the People's Republic of China is inviolable" and "unlawful deprivation or restriction of citizens' freedom of person by detention or other means is prohibited." Further, "citizens who have suffered losses through infringement of their civil rights by any state organ or functionary have the right to compensation in accordance with the law."

Consistent with international norm, victims of police abuse can expect compensation as a matter of right under the P.R.C. Criminal Law and Civil Law. The Criminal Law of the P.R.C. (1997) established legal grounds for crime victims to sue for compensatory damages where the victim has suffered an economic loss as a result of a criminal act; the criminal, in addition to receiving criminal sanctions according to law, shall in accordance with the circumstances be sentenced to pay compensation for the economic loss. More specifically, the law creates a legal liability on part of the officer to address official wrongdoings. Finally, the Law of the People's Republic of China on State Compensation (1995) creates a special cause for action against police for harm caused by unlawful use of firearms: "The victim shall have the right to compensation if an administrative organ or its functionaries, in exercising their administrative functions and powers, commit any of the following acts infringing upon the right of the person of a citizen: . . . Unlawfully using weapons or police restraint implements, thereby causing bodily injury or death to a citizen . . . " In order to recover damages, victims of police abuse must prove the following:

1. The police must be acting in official capacity (e.g., under "color of law," and in the line of duty, not off duty);
2. The police's exercise of authority is illegal;
3. The police action must cause harm.

In cases of injury or death, compensation can include out- of pocket-medical expenses, loss of income due to missed working time (up to five times the State average of yearly salary of staff and workers in the previous year), and loss of working capacity in whole or in part (with a maximum of ten times State average salary). For total loss of function, the maximum penalty is twenty times the State average salary, plus living expenses for life. If death results, compensation for death and funeral expenses shall be paid, with the total amount being 20 times the State average yearly salary, or living expenses covered for a dependent with no working capacity (Jin 2006).

CONCLUSION

This chapter provides a first look at P.R.C. legal control of the police use-of-force framework. This chapter is about police laws on the book, not in the court or street. The question of how legal control works in practice and with what impact is not the objective of this study. Nevertheless, the outlining of legal framework governing police use of force and deadly force should help us to understand what the P.R.C. policymakers believe to be the best way to control the police and their firearms.

The lessons we learned here is that, consistent with Chinese comprehensive crime control thinking, the MPS control of police use of firearms is conducted in a comprehensive, systematic, and holistic manner. As a result, the MPS spends much time in regulating gun availability for the police (e.g., how many guns are available and entitlement, who can bear arms, how guns are used, and how offenders are sanctioned). Another point to note is that internal administrative control is given more weight than external legal control. Finally, it is clear that to the Chinese administrator, prevention is better than a cure.

In the process of investigations, we find that the MPS has taken robust and resolute steps to remedy police misuse of firearms. This is evidenced by a zero tolerance gun use policy and generous compensation for police shootings. Such highly charged counter-measures, however, come with a high price. Police are increasingly anxious about the use of arms for fear of administrative discipline and legal punishment (*Southern Weekly Magazine* 2008). Violent criminals and belligerent citizens are, in turn, emboldened. This is evident in increased challenges to police exercising authority (e.g., mass incidences and more blatant attacks on police in the line duty, including forcefully resisting arrest).

The way forward, to improve the regulatory framework, is to move in two directions. First, there is a need to remove legal ambiguities. This can be achieved by refining the laws to make room for more structured and guided police discretion in the use of arms (e.g., detailing what critical risk factors to be used in shooting decision, or specifying what warning steps need to be taken before use of force is allowed). Second, there is a need to provide for more legal protection for street officers from belligerent citizens and violent attacks. This can be done by introducing a "citizen accountability" doctrine and system, such as adopting contributory negligence concepts in deciding compensatory damages cases against wrongful shooting cases.

14

Deadly Force in the United States

Gregory B. Morrison

ABSTRACT

Though the United States is a "gun culture" that is owed to its unique combination of historical developments and long-standing constitutional protections, police use of firearms attracted little scholarly, legal, and practical attention until the tumultuous 1960s. This chapter therefore begins with pertinent historical context surrounding the police-firearms nexus before summarizing major research findings that influenced police policies, programs, and practices in the late 20th century. The chapter then turns to two prominent challenges that scholars and practitioners face and which revolve around training and technology. One is state-based standards for initial or "recruit" firearm training that dramatically vary across the United States. This situation is then compounded by the idiosyncratic approaches that the thousands of state and local police departments take in designing and delivering in-service programming for officers throughout their periods of employment. This combination of latitude at both state and local levels produces a dizzying array of approaches to firearms training. Interestingly, police appear to assume that disparate approaches achieve similarly utilitarian ends in terms of the many capabilities that officers ostensibly should possess in order to prudently prevail in these highly demanding encounters. Importantly, the nature and extent of these differences make it highly unlikely that programs produce comparably (in some cases perhaps not even adequately) prepared officers. A second, closely related challenge involves the technology and methods associated with the widely popular computer-based simulation equipment for judgment/decision-making training, but which has not yet been validated. The impact of this form and other forms of experiential training on officer performance in field encounters needs research aimed at identifying and developing best practices.

Gregory B. Morrison, Ball State University

INTRODUCTION

United States police departments primarily operate at the municipal and county levels and generally do not take direction or priorities from state or federal departments. This makes firearms use, along with responsibility for it, a largely local phenomenon. Deadly force is a rare but serious matter for police and the communities they serve, but there is no serious argument as to whether police officers should be armed and able to protect themselves and the public. As has been the case since the mid-19th century, the officers most often involved in shootings are uniformed patrol officers. The principal firearm remains the handgun, because its light and compact features facilitate holster carrying for immediate use in an emergency.

This chapter is divided into four sections. First, it briefly examines historical context surrounding the police-firearms nexus and then, second, summarizes some key findings that emerged from early research. Third, the focus then turns to recent research and the implications for policy and practice. Finally, the chapter concludes with a discussion of several worthy research challenges aimed at identifying training technologies and evaluative approaches that might measurably improve officer field performance and thereby contribute to improvements in both officer and public safety. At present our understanding of officer field performance is far too anecdotal and too heavily dependent on speculative or desirable results, as opposed to conclusions grounded on a firm empirical foundation.

HISTORICAL PERSPECTIVE

Police firearms use in the United States dates to the mid-19th century when several large urban cities began experimenting with modern policing. The catalyst for creating those departments was civil disorder and the occasional major riot, and that typically left what now are common missions and capabilities both poorly conceptualized and executed. Reform efforts in the early 1900s focused on instilling the crime-fighting mission, along with enhancing the public image of police work. One avenue for achieving improved capabilities included implementing training, and this extended to rudimentary target shooting with handguns. Despite the promise of change, police executives, the local governments they reported to, and their respective legislative bodies afforded few resources for officer firearm proficiency, though this obviously was preferable to none. Attention to basic tactical procedures and sound decision making during field encounters languished until the late 20th century. To further compound matters, the practical benefits accruing to trainees from the prevalent mid-20th-century models of marksmanship and gunhandling would have been quite modest (Morrison and Vila 1998; Morrison 2008).

This is fascinating on a number of levels, not the least being the rather unique historical developments and constitutional guarantees that leave the United States perceived as *the* world's gun culture. Such a country might be expected to have a complement of modern police officer "gunfighters," but historically this is far from reality. In terms of the handgun itself, it is interesting that police did not embark on a large-scale transition to the now ubiquitous semiautomatic pistol until rather recently (Reaves and Hickman 2004). Neither firearms proficiency training nor the prudent use deadly force, however, attracted more than scant scholarly, legal, or practitioner attention until the 1960s (e.g., see Geller and Scott 1992).

PIONEERING RESEARCH

Civil unrest during the 1960s sometimes brought urban police and black communities together under highly charged circumstances. Long-standing tensions between police and blacks in some cities had resulted in a chronically tense environment which police use of force, particularly deadly force, further exacerbated. A racial dimension to the use of deadly force seemed obvious to many observers, and early scholars did find a disproportionate use of deadly force against blacks given their relative percentage in the general population (e.g., Robin 1963; Faison and Clark 1974 as cited in Fyfe 1978; also see Geller and Karales 1981). Blacks and Hispanics were killed at sometimes highly disproportionate rates compared to whites. Subsequently, however, researchers discovered that this frequently was tied to indirect measures of workplace danger as reflected in community homicide and other violent crime rates, officers' assigned patrol areas, and their activity levels, as well as suspect weapon possession or use during encounters (consider National Institute of Justice 1999).

Constitutional provisions, state laws, and department policies all benefited from scrutiny, and no longer was the norm either no written policy or one not far removed from this classic example that refers to the handgun itself: "Never take me out in anger; never put me back in disgrace" (Chapman 1967 as cited in Milton et al. 1977, 47). Importantly, restrictive policies implemented during the 1970s and 1980s led to decreases in the number of fatal shootings (Fyfe 1978), and early in the 1980s researchers already were able to detect shooting rate decreases of approximately one-third (Sherman and Cohn 1986). Interestingly, this coincided with heightened concerns over "officer survival" driven by increased violence toward police, particularly in the form of felonious line-of-duty deaths. During the 1960s, the rate leapt from 14 slain officers per 100,000 sworn personnel to 38, and this understandably riveted the attention of police to improving workplace safety (FBI 1972; for more discussion see Fridell and Pate 1993; Geller and Scott 1992).

The landmark 1985 U.S. Supreme Court case of *Tennessee v. Garner* shares credit for speeding change in deadly force policies with the growing influence of professional standards, efforts to improve public perceptions and relations, and the reality of civil lawsuits and monetary awards to plaintiffs. Externally, skepticism over police departments investigating their own shootings brought scrutiny. When used wisely, department culture can positively influence the degree to which police officers adhere to restrictive deadly force policies through executive-level clarity when coupled with rigorous internal investigative processes (Uelmen 1973; White 2001). Human nature suggests that police generally will avoid behaviors that bring certain, swift, and appropriately severe consequences for them professionally and personally. Importantly, and rather counterintuitively, strict policies combined with thorough post-shooting investigations have *not* been associated with increased felonious deaths or serious injuries. Indeed, police work is now at its safest levels in four decades when measured by felonious line-of-duty deaths; the rate is now one-fourth of that experienced at the peak in the early 1970s (FBI 2008; Fridell and Pate 1993; Morrison 2008).

RECENT RESEARCH

An appropriate starting point for this section is what we know about the volume or number of civilian fatalities attributed to police use of deadly force. This has been estimated at between 300 and 1,000 per year (e.g., see Fyfe 1999; Geller and Scott 1992; Sherman and Cohn 1986). Yet, because only around one-half of the suspects shot at by police are struck by at least one bullet, and only around one-third of those are killed, the volume of shootings in the United States each year probably is between 2,000 and 6,000. These figures might seem high until factoring in the violent nature of some police work that results in around 60 felonious line-of-duty deaths and 17,000 injuries annually, the sheer volume of police-public contacts of approximately 44 million face-to-face encounters annually, the large number of encounters where police display firearms in response to patent threats or ones that reasonably might develop yet do not fire, violent crime levels (e.g., 17,000 murders or non-negligent homicides in 2006), and the estimated 250 million firearms owned by the general population (Durose, Schmitt, and Langan 2005; FBI 2008; Hepburn et al. 2007). Given these facts, perhaps most surprising is the infrequency of police shootings. Indeed, researchers have repeatedly confirmed that police use of force of any kind is rare and that deadly force is extremely rare (e.g., International Association of Chiefs of Police 2001; and for an excellent summary see National Institute of Justice 1999). Furthermore, researchers long have noted the hesitancy of police to use deadly force even when justifiable under applicable constitutional, statutory, and policy provisions (Geller 1985; Klinger 2004). James Fyfe, the leading researcher on the use of deadly force by police from the 1970s through the early 2000s, identified three prominent sets of factors—environmental, organizational, and situational—that he found to influence police shooting behavior (e.g., see Fyfe 1978; 1979; 1999; also see Geller and Scott 1992 regarding Fyfe's many contributions). Michael White has extended Fyfe's work by exploring a number of research questions using official records and summary reports on nearly 1,000 Philadelphia shootings for 1970–1992. He first (White 2001) examined the effects of various legislative and policy impacts on police shooting behavior in Philadelphia, finding that shooting rates remained consistently high until policy changes implemented in 1980 cut the rate roughly in half during the 1980s when compared to the 1970s. The linchpin was thorough post-shooting administrative investigation coupled with appropriate administrative sanctions.

White (2002) pursued situational characteristics that emerged as being potential predictors of "non-elective" deadly force incidents, while narrowing his scope to encounters with "assaultive suspects armed with guns." As one might imagine, the type of incident (e.g., man-with-gun, robbery, and disturbance) was an important predictor of shooting likelihood. The presence of multiple officers also made a difference, likely because operational policies typically call for dispatching more than one officer on potentially dangerous calls-for-service. Shootings involving gun-assaultive suspects also tended to occur soon after arrival at the scene or in making initial contact. Despite the previously mentioned pioneering research that often suggested racial influences—in particular, white officers disproportionately using deadly force against minority, especially black, citizens—White found the tendency for officer and suspect race in Philadelphia to be non-white as well as intraracial.

White (2003) also probed the role of external factors in Philadelphia, finding that neither population levels, nor arrests for violent felonies and homicides, were associated with shooting rates. Much of his analysis focused on the possible contributions to shooting behavior made by the 1974 federal district court injunction and federal appellate court's concurrence attributed to the previously mentioned prevailing operational norms within the Philadelphia Police Department; the 1976 U.S. Supreme Court's overturning of these lower court decisions (also an artifact of departmental culture); and the 1985 U.S. Supreme Court landmark decision in *Tennessee v. Garner*. Changes in state law during the study period did not have a measurable effect, though two minor impacts related to department policy were in the opposite directions of that which was expected. As for *Garner*, the department had instituted similar provisions in 1980 and, thus, before the 1985 case, and that essentially eliminated it as a likely influence.

Most recently, Michael White and David Klinger (2008) used the 1970–1992 Philadelphia data to empirically test long-standing, anecdotal-based assertions about "contagious" or reflexive firing wherein an officer's initial shots precipitate firing by multiple officers. In addition to finding these highly publicized accounts to be extremely rare, they did not find empirical support for a contagion effect. Klinger's (2004) earlier and fascinating work explored officers' perceptions of training, patrol, and special teams environments through the experiences of officers who used deadly force under a wide variety of circumstances, as well as those who under certain conditions held their fire. Klinger conveyed through that work many practical insights into officers' thoughts on the complexities and implications of these high-stakes encounters for them professionally and personally.

In addition to critically analyzing the historical (Morrison and Vila 1998; Morrison 2008) and exploring field performance (Schade, Bruns, and Morrison 1989; Vila and Morrison 1994) dimensions to firearms use, my own research has focused on establishing an empirical foundation for understanding the wide variety of approaches that departments take in preparing and certifying officers for performing during dangerous encounters. This is important because of two steady themes from prior research. First, combat shooting performance varies dramatically between departments (e.g., bullet hit rates range from around 15%–60% across departments), yet typically is relatively low (e.g., most police bullets miss their target because hit rates rarely exceed 30%). Second, both anecdotal and empirical evidence from early research (e.g., see McManus et al. 1970) indicate that firearms training and qualification policies and processes differed across departments in important ways.

The first two comprehensive surveys of training and qualification were conducted in the late 1990s in Washington State (hereafter "smaller departments") with the support of the state's Criminal Justice Training Commission and the assistance of the Washington State Law Enforcement Firearms Instructors Association (Morrison 2003). A similar, but briefer survey was administered in 2001 to major municipal and county departments, along with state police and highway patrol departments (hereafter "larger departments") (Morrison 2006a). A few highlights suffice to convey some fundamental difference in the areas of training, qualifying, and assessing field performance (also consider Morrison 2006b).

Instructors: Large municipal departments are more likely to rely on full-time instructors, whereas state police and highway patrol departments usually rely on collateral-duty instructors who hold other primary responsibilities (e.g., as patrol officers or investigators). Around three-quarters of the larger departments reported requiring periodic update training, but only half did so at least annually. Departments with full-time cadres also were much more likely to invest in higher numbers of hours for their own update training. Among smaller departments, firearms instruction was an overwhelmingly collateral-duty assignment. Though this approach need not be inherently inferior to a full-time cadre, nearly half of the instructors among the smaller departments reported that they were not provided with on-duty time to prepare for conducting training and requalification sessions. Furthermore, not quite one-third of these smaller departments required instructor refresher training.

Training: The larger departments typically provided around eight hours of handgun activity hours a year, though many provided far fewer. For judgment and tactics training, which today are principal components to these critical programs, computer-based and role-playing simulations were the two primary formats. Yet officers most often participated in only around five scenarios over a two-year period, and only around half of the departments documented any aspect of those sessions. As such, activities that have come to be perceived as vital to acceptable officer performances in dangerous encounters remain largely practice or experiential and, thus, rarely comprise a key component to their continuing certification.

Among the smaller departments, activity hours ranged widely from 0 to 64, with a mean of 13, a median of 10, and a mode of 8. Three-in-five departments provided from 8 to 16 hours. While training was most often conducted quarterly, there were departments relying on annual, semiannual, bimonthly, and monthly intervals. Finally, in terms of shots fired, 29% of departments provided 750 or more cartridges annually, yet a very similar 32% provided only between 100 and 499. It is unlikely that these two vastly different levels produce similar outcomes for officers in terms of the numbers and/or levels of skills.

Requalification: The two major in-service firearms activities—training and requalification—attracted highly varied resource allocations among larger departments. Requalifying consumes a large portion of annual handgun activity hours even though more and varied training does occur today. On average there were slightly more hours reserved for training than requalifying, but at least one department of each type (city, county, and state) used *all* (100%) of its annual hours for re-qualification, while at the other extreme one of each type used 5% or less for this purpose Among the smaller departments, and as with the larger departments, officers with the vast majority could requalify despite missing with numerous shots as long as their point scores cleared the percentage threshold score. That figure typically falls between 70% and 80% despite considerable differences in terms of target(s) size and scoring zones, target distances, time limits, and related gunhandling. The single most common policy response (40%) for when officers failed to requalify on their first attempt was to have them repeat it that day until a passing score resulted.

Field assessment: Nearly two-thirds of the larger departments reported that their firearms training units had no role in post-shooting investigations. Around half did not receive information from those investigations, while two-in-five did not even have formal access to the resulting files. This raises serious questions about the type and extent of applicable insights to meaningfully inform the evolution of firearms and deadly force training—in the past or presently. This is disconcerting because these programs are expressly intended to prepare police officers to competently perform during high-risk, challenging encounters in which they might have to use deadly force.

RAND Corporation recently completed a study for the New York City Police Department (NYPD) in which it focused narrowly on the firearms training program and the shooting investigation process (Rostker et al. 2008). The study generated many recommendations, and there are ones worth noting here. For instance, RAND recommended that NYPD develop recruit training performance standards requiring that recruits demonstrate their knowledge and skills at a "mastered" level. In terms of application (e.g., simulations or role-playing scenarios) training, the department should add simulation equipment, update the vignettes, and involve recruits in a wider range of scenarios. The RAND research team encouraged the department to reconsider the current "firearm-qualification paradigm" (a long-standing one shared with depart-ments around the nation) that it characterized as underemphasizing the wide array of proficiencies needed for performing competently in armed confronta-tions (in this regard also see Vila and Morrison 1994; Morrison and Vila 1998). In terms of the firearm-discharge investigative process, there was a recommendation that reviews extend to "the tactics used." RAND even recommended a pilot study to determine the effect of increasingly popular handgun-mounted laser sighting systems and flashlights on various aspects of field performance, such as the impact of light levels on officer decisions to use deadly force and, in the event of a shooting response, shooting accuracy.

FUTURE RESEARCH

The deadly force literature reveals that early research that was limited to fatal-ities and/or woundings soon expanded to include all incidents in which police and/or suspects fired a weapon, regardless of whether anyone was struck by bullets. The effect was a dramatically increased capture of relevant data for understanding of these complex encounters. We now should extend this even further to include encounters in which police reasonably *could* have used deadly force (consider Klinger 2004). This would include calls-for-service with obvious potential for extreme violence and officer initiated contacts of a risky nature. This would enable an even more detailed examination of deci-sion making, tactics, and firearms proficiency that includes both marksmanship and gunhandling skills that are central to police-citizen encounters that feasi-bly could lead to the use of deadly force.

Another challenge presents itself in the form of statewide police training commissions and professional associations whose standards vary considerably with regard to recruit and in-service firearm and deadly force training. This is especially relevant because of the previously discussed wide latitude that departments exercise in their programs, ones that seem highly unlikely to achieve comparable ends. In an era of reduced resources—not only state and local budgets, but also currently skyrocketing raw materials such as copper and lead for ammunition—matters as basic as the number of training sessions, hours, and number of cartridges fired will come under increased pressure. Police need an empirical foundation for recommendations in these areas, this as opposed to simply relying on convenient divisions of the calendar year, long-standing personal preferences, and the understandable desire to train as much as possible.

A third challenge involves technology, instructional methodologies, and assessment models. The impact of firearms and deadly force training on officer performance in field encounters would greatly benefit from research aimed at identifying and validating best practices in this critical training. Why? Because while there are many opinions, we actually know very little about the advantages and disadvantages of the three primary formats: live-fire scenarios at a conventional range, role-playing with non-gun props or ones fitted to fire marking cartridges, or computer video-based simulations. Presently, these three formats are treated with relative equivalency, leaving one to wonder about their effectiveness. Do police really perform better as a result of these experiences? Which format produces the most desirable results? What is the impact of instructor expertise and approach to conducting this training? It is my hope that within a decade we can confidently answer these and many related questions about the impact of training on field performance.

Finally, and of utmost importance it seems to me, is our need for comprehensive program evaluation—conceptualization, process, output, and impact— that meaningfully informs executives, managers, and trainers about value added by their efforts to prepare their officers to competently perform in dynamic, high-risk encounters against determined suspects. Evaluation should be at the core of future policy making and the identification of best practices. This is because it should heavily influence the content and delivery of training, what we need to glean from post-shooting investigations, and how best to evolve police firearms and deadly force training in the United States and elsewhere. Doing so will make important contributions to, on the one hand, minimizing the use of deadly force by police officers while, on the other hand, maximizing officer performance under those circumstances when their use of firearms is a reasonable and appropriate response.

15

An Exploration of Police Use of Firearms in Australia

David Baker

ABSTRACT

POLICE USE OF FIREARMS in Australia remains problematic and contentious. In recent decades, a disproportionate number of fatal police shootings have involved the mentally ill. The state of Victoria has experienced a spate of police shooting fatalities. Victoria Police implemented Project Beacon, an on-going training program designed to develop defensive tactics in order to limit dependence on firearms. A substantial decline in police shootings resulted, although recent years have witnessed intermittent rises in police shooting fatalities. Despite considerable debate, alternative weapons—OC spray and TASERs—have been introduced across much of Australia. It is argued that a range of options is needed, especially appropriate training and negotiation skills, in order to ensure that use of the gun remains very much the last resort.

INTRODUCTION

In a democratic society, lethal force, both theoretically and legally, is the option of last resort for police. Victoria's Office of Police Integrity's (OPI) director highlighted the consequences of lethal force: "A fatal police shooting is a tragedy in itself and the impact profound and lifelong, for both police and the families of the victims." Inappropriate force can also harm public confidence in police (Brouwer 2005, 55). This chapter examines police use of firearms across Australia, but Victoria is the focus because this state has experienced a disproportionate number of fatal police shootings in the late 20th century.

Despite the hazards of trying to estimate police violence against citizens (Chan 1997), it must be emphasised that the vast majority of citizen-police

David Baker, Monash University

interactions in Australia do *not* involve the use of force or even the threat of force (Goldsmith 2006). The use of police lethal force is an uncommon event, but excessive force by police often attracts critical scrutiny by the media, politicians, concerned libertarians, and the police themselves. In reality, police in Australia do not often resort to the use of force, and they identify service and crime prevention as paramount in community interaction (Findlay 2004). Firearms are typically not present at crowd management situations such as picketing, protests, sporting and festive events.

Much Australian research focuses on excessive use of force by police (Coady, James, and Miller 2000; Findlay 2004; McCulloch 2001), rather than justifiable use or avoidance of force. As P. A. J. Waddington (1999a) argues, "cops usually ask or command people to do something and those people usually comply" (30). However, police operate in volatile, unpredictable, and sometimes dangerous contexts (Sarre 1993). Approximately 190 police officers have been murdered in Australia since English-style law enforcement was established in the 19th century (Webster 2004). Dangers were highlighted in April 2005 when an experienced senior constable, on a solo ("one-up") patrol in the outskirts of eastern Melbourne, was shot with his own service revolver by a man who later turned the pistol on himself. The Victoria Police Association (VPA) subsequently initiated a campaign against solo police patrols.

According to ethicist Seamus Miller (2000), Australian society accepts police use of deadly force as a last resort if the offense is a serious one and if the offender is prepared to use deadly force to avoid arrest. The issue for police and the public is how serious the offense needs to be to justify use of deadly force. Findlay (2004) argues that the media regularly neutralizes police violence, including fatal shootings, through justifications such as self-defence and the necessity of police operations. He claims that the media in Australia is reluctant to challenge the independence of the police and demand accountability for police behavior. This is not necessarily so. *The Age* newspaper, for instance, led with numerous investigative reports of police malfeasance and fatal shootings in Victoria in the 1990s. The unacceptable and deviant actions of two police officers shooting Roni Levi on Sydney's tourist Bondi Beach on June 3, 1997, were exposed through media outrage. In a suicidal state and armed with a kitchen knife, Levi, surrounded by six police, was shot four times at close range during an acute psychotic episode. The coroner recommended that the Director of Public Prosecutions (DPP) investigate laying charges against the two officers, but the DPP eventually announced that no charges would be laid (J. Miller 2000, 157).

HISTORICAL USE OF FIREARMS

Police use of firearms has been a contentious issue since convict settlement under military control. In the 19th century, the six Australian colonies all established independent police forces organized and supported by centralized bureaucracies. The colonial police forces adopted similar policy and administrative control mechanisms and replicated the English policing principles and institutions. Although in theory policing was meant to be civil in nature, both in organization and operation, it often was militaristic (Haldane 1995; McCulloch 2001). Police departments adopted many procedures and symbols of the military including uniforms, ranks, batons, firearms, drills, ceremonies, and procedures. Colonial policing featured many confrontational, armed clashes (e.g., 1850s goldfields, 1873 Clunes Riot, 1890s Great Strikes) (Baker 2005).

The failure of governments to hold police accountable for alleged excesses and violence, including shootings, was a common characteristic of Australia's colonial and pre-World War II history. A few notorious examples of police firearms excesses during industrial disputations include:

- On February 2, 1912, "Black Baton Friday," in Brisbane about 15,000 demonstrating workers were confronted by police and special constables, armed with rifles and bayonets (Johnston 1992).
- On "Bloody Sunday" at Fremantle wharf, May 4, 1919, police and wharfies fought a bloody, pitched battle. Edward Brown was shot by police and Tommy Edwards died from police batoning (Oliver 2003).
- On June 29, 1919, at two Townsville meatworks, police panicked and opened fire on workers. Seven people were injured as a result of police bullets (Cutler 1973).
- On November 2, 1928, constables fired approximately 100 bullets at fleeing stevedores at Port Melbourne. An unarmed stevedore, Alan Whittaker, "got shot right through the back of his neck. The bullet came out through his mouth" (Baker 2005, 38–43).
- In late 1929 and early 1930, the New South Wales police "flying squad" terrorized the northern NSW coal-mining communities. Miner Norman Brown died as the result of a ricocheted police bullet (Comerford 2006).

More recently, accountability mechanisms from the 1970s onwards—Royal Commissions, internal police investigations, civilian oversight bodies and mobile cameras—have had a far-reaching effect on overt police operations, including use of firearms.

Allegations of excessive police coercion, including inappropriate use of firearms, have tainted the police image of community protector. Questions have been voiced about police use of force, especially in relation to Indigenous peoples (deaths in custody revelations), the unemployed, gay men, drug users, radical extremists, strikers, youth, and the socially marginalized (Baker 2005; Coady, James, and Miller 2000; Findlay 2004; White and Perrone 2005). Findlay (2004) argues that police in Australia, akin to many police counterparts, have acted within an atmosphere of "selective coercion" as they have confronted such marginalized and isolated groups (12). Police also vigorously enforced the law that dispossessed Aborigines of their land, suppressed Aboriginal resistance, and enforced segregation (Finnane 1994).

USE OF FORCE: PRINCIPLES AND GUIDELINES

With the advent of the Federation of Australia in 1901, each of the six states maintained its policing autonomy under a centralized, disciplined, bureaucratic system. These centralized public police departments are large-scale organizations: the NSW Police Force numbers more than 15,000 sworn members; Victoria Police numbers approximately 11,500. Unlike New Zealand, there is no unitary police administration in Australia. Today, all six state police organizations espouse the principle of minimum force and identify service and crime prevention as paramount in community interaction and intervention. Officers support "Safety First" principles that advocate a cautionary and suspicious approach.

The National Guidelines on Police Use of Lethal Force (1994) clearly advocate that "intentional lethal use of firearms may only be made when strictly unavoidable in order to protect life" (5). The first principle of the *National Guidelines for Incident Management, Conflict Resolution and Use of Force* (Tuckey 2004) explicitly states that police management should "promote the policy that the police will use the minimum amount of force appropriate for the safe and effective performance of their duties" to effect arrest and apprehension (v). Any force used should be proportional to the level of risk involved. Emphasis is placed on "the over-arching importance of effective communication and conflict resolution as means to resolve incidents" (Tuckey 2004, vii). Tactical preferences range from police presence, tactical disengagement, negotiation, empty hand tactics, cordon and containment, lethal force, and various less-than-lethal options. Operational police can only carry operational safety equipment "for which they are fully trained and deemed competent" (Tuckey 2004, 2). Police organizations and individual police are conscious that they can be held vicariously liable for the unnecessary use of force as well as failing to perform required duty.

The Australian guidelines fit Waddington's mantra (1990) that force should not be employed until it becomes essential, normally in response to the threatening actions of an adversary, and then only sufficient force to overcome the perceived resistance by being reasonable in the circumstances. Therefore, the use of firearms is only justified when there is an immediate threat to life. The recognized situations where police are justified in using firearms and potentially killing a citizen constitute in self-defence and in defense of lives of others (not property) (Miller and Blackler 2005). The guiding common law principle remains that of "minimal" force (Sarre 1993).

"WEAPONS OF WAR" AND ELITES

In the early 1970s, NSW Police was the only routinely armed force in Australia, but somewhat unobtrusively and swiftly the carrying of firearms evolved across the nation. Today, police in all states normally carry a firearm that is visible and available; it is mandatory on operational duty. Police performing uniform duties carry the "weapons of war:" the Victoria Police Manual stipulates a firearm (Smith and Wesson .38 caliber revolver), oleoresin capsicum (OC) spray, an extendable baton (ASP band 21 inch), Hiett brand handcuffs, and an equipment belt.

Within Australia, Victoria and South Australia rely on revolvers and are the only two states without semiautomatic pistols (*Herald-Sun* 2004). The VPA is campaigning for the replacement of the present issue of Smith and Wesson .38 revolvers with semiautomatics: "Most police and military units around the world are switching to semiautomatics with no known cases of the reverse scenario" (The Police Association 2007, 14). Ten million dollars was allocated to Victoria Police in the 2008–2009 Victorian State Budget for this change, and about 6,500 semiautomatic handguns will be introduced (*The Age* 2008).

When firing a weapon, police are instructed to aim for the largest body mass, the chest region, until the threat no longer exists. Between 1990 and 2006 in Australia, 82 people were fatally shot by police when they were attempting to "detain" them, and 58 others shot themselves in the presence of police (Joudo and Curnow 2008). All police shootings are recorded as "deaths in custody." "Suicide by cop" may have accounted for some of the deaths. Many of those killed were highly disturbed people (under the influence of alcohol and/or drugs, depressed, psychiatric histories, domestic altercation before police encounter). Coronial inquests examine the appropriateness of police approaches and alternative options. An Australian Institute of Criminology study highlighted the significance of negotiations skills and appropriate weapons training in managing dangerous and unpredictable encounters (Dalton 1998).

All state police agencies have special paramilitary response units. Victoria boasts an elite Special Operations Group (SOG) and a specific crowd control unit, the Force Response Unit. The SOG provides the state with an armed offender and counterterrorism response capability as well as responding to critical incidents including sieges, hostage situations, and the arrest of dangerous suspects. It is modeled and trained on a military commando unit. Critics allege that the SOG adopts a military rather than a civilian operational approach (McCulloch 2001).

In 1994 Task Force Victor, the only publicly released internal review of Victoria Police firearms tactics, recommended a reduction on reliance on the SOG in certain circumstances by establishing armed response groups capable of undertaking "all but the most demanding operations." Like SWAT teams deployed in high-risk situations in America, Victoria's SOG trained elite, whose role includes dealing with those with a mental disorder and exhibiting violent behaviour, are more likely to use weapons than street police. Since America's 9/11 and the "Bali bombings" on October 12, 2002, combined counterterrorist police and military training exercises have been conducted that further obscure the distinctions and functions between civil police and the armed forces (McCulloch 2001).

TAKING A "BEACON" TO FATAL POLICE SHOOTINGS IN VICTORIA

The VPA, the union boasting 98% officer affiliation, proudly asserts that Victoria Police is often touted "as the world's best" (The Police Association 2007, 14). Crime reporters alleged that Victoria Police was "the most popular and respected force in the country," but also "the most deadly" (Silvester, Rule, and Davies 1995, 1). In recent decades, Victoria, with approximately one-quarter of the nation's population, has had the worst record in terms of fatal police shootings (Silvester, Rule, and Davies 1995). Thirty-three fatal police shootings took place in Victoria from 1984 to 1995, which was double that of the rest of Australia and was very difficult for the police hierarchy to explain. The issue of lethal use of force by police has been an ongoing saga in Victoria. (See Table 15-1 for a state-by-state comparison of police shooting deaths.) Sarre (1993) questions whether or not the use of lethal force by police officers has made Victoria a safer place.

Table 15-1 Police Shooting Deaths in Australia from 1990 to 2004

Year	NSW	Vic.	QLD	WA	SA	Tas.	NT	ACT	Total
1990	1	2					1		4
1991		2	1	1		1			5
1992	2	2							4
1993	1	1				1			3
1994		9	1	1	1				12
1995		3	1					1	5
1996	1						1		2
1997	3	2					1		6
1998	3	3							6
1999			1	1	2		2		6
2000	3	1	1	1					6
2001	1				2				3
2002		1	3				1		5
2003	1		2						3
2004	2	3	1						5
Total	18	29	11	4	5	2	6	1	76

Source: Australian Institute of Criminology, National Deaths in Custody Program 1990–2004.

The police shootings need to be considered in the context of the death of 19-year-old Constable Angela Taylor and 22 others injured in the Russell Street Police complex bombing on March 27, 1986, and the ambushing of two young constables in an inner suburban Melbourne street on October 12, 1988 (Hoser 1999; Silvester, Rule, and Davies 1995). Officers perceived that they were subject to a high level of physical threat. The police shootings coincided with the gradual diminution in the training of officers in controlling situations without physical confrontation (Brouwer 2005). While public order issues in Victoria challenged police use of collective force (Baker 2005), the police shootings focused attention on police strategy, behavior, and decision making. When he reported on seven police shootings in 1988–1989, state coroner Hallenstein criticized a "police ethic and culture of public duty requiring courage in physical exposure to personal risks" (*The Age* 1994). He concluded that no police were criminally responsible for any of the deaths, but they were partly to blame for engineering situations where there was little alternative but to shoot the offender. Hallenstein asserted that Victorian police considered it a public duty to risk their lives in confrontations and that they did not have adequate training in alternatives (*The Age* 1994). Police maintained an attitude that they could, and should, resolve any potentially violent situation and do so immediately. For both public and police expectations, "deserting" the scene was not an option (O'Loughlin and Billing 2000). After community outcries, coronial inquiries, increasing calls for an external inquiry, and considerable consultation with other policing agencies, Chief Commissioner Comrie announced the implementation of Project Beacon, which was designed to train operational police to control dangerous incidents that involved potential confrontation by developing defensive tactics to limit dependence on firearms. Comrie emphasized that the success of Project Beacon "will primarily be judged by the extent to which the use of force is avoided or minimized" (*Victoria Police Gazette* 1997).

Between mid-1994 and the end of 1995, more than 8,600 operational Victoria Police undertook intensive Operational Safety and Tactics (OST) training, "Safety First" training in communication and conflict resolution, incident planning, defensive tactics, dealing with the mentally impaired, and the use of firearms and scenario training. Police attended a five-day operational safety and training tactics course, with a two-day follow-up course every six months (Victoria Police 1997). Such training, focusing on life-and-death scenarios, remains part of current police training. The Tactical Options Model, which was implemented with Beacon, is a situational model, involving continual assessment of the scenario and randomly arranged tactical options, designed to react or initiate action with the objectives of minimum force and a safe resolution. Victoria was the first state in Australia to establish a Use of Force Register to monitor the extent of the use and the effectiveness of less-than-lethal equipment options. The introduction of OC spray in April 1996, as compulsory apparel for street police, was a feature of Beacon. The Beacon principles have also been extended to training for public order situations.

Beacon facilitated a significant decrease in fatal police shootings in Victoria. In the 10 years after Beacon's implementation, there were 16 fatal police shootings, half the number of the previous decade (Brouwer 2005). Further, 1996 was the first year in 13 years in which there was no fatal police shooting. The "Safety First Philosophy" and "Operational Safety Principles" were applied in practice. For instance, a man with a mental disorder and brandishing a gun disrupted traffic at the Westgate Bridge for eleven hours on September 16, 2003, before police restored order. This was despite some irate talk-back radio callers who demanded that the police shoot the man (*The Age* 2003).

The incidence of police shootings escalated again in Victoria in 2004–2005 outstripping the rest of Australia (*The Age* 2005). From March 2004 to April 2005, six people were fatally shot by police in Victoria. The OPI conducted an investigation into these fatal police shootings: four by operational police and two by SOG members. The inquiry concluded that the operational police shootings stemmed from "poor command and control, inadequate risk assessment, limited understanding of the symptoms of mental disorder and police being unprepared when OC spray proves ineffective" (Brouwer 2005, 16). In five of the six fatal shootings, officers failed to follow correct procedures. Improvements in training, policies and procedures were recommended. Acting Deputy Commissioner Ashby refused to comment on the OPI's report but stated that "during the period there's been 8,500 use-of-force incidents . . . with something like 5,500 assaults on police at the same time" (Moor 2005).

THE MENTALLY ILL

The November 2005 OPI report of fatal police shootings was highly critical of a number of police shootings involving the mentally ill, and also of inadequate training and lack of negotiation skills. Approximately 30% of incidents that Victoria's Critical Incident Response Teams attended to within an 18-month period involved persons in mental health crisis (Brouwer 2005). The OPI's review concluded that 53% of all fatal shootings between 1990 and 2004 concerned individuals with a mental health problem (Brouwer 2005). In most cases, police were subjected to threatening behavior prior to the police shootings (Dalton 1998).

The OPI's report alleged that officers had limited knowledge and understanding of people suffering from mental disorders, a failing that demanded skills in identifying, communicating with, and managing such people. OST training had last addressed the mentally ill in January 2002 (Brouwer 2005). Since 1990, nine of the sixteen people with a mental disorder that were fatally shot by police possessed an edged weapon at the time. Edged weapons (knives, swords) increasingly became the weapon of protagonists rather than firearms. In 2004, police shot a man in an inner suburb who was wielding a shield that he had used to attack lamp-posts (Walters 2005). OST training continues to teach that the first reaction to an individual armed with an edged weapon should be to disengage, cordon, contain, and negotiate. A full range of options and tactics was promoted in response to an edged weapon threat (Brouwer 2005).

The OPI's director believed that since 1994 "a gradual shift in attention . . . could allow the re-emergence of a culture among police which is overly reliant on firearms" (Brouwer 2005, ii). The report speculated that Victoria Police "has lost some of the strategic focus on safety and avoiding the use of force which it developed during Project Beacon" (Brouwer 2005, 55). The OPI review identified police failures in implementing safety principles, especially failure to cordon and control incidents and failure to train officers adequately to deal with people with mental illness. Police need protection and resources, including access to trained medical health professionals when dealing with disturbed people (*The Age* 2005). A police spokesman stated that members "may only draw their firearm when they anticipate extreme danger" (*Sunday Age* 2008). Although Project Beacon emphasized conflict resolution and verbal negotiation, police routine wearing of firearms may add to potential confrontation (Walters 2005).

Australia's mental health system has been described as "failing" and "in crisis" (Sced 2006, 1). Police are often the first respondents to mental health crises. In all states and territories of Australia, legislation allows police to intervene in situations involving the mentally ill (Sced 2006). In NSW in 2004, police responded to 18,000 calls involving individuals with mental health issues, almost 50 calls a day. Deinstitutionalization and a community-oriented policing ethos have increased interaction between police and the mentally ill on the streets. Two national inquiries (Whiteford Report 1998 and Wooldridge Report 2000) emphasized police responsibility to protect the safety of all parties and recommended improved information sharing between police, health professionals, and mental health and emergency services. All police agencies have instigated training initiatives to improve officer knowledge of mental illnesses, especially in rural areas where specialist assistance may not exist (Sced 2006).

ALTERNATIVES TO LETHAL FORCE

The police shootings have prompted debate about deployment of alternative weapons, including OC spray and TASERs, when apprehending suspects. Between 1998 and 2007, the use of OC aerosol in Victoria increased 16 fold. Senior police determined that capsicum foam should be standard issue and all patrol vehicles have been equipped with large support canisters. Victoria Police in 2008 were using OC spray and foam an average of seven times a day (Silvester 2008a). In two of the six fatalities investigated by the OPI, capsicum spray failed to subdue the alleged offender. In these situations, the two SOG Inspectors and three SOG operatives were not OST qualified despite being armed with complete OST equipment (Brouwer 2005). Debate about OC spray ignited during the January 2008 Australian Tennis Open when a policeman, seeking crowd compliance, erratically sprayed rowdy and unruly Greek spectators. Some innocent bystanders were adversely affected (Silvester 2008a).

Ryan (2008) argues that while TASERs are being advocated by police in Australia, "international experiences indicate that this move is likely to be problematic" (1–5). These stun guns, with 50,000-volt charges to disable suspects, are promoted instead of lethal force, but scrutiny is required that they are not used in non-dangerous situations in order to secure compliance and that "usage creep" is avoided.

All states except Tasmania have issued TASERs to specialist response units. TASERs are currently general issue for 1,500 Western Australia operational police and more than 5,000 general duty Queensland officers. Despite warnings of the state's Ombudsman, NSW Police is debating a full roll-out of TASERs. The VPA has repeatedly called for the introduction of M26 Air TASER guns for all frontline police, but the Victorian government and Chief Commissioner Overland maintain that the situation is still under review. The elite SOG and the Critical Incident Response Teams, who have conducted a 12-month trial of X-26 stun guns, are currently campaigning to test TASER shotguns that can strike at 20 meters using a wireless electronic projectile (*Herald-Sun* 2009). TASERs could avert the need to shoot, but other options, depending on the circumstances, on better training, incident planning, and application of the cordon, and control principle may be more desirable.

RECENT FATALITY: TYLER CASSIDY

According to Liberty Victoria, Victoria continues to have a major problem with police shootings, outstripping all other states combined. Between September 2006 and January 2008, there were six Victoria Police shootings (*Australian* 2008b). On December 11, 2008, a 15-year-old Melburnian youth, Tyler Cassidy, armed with two knives in a suburban skate park, was killed when confronted by four police who fired six bullets. This was the fourth such shooting in the year and, for some, it indicated a further escalation of excessive police use of force. The officers attempted to negotiate with the agitated teenager who was a threat to himself and police. Cassidy was twice sprayed with capsicum foam which proved ineffective. An officer claimed that OC spray "does not work against people who are mentally disturbed or high on drugs" (Silvester 2008b). A warning shot was also fired before three of the four officers shot Cassidy. The coroner is investigating his death.

There is no clear-cut process in police decisions on whether to shoot or not. The VPA questioned whether Cassidy would still be alive if uniformed police in Victoria, like WA, NSW, and Queensland, carried TASERs (*Australian* 2008a). The VPA secretary regretted that, without TASERs, police level of force "escalates directly from OC spray to a firearm—there's nothing in between" (Russell 2009). Eight years earlier, coroner Graeme Johnstone had recommended that police be armed with TASERs. Similarly, the Queensland coroner recently asserted that four men, who were long-term sufferers of mental illness and who were legally shot by police, could have been saved if officers had been armed with TASERs (McKenna 2009).

CONCLUSION

As police in Australia confront volatile and unpredictable situations, the issue of police use of force, especially lethal force, is vexed and problematic. Planning, training, negotiation skills, supervision, equipment, review, and accountability mechanisms are needed to ensure that firearms are only utilized as a last resort. Little debate questions whether or not operational police in Australia should be armed, but the actual deployment and use of firearms remain contentious. Police use of firearms receives scant attention and commentary, except when someone is fatally shot. Police often need to assess spontaneously whether any other less-than-lethal alternatives are available and their likely effectiveness.

During the past two decades, police have explored strategies both to limit reliance on lethal weapons in dangerous situations and to broaden the vision of police responses through communication and negotiation skills training, education programs, and collaboration with health professionals. As the array of police armed apparel continues to expand, accountability mechanisms must be rigorous. The new Victorian Human Rights Charter advocates that if fatal force is used, the Charter requires a prompt, comprehensive, and independent investigation. Police use of firearms needs scrutiny like anyone else's use of a firearm. The Cassidy death is a case in point.

16

The Consequences of Using Deadly Force

David A. Klinger

ABSTRACT

THE LITERATURE ON the use of deadly force by police officers includes a limited body of research that examines how being involved in shooting incidents affects officers who pull the trigger. This research indicates that police officers who shoot citizens may experience a variety of short- and long-term reactions that can include recurrent thoughts about the incident, a sense of numbness, trouble sleeping, sadness, crying, and frayed relationships. This chapter reviews the research on officers' post-shooting reactions, offers information from case studies of officers' experiences in the wake of shootings, traces changes in officers' reactions over time to provide the reader with an overview of what is known about the personal consequences of using deadly force in police work, and offers some brief suggestions about how this information might inform police agencies' treatment of officers who pull the trigger.

INTRODUCTION

All sworn police officers in the United States carry firearms, but the vast majority of them—some 90%—never shoot anyone during their law enforcement careers (see, e.g., Klinger 2004). For the small minority of officers who do shoot citizens, however, the experience can be a rough one. In the aftermath of shootings, officers may experience a variety of negative mental, emotional, and physical symptoms such as guilt, anxiety, and sleep disturbances. Such reactions have led mental health professionals who work with the police to note that officers who shoot are subject to experiencing a type of post-traumatic stress response commonly referred to as "post-shooting trauma." While the notion that involvement in shootings can negatively affect officers is well developed in law enforcement circles, the body of empirical research on what after effects

David A. Klinger, University of Missouri at St. Louis

officers experience following shootings is sparse. Much of it, moreover, is limited in scope and thus offers little insight. This chapter provides an overview of current knowledge about how shootings affect officers by briefly reviewing the initial research on the topic, and then presenting findings from a more detailed study of post-shooting reactions that the author conducted a decade ago.

EARLY RESEARCH

Empirical research on how shootings affect police officers first appeared in 1981, when Eric Nielsen (1981) published the results of his survey of post-shooting reactions among 63 municipal, county, and state law enforcement officers who had shot citizens. Over the next eleven years, four additional studies of officers' post- shooting reactions were published; John Stratton, David Parker, and John Snibbe's (1984) survey of 60 Los Angeles sheriff's deputies; Roger Solomon and James Horn's (1986) survey of 86 Rocky Mountain officers; Berthold Gersons' (1989) survey of 37 Dutch officers; and John Campbell's (1992) survey of 167 FBI agents. Together, these five studies developed an initial empirical outline of officers' post-shooting reactions by reporting information about how frequently the surveyed officers experienced specific emotional, psychological, and physical phenomena in the wake of shootings.

Nielsen, for example, reported that in the first week following shootings more than 90% of the study officers experienced at least one *physical* symptom, such as nausea and headaches, and that nearly 90% of them experienced at least one *emotional* or *psychological* symptom, such as anxiety. Among the highlights of the Stratton, Parker, and Snibbe study were that the average deputy "occasionally" experienced recurring thoughts (flashbacks) about the shooting and had "some" problems sleeping during the week immediately after the incident. They also reported that 63% of the deputies surveyed either cried or experienced feelings of depression, anger, and/or elation at some (unspecified) point following the shooting.

Solomon and Horn provided a bit more detail about officers' post-shooting reactions, reporting that 58% of the officers they surveyed felt a notable degree of anger at some (unspecified) point after the shooting, 46% experienced substantial sleep difficulties, and 44% had bothersome intrusive thoughts. Gersons also provided data on how frequently officers reported specific reactions, reporting, for example, that 76% experienced recurrent thoughts about the event, 68% had a sense of "hyper-alertness," and 43% suffered disturbed sleep at some (again, unspecified) point after their shooting. Campbell was more specific in his work, noting that he inquired about agents' reactions during the first week following their shootings, and reporting that during this time frame 62% of the agents experienced recurrent thoughts, 29% had dreams about the shooting, 32% had problems sleeping, 24% were fatigued, and 25% had some sense of anxiety and/or tension.

Two of the studies also provided a bit of information about changes in officers' reactions over time. Nielsen asked his officers whether they experienced any attitude changes during the first three months following their shootings; nearly 80% reported that they experienced at least one (most frequently, increased apathy and cautiousness). Stratton, Parker, and Snibbe also provided information about changes during the first three months following shootings, reporting a modest decrease in the frequency of flashbacks and sleep disturbances that deputies experienced. Neither study provided any information about officers' reactions after three months.

In sum, the first five studies on the topic established that officers often experience negative reactions following shootings and suggested that such reactions are liable to change as time passes. But these studies provide little detail about the specific reactions officers' experience and very little data on changes over time. The remainder of this chapter focuses on findings from a study that developed a good bit of detail about officers' reactions following shootings and how those reactions changed as time passed.

THE KLINGER STUDY

Between 1997 and 1999, the author of this chapter interviewed 80 police officers and sheriffs' deputies from 19 municipal and county law enforcement agencies in four states who had shot citizens in the line of duty (see Klinger 2001a for study details). The interviews included two parts. The first was the administration of a questionnaire that included items about officers' physical, psychological, and emotional experiences during four distinct post-shooting time periods: 1) within the first 24 hours after the shooting; 2) from the second to the seventh day; 3) from the beginning of the second week after the shooting to the end of the third month; and 4) after three months had passed.

For each of these time periods officers were asked to report whether they experienced each of the following physical responses: 1) nausea; 2) loss of appetite; 3) headaches; 4) fatigue; 5) crying; 6) sleep disturbances; and 7) other physical symptoms. They were also asked to report whether they experienced each of the following psychological/emotional phenomena: 1) sadness; 2) anxiety; 3) numbness; 4) recurrent thoughts about the shooting; 5) fear for their physical safety; 6) fear of legal and/or administrative problems; 7) nightmares; 8) elation; and 9) other thoughts/feelings.

Elation was included in the list of emotional/psychological reactions, because Stratton, Parker, and Snibbe had included it as a possible reaction, and because the author—a former police officer—had been told by some colleagues who had been involved in shootings that they experienced high spirits afterward. This indicated that 1) not all post-reactions are negative and 2) a comprehensive study of post-shooting reactions should include elation as a possible response.

After completing a separate questionnaire for each incident in which they shot citizens, each officer sat for an individual directed interview. These interviews covered several topical areas, including what occurred after the shooting—moving sequentially through the four time frames addressed in the instrument—in order to let the officers describe in their own words the thoughts, feelings, and other reactions they had as time passed.

In the end, the interview process yielded detailed information about 113 shooting incidents in which the 80 study officers were involved. Fifty-six of the officers were interviewed about a single shooting, sixteen were interviewed about two, seven were interviewed about three, and one officer was interviewed about four shootings. With this background information in hand, attention now turns to a look at the sorts of reactions officers experienced and how they evolved as time passed. To provide some sense of how these data compare with those reported in previous studies, this examination includes information on how frequently officers experienced each sort of reaction at any point following the incidents in question.

PSYCHOLOGICAL/EMOTIONAL REACTIONS

Recurrent thoughts about the incident in question were by far the most commonly reported psychological/emotional reaction officers experienced, occurring in 83% of the cases. The directed interviews indicated that few of the officers viewed such thoughts as a negative, however. Indeed, most officers described the thoughts they had about the shooting in positive or neutral terms (see discussion of elation below). This finding suggests that as a generic category of post-shooting reaction, recurrent thoughts should not be viewed as a part of the stress reaction that previous work has identified as "post-shooting trauma."

Anxiety was the next most frequently experienced reaction, with officers reporting feeling anxious following 42% of the shootings. Many of the officers who had this response reported that they were anxious about the prospect of being involved in additional shootings. One officer who was involved in a shoot-out fairly soon after graduating from the police academy, for example, figured that having a shooting early in his career meant that he could be destined to be involved in others, and was therefore anxious about the prospect of future shootings. Other officers felt trepidation about dealing with third-party responses to their actions, linking their anxiety to concerns about sharing what happened with others, press coverage, and/or investigations into the shooting.

Concerns about investigations were also salient for officers who reported fear that the shooting might create administrative and/or legal problems for them. Officers reported such fears in 35% of the cases, worrying that they might be punished by their agency, sued, and/or charged with a crime. For some officers, such fears emanated from the shooting itself (e.g., two officers who shot unarmed citizens whom the officers believed were about to shoot them became quite worried after it was determined that the suspects were, in fact, unarmed). For other officers, fears of legal and/or administrative entanglement came from things that occurred after the shooting (e.g., an officer who was initially confident that he had acted properly became quite concerned about legal and administrative matters when he saw his attorney in a heated argument with the homicide division supervisor who was in charge of the investigation into the incident).

The next most frequently occurring thought/feeling reported was elation, which officers experienced at some point following 29% of the shootings. The directed interviews identified three types of elation among the officers who reported experiencing it. The first was a sense of joy about having survived a life-threatening situation. The officers who experienced this form of elation reported a profound satisfaction about being alive following an event that could have left them dead. The second type of elation reported was exhilaration that appears to be a type of residual emotion from the sheer excitement of the situation in which they fired. As one officer put it, he was "hyped-up" for a while after his shooting. The third type of elation officers described was deep satisfaction about doing their job properly. Several officers reported that they were elated they had passed what they described as the utmost challenge in a law enforcement career—an encounter where deadly force is necessary. In sum, none of the various sorts of elation that officers reported involved pleasure taken from hurting or killing the person they shot, but rather described feelings of excitement about the event, joy about being alive, or accomplishment about doing a tough job properly.

Officers reported having a sense of sadness following 26% of the shootings. The sadness felt was often over the fate of the person they shot, though not always in relation to the injury their bullets caused, *per se*. Several of the citizens shot were, in the minds of the officers, tragic figures whose lives came to tragic ends. Some of the citizens, for example, were suicidal and chose to end their lives in a hail of police gunfire (a phenomenon often referred to as "suicide by cop" in police circles; see, e.g., Klinger 2001b) while others were lost souls whose long-standing substance abuse had led them to the deadly confrontation with authorities. Officers who expressed such sadness often spoke of feeling bad that a fellow human could devolve to the point of being on the wrong end of police guns. Other officers expressed sadness for the members of the family of the person they shot, feeling sorry for them to have lost a loved one. Still other officers reported sadness over having scared *their* loved ones, because the shooting led their parents, spouses, or other family members to worry about their safety. Finally, some officers reported feeling sad for innocent people who were injured or killed by the person they shot moments before they fired.

Officers reported a sense of numbness at some point after 20 percent of the shootings. They often described this numbness in terms of being so overwhelmed by the shooting and its aftermath that they were mentally, emotionally, and/or physically spent. For example, one officer felt as if "he had used up all of his brain cells" dealing with all that had happened during the shooting, the events it had set in motion (e.g., the investigation), and the other post-shooting reactions he was experiencing.

Officers reported having nightmares after 18% of the shootings. In most cases these nightmares revolved around police shootings, and took two forms. The first sort in some fashion replayed the shooting incident. In one case, for example, an officer had repeated dreams of the thief she shot charging at her. The second sort of shooting-related nightmare consisted of dreams where the officer was involved in a different shooting. In this type of nightmare, officers were typically unable to defeat their opponent, either because their gun would not properly function or because the bullets they fired into opponents had no effect. Finally, in dreams with no linkage to shootings, officers often had visions of monsters and similar entities.

Officers were fearful for their safety at some point following 18% of the shootings. For most officers, the fear took the form of a realization that they could have been injured or killed during the incident in question. For other officers it was fear of becoming involved in another incident that might not end as favorably for them as the shooting they survived. The fears that officers expressed typically had less to do with being harmed and more with worry about what their loved ones would do if something happened to them. One example of such fear arose in an officer when the person he shot was released from custody and began to stalk and threaten the officer and his family. The officer became fearful that if he were incapacitated that his family would be at the mercy of a dangerous lunatic.

Officers experienced some sense of guilt in 12% of the cases. For example, one officer who shot an individual armed with a toy gun felt guilty over having hurt someone who posed no actual threat. In a related vein, some officers expressed guilt over having harmed or killed the person they shot, even though the individual had engaged in actual life-threatening action. Finally, other officers experienced guilt for not having done their job as they perceived they should have during the shooting. One officer who reported this sort of guilt felt badly that he was not able to capture any of the four body armor-clad robbers with whom he engaged in a wild shootout (one suspect escaped only because his body armor prevented incapacitating injuries from bullets the officer fired, which allowed him to scramble into the getaway car).

In addition to specific psychological/emotional responses listed on the instrument, officers frequently—in 42% of the cases—reported experiencing some "other" thought or feeling. The most common of these miscellaneous reactions was anger, which officers reported in 15 cases. The object of the anger was often the person they shot. In some such cases officers were angry at their opponent for trying to kill them, while in others they were upset at their target for forcing them to shoot. One officer, for example, was angry at the suicidal citizen he shot for involving him in a demented death drama. Other officers were upset with fellow officers. One such officer—who shot a gunman

after dozens of other officers failed to do so during a tense stand-off—
expressed anger at his colleagues because he felt the suspect should have been
shot long before he arrived on scene. Still other officers were upset with
detectives and other law enforcement officials (e.g., district attorney personnel) over some aspect of how the shooting was investigated and reviewed.
Finally, some officers expressed anger at the news media for what they
viewed as anti-police bias in coverage of the shooting.

Half a dozen officers reported a sense of pride or satisfaction over the
actions they took during the shooting, a response closely related to the satis-
faction-based elation discussed above. Information collected during the
directed interviews suggests that the difference between the two types of
responses is in the nature of satisfaction or pride felt. The officers who felt
satisfaction or pride and who checked the "elation" response category seemed
to have had a more visceral response than their peers who checked the
"other" category to register their more cerebral sense of accomplishment.
Whatever the case, the information from the "other" category indicates that
more officers experienced some measure of satisfaction about their actions
than was indicated by responses to the "elation" item.

Also counted among the "other" thoughts or feelings reported were a
few that could be viewed as the flip side of the satisfaction coin. One officer,
for example, reported a sense of disappointment that the shots she fired did
not strike her opponent where she had aimed, while another said he was
embarrassed about his inability to appropriately assess the actual threat posed
by the person he shot: an emotionally disturbed individual armed with a toy
gun. Other responses included the desire to withdraw from other people, an
increase in the frequency of benign dreams, second-guessing the decision to
make police work a career, difficulty focusing on tasks such as reading, and
wondering if there was something wrong with them because they did not feel
bad about killing another human.

PHYSICAL RESPONSES

The most commonly reported physical response was trouble sleeping, which
officers experienced following 49% of the shootings. Sleep problems included
not being able to fall asleep, sleeping and waking in starts and fits, and
waking up in cold sweats. One officer reported that the sweats he experienced
were so severe that he would have to strip and re-sheet his bed, take a
shower, and put on fresh sleep clothes before seeking more slumber. Logically
enough, the next most frequently reported response was fatigue, which officers
experienced in 46% of the cases. Officers reported that they cried at some
point following 24% of the shootings, experienced a noticeable appetite
decline in 17% of the cases, got headaches in 8 cases, felt nauseated in 5, and
reported experiencing some other physical reaction in 21.

These "other" physical reactions were a diverse bunch with no single type reported in more than a handful of cases. Officers experienced elevated levels of energy in five cases. In three other cases officers reported trembling or shaking at some point following their shooting, including a SWAT marksman who began to tremble at the conclusion of the first call-up after the shooting in question. Just one other response was reported in more than one case: an increase in appetite, which occurred in two cases. Among the responses reported in a single case were a marked increase in sex drive, increased alertness, bouts of diarrhea, and a compulsion to exercise.

TEMPORAL VARIABILITY IN POST-SHOOTING RESPONSES

Tables 16-1 and 16-2 present the percentage distributions of cases where officers experienced each of the several emotional/psychological and physical responses during each of the four post-shooting time periods measured. Perhaps the most striking information conveyed in these tables is a strong tendency for the proportion of cases in which officers experience any given response to diminish over time. Across the 51 possible adjacent time comparisons (e.g., first day to first week, first week to three months, three months to post three months = 3 comparisons x 17 response categories = 51), the figures drop in 43 of them, are equal in 5 others, and increase by a single percentage point in the other 3. By the time 3 months have passed, moreover, the

Table 16-1 Percent of Cases Where Officers Experienced Particular Thoughts or Feelings During Four Post-Shooting Time Periods

Thought/Feeling	First 24 Hours	First Week	Within Three Months	After Three Months
Elation	26%	19%	11%	5%
Sadness	18%	17%	5%	5%
Numbness	18%	7%	4%	3%
Recurrent Thoughts	82%	74%	52%	37%
Anxiety	37%	28%	13%	10%
Guilt	10%	5%	6%	2%
Nightmares	13%	13%	10%	6%
Fear for Safety	9%	10%	9%	8%
Fear of Legal Administrative Problems	31%	25%	19%	11%
Any Other Thought or Feeling	33%	23%	20%	14%

Table 16-2 Percent of Cases Where Officers Experienced Particular Physical Responses During Four Post-Shooting Time Periods

Physical Response	First 24 Hours	First Week	Within Three Months	After Three Months
Nausea	4%	4%	0%	0%
Appetite Loss	16%	8%	2%	1%
Headache	6%	4%	1%	1%
Fatigue	39%	26%	7%	5%
Crying	17%	7%	2%	2%
Trouble Sleeping	46%	36%	16%	11%
Other Physical	18%	11%	12%	6%

proportion of cases in which officers experienced given reactions decreased by at least 50% in 16 of the 17 response categories, with 12 of the 16 falling by at least two-thirds.

The tables also show that the temporal decrease is so pronounced that by the three-month post-shooting mark very few of the responses were manifest in even 10% of the cases. Only one specific reaction—recurrent thoughts— persisted in more than one-third of the cases, and only two others broke the 10% mark—fear of legal problems and trouble sleeping—both of which were reported in 11% of the cases. Because, as noted above, the directed interviews disclosed that few of the officers who reported recurrent thoughts defined them as negative, the percentage distributions clearly indicate that specific negative post-shooting reactions were quite rare after three months had passed. These low rates indicate that only a small proportion of the officers inter- viewed suffered any remarkable long-term detrimental consequences from the shootings in which they were involved.

This is confirmed by additional analysis that looked at the number of neg- ative reactions each officer experienced at each time period (elation, as well as positive and neutral "other" responses, were not counted). This analysis shows a marked drop in the average number of negative responses officers reported as time passes, from 2.88 in the first 24 hours, to 2.05 in the first week, to 1.06 within 3 months, and finally to .77 by the time 3 months had passed. Finally, this analysis indicates that 63% of the time officers reported zero negative reactions by the time 3 months had passed after their shooting.

CONCLUDING COMMENTS

That nearly two-thirds of study officers reported no negative reactions at the three-month mark following a shooting indicates that the act of shooting another human being typically does not produce lasting disruption in the lives of police officers. On the other hand, the evidence that officers only infrequently experience notable long-term problems should not be taken as evidence that shootings are no big deal for police. In the first place, the research clearly indicates that most shootings do lead to notable short-term disruptions (on average, nearly three negative reactions in the first 24 hours). In the second place, it also clearly indicates that shootings can and do lead to substantial long-term tumult for some officers. When officers suffer from combinations of phenomena such as sleep disruption, fatigue, and anxiety more than three months after a shooting, the incident has plainly taken a substantial toll. While such reactions are mercifully infrequent, they are by no means rare and thus constitute a prominent part of the picture of what happens to police officers who shoot.

Another prominent part of the post-shooting picture is that many officers experience positive reactions (e.g., elation and satisfaction) following shooting incidents. This—coupled with the relative infrequency of negative reactions in the long term—indicates that the long-standing emphasis on the negative impact of shootings should be leavened with recognition that many officers will do just fine following their use of deadly force, and that some will even take something positive from the experience.

Finally, the directed interviews indicate that generic categories of post-shooting reactions mask a good deal of variability in how officers respond to shootings. Officers who experience anxiety, for example, may be anxious about a variety of things; those who have nightmares have different sorts of dreams, and so on. Because officers reactions can vary in so many ways— from negative to positive, the number of reactions each officer will experience, how reactions unfold over time, and even how specific classes of reactions are manifest—it is clear that there is no typical response pattern among police officers who shoot. Based on the available evidence then, it seems fair to conclude that while there are some patterns in officers' post-shooting reactions, the consequences of using deadly force are as individualistic as the officers who pull the trigger.

The evidence that officers' experiences in the wake of shootings are idiosyncratic has implications for how police agencies might want to deal with officers who have shot someone. Many agencies in the United States provide standardized mandatory mental health debriefings based on the knowledge that officers who shoot citizens are susceptible to suffering negative reactions. While concern for the emotional and psychological well-being of officers is commendable, police agencies should endeavor to ensure that the services they provide are not of the "one size fits all" sort. They should do all they can do to provide each officer with whatever level and type of support he or she needs, based on the reactions each individual is experiencing. By paying attention to what research on the topic shows, police departments can move away from standardized programs and towards post-shooting services that truly seek to meet officers' needs.

PART III

Police Use of Non-Lethal Weapons

Introduction

Joseph B. Kuhns

USE OF DEADLY force (firearms and other lethal tactics) remains a last resort for police around the world. Nevertheless, in many countries there is a clear movement to restrict the use of firearms and deadly force through legal decisions, departmental policies, and officer training. Further, law enforcement agencies continue to broaden the range of alternatives to deadly force through advancements in less-than-lethal tactics, technologies, and tools. Adoption of these tools, however, can have negative effects including police use of excessive force (e.g., deploying a TASER when it may not be necessary or when lesser force might still accomplish the job) or using these weapons to punish uncooperative suspects.

The last section of our book focuses attention on some of the currently used less-than-lethal weapons and looks forward to the further development and, perhaps eventual adoption, of other such technologies on the horizon. It is important to note that "less-than-lethal" does not equate to "non-lethal;" both OC spray, the focus of the first chapter in this section, and TASERs, the focus of the next, have contributed to deaths with certain suspects and under certain conditions. That said, batons, flashlights, and fists have also been used lethally by police officers for generations, but the general intention of all of these devices, first and foremost, is not the exercise of deadly force.

Robert Kaminski and Otto Adang begin with a critical analysis of the adoption of oleoresin capsicum (OC or "pepper spray"). They identify some of the strengths and criticisms associated with this fairly common police tool and pay particular attention to the adoption of OC in the Netherlands, which provides some important lessons learned for other countries that might be interested in integrating this technology into their policing processes and use of less-than-lethal force options. Specifically, the authors remind readers of the importance of thorough advanced planning, developing specific policies for acceptable use and misuse, and the need for ensuring availability of after-care and medical attention (if needed) following spraying incidents.

Michael White and Justin Ready then turn a critical eye toward the widespread, yet incomplete, adoption and implementation of TASERs in the United States law enforcement community. By focusing attention on this controversial, yet seemingly effective, "stun gun" device, White and Ready provide our readers with some suggestions for when and how the device should be used and also assess the effectiveness of TASERs in reducing injuries to officers and suspects. Their critical analysis considers the relative placement of the TASER on the use-of-force continuum, which can vary from one department to the next in North America. Finally, this chapter recognizes and explores the (minimal, but nevertheless apparent) risk of death when the TASER is used under certain conditions and with certain individuals. Given the rarity of lethal consequences associated with the TASER, current evidence tends to warrant continued use of this technology.

Finally, Diana Summers and Joseph Kuhns again consider the United States law enforcement community. This chapter examines the past, to some degree, and then looks forward and identifies and discusses some emerging less-than-lethal technologies that are being further refined to reduce the likelihood of lethal outcomes (e.g., rubber/plastic bullets, beanbag and plastic baton projectiles, and K-9 units) or are in the earlier stages of development (acoustic devices, directed energy devices, and advanced disorientation technologies that disrupt sensory input). Many of these devices are either designed or are being redesigned to increase the relative distance between officers and suspects, which should theoretically reduce injuries to both. Summers and Kuhns again recognize and reiterate the importance of safe use procedures and extensive training, but they also raise concerns with fragmented adoption of past less-than-lethal weapons in the United States and in other countries that do not have centralized policing. Such fragmentation has important consequences for departments, officers, policy, and law, but also provides a sort of "field test" for agencies that may want to consider newer alternatives before adoption.

Pepper Spray: Practice, Policy, and Research in the Netherlands

Robert J. Kaminski and Otto Adang

ABSTRACT

DURING THE LAST two decades personal issue handheld canisters containing ole-oresin capsicum (OC) or "pepper spray" have been adopted as a less-than-lethal force option by law enforcement agencies in the United States, Canada, the Netherlands, Switzerland, Austria, Belgium, Russia, and elsewhere. A major reason for its widespread adoption is that it provided several advantages over other chemical agents, such as CS/CN or "tear gas." Specifically, OC works more rapidly, has fewer cross-contamination problems, is easier to neu-tralize, is effective against dogs, and is more effective on persons impaired by drugs or mental illness. Further, early reports indicated that OC was extremely effective at incapacitating subjects and that its adoption by law enforcement agencies led to significant reductions in assaults on police, incidences involv-ing use of force, officer and suspect injuries, and excessive force complaints. Subsequent evaluations, however, called into question some of the seemingly exaggerated claims of OC's incapacitating effects. There also were concerns about potential health risks associated with OC exposure, most notably that it may have been a contributing factor in a number of in-custody deaths. Others questioned the appropriateness of offensive tactical use of OC on subjects pos-ing no danger to themselves or others (e.g., passive resisters). Even designat-ing pepper spray as the preferred force option in situations where suspects are verbally resistive may be deemed unreasonable and viewed as a form of police abuse. Thus, although there is little doubt that OC is useful during forceful encounters, appropriate training and policies governing OC are criti-cal. In this chapter we review the history of OC as a less-than-lethal weapon,

Robert J. Kaminski, University of South Carolina
Otto Adang, Police Academy of the Netherlands

we present a brief summary of the related empirical research and we discuss the major controversies regarding OC. We conclude with a review of the Dutch experience in adopting OC for its police forces.

INTRODUCTION

Throughout history, police have continuously sought more effective less-than-lethal methods and technologies for subduing resistive and combative subjects. These methods have included improved 1) empty-hand tactics (e.g., pressure-point controls); 2) handheld impact devices (e.g., side-handled batons; tele-scoping batons); 3) impact munitions (e.g., bean bag rounds); 4) chemical agents (e.g., pepper spray); and 5) electronic control devices (e.g., stun guns). Although the development of each these methods and technologies was impor-tant, the widespread adoption of oleoresin capsicum (OC) or pepper spray by law enforcement agencies during the last two decades represented a "paradig-matic shift" in how street-level police officers in many countries responded to violent and potentially violent encounters. Although policies governing when officers are authorized to use OC can vary within and across countries, police for the first time had a readily available and reasonably safe and effective means for incapacitating persons during confrontations in which the use of deadly force would be inappropriate. Further, despite the recent development and adoption by some law enforcement agencies of next-generation electronic control devices (ECDs) such as the TASER™ and Stinger™, OC continues to play a significant role in the use-of-force arena. However, the adoption and deployment of OC by police did not occur without controversy. In this chapter we review the history of OC as a less-than-lethal weapon and present a brief summary of the related empirical research. We also discuss the major contro-versies regarding OC. We conclude with a review of the Dutch experience in adopting OC for its police forces.

BACKGROUND

Collectively known as capsaicinoids, the active ingredient in pepper spray devices is either OC (oleoresin capsicum), a multi-component oily extract from the capsicum (cayenne pepper) plant, or PAVA (pelargonic acid vanil-lyamide), a trace component of OC than can be made synthetically as a single pure compound (Downs 2007) (an additional synthetic version of pepper spray containing pelargonic acid morpholide is apparently in use by Russian and Ukraine police). Although other delivery systems exist (e.g., pepper ball gun), police most commonly carry small pepper spray canisters that contain a cap-saicinoid, a solvent, and a propellant to disperse the spray as an aerosol or liq-uid stream. Aerosols disperse small particles that primarily affect the lungs whereas liquid streams primarily impact the eyes. Because of the wider dispersal pattern, accuracy is less of an issue with aerosols but a greater likelihood of secondary exposure is a disadvantage. Liquid streams are effective from longer distances and the risk of secondary exposure is reduced, but streams require greater accuracy. In all cases, the capsaicinoid acts as an inflammatory agent that irritates the skin, eyes, and mucous membranes of the upper respiratory tract. Although certain effects depend on the delivery method (e.g., aerosol vs. stream), symptoms include intense burning and tearing of the eyes; eye spasms (ranging from involuntary blinking to sustained closure of the eyelids); a burning sensation of the skin; coughing; gagging; shortness of breath; rhinorrhea (runny nose); and congestion (Vilke and Chan 2007).

As noted by Theodore Chan and colleagues (2001), the properties of the pepper plant have been known for centuries. Chinese soldiers, for example, heated red peppers in hot oil to create an irritant smoke that was blown over enemy lines. However, feudal police officers in Edo-era Japan were probably the first to use a handheld pepper spray device to incapacitate resistive and combative suspects. Worn like a necklace, the device consisted of a small canister (sokutoku) containing fine sand boiled in a solution of red peppers. Designed to temporarily blind criminals by "attacking the eyes" (metsubushi), officers removed the sokutoku's plug with a short tug on its cord and blew sharply into the device's mouthpiece to propel the mixture into an offender's face (Cunningham 2004).

Oleoresin capsicum was first extracted as an incapacitating agent by the Army Chemical Research Unit at Aberdeen Proving Ground in the 1930s, but it was not adopted for military purposes at that time. An aerosolized version developed in 1960 for stopping attacking dogs became popular with mail carriers. It was first sold commercially in 1963 as Halt Animal Repellent™. Efforts during the 1970s to market pepper spray devices for law enforcement officers were unsuccessful, but commercial successes were later realized during the 1980s (Ijames 2005). By the mid-1990s, over half of the law enforcement agencies in the United States authorized the use of pepper spray for their officers (Kaminski, Edwards, and Johnson 1999) and by 2003 98% of American police forces surveyed by the Bureau of Justice Statistics (2003) did so. Police in several other countries also have authorized the use of pepper spray for their officers, including Canada, the Netherlands, Switzerland, Austria, Belgium, and Russia.

EMPIRICAL RESEARCH

During the early 1990s, when OC began to be widely adopted by law enforcement agencies in the United States, Pilant (1993, 5) noted that the lack of research on OC and "the novelty of OC spray and manufacturers' product

claims that range from the credible to the ridiculous, have left many administrators frustrated and confused, not knowing whether their officers should be
carrying CS/CN, OC, or nothing at all." Subsequent early studies suggested
that OC was highly effective in helping officers subdue resistive and violent
suspects, and several evaluations concluded that the adoption of OC by police
departments led to reductions in the incidence of more serious forms of force
(e.g., deadly force, use of impact weapons), fewer assaults on officers, fewer
officer and suspect injuries, and fewer excessive force complaints (Bobb et al.
1996; Bonar 1994; Gauvin 1994; IACP 1995; Kaminski, Edwards, and Johnson 1998; Lumb and Friday 1997; Morabito and Doerner 1997; Williams
1994). However, most of the early studies suffered from methodological limitations that cast doubt on their findings (Kaminski, Edwards, and Johnson
1998; 1999). Later studies employed quasi-experimental designs that suggested the adoption of OC did indeed lead to fewer assaults of police and
fewer injuries to officers and suspects (Bowling and Gaines 2000; Kaminski,
Edwards, and Johnson 1998). Others studies improved on assessments of the
incapacitating effects of OC through the use of multiple and explicit definitions of "effectiveness" and dependent variables that moved beyond simple
effective-ineffective dichotomies used in previous research (Adang et al.
2006; Kaminski, Edwards, and Johnson 1999). These studies, conducted in
the Netherlands and the United States, found that OC was effective between
70% and 85% of the time, depending on the definition of effectiveness used.
These estimates were substantially lower than those reported in most prior
evaluations. Importantly, both studies found that perceived drug use by suspects was the strongest predictor of OC ineffectiveness. Finally, a recent study
that controlled for all types of force used by officers and suspects during
encounters found that, even after the adoption of ECDs, OC continued to be
associated with reductions in suspect injuries (Smith et al. 2007).

CONTROVERSIES

The adoption of OC spray by police did not occur without substantial controversy. For example, there were concerns about the appropriateness of offensive tactical use of OC on subjects posing no danger to themselves or others
(e.g., passive resisters), and the potential for disparate use of OC on minority
groups (ACLU 1993; *Associated Press* 1977; Derbeken 1997; Phillips 1994).
Much of the controversy, however, focused on the potential health risks associated with exposure to OC. Reports indicated that OC could cause skin irritation, corneal and vocal cord damage, breathing difficulties among asthmatics,
and that it might have carcinogenic and mutagenic potential in humans
(Brown 1997; Brown, Takeuchi, and Challoner 2000; Doubet 1977; Petty
2004). More importantly, OC exposure was implicated as a potential contributing
factor in a number of police in-custody deaths (ACLU 1993; Steffee et al. 1995).

Reviews of the medical literature, however, suggest that the risks are minimal (Brown 1997; Petty 2004; Ruddick 1993; Vilke and Chan 2007) and that other factors, such as drug intoxication, positional asphyxia, and pre-existing health conditions are the major contributors to in-custody deaths (Granfield and Petty 1994; Petty 2004; Steffee et al. 1995; Vilke and Chan 2007).

Although the evidence indicates OC is a reasonably safe and effective means for gaining compliance from uncooperative, resistive, and combative subjects when used properly, issues remain regarding police policy and practice regarding OC (Adang et al. 2006; Smith and Alpert 2000). A number of these issues are highlighted in the following case study of the Dutch experience in field-testing and ultimate adoption of OC.

OC USE, PRACTICE, AND POLICY: THE DUTCH EXAMPLE

In the Netherlands, the introduction of OC took approximately six years from the start of exploratory research into the feasibility of different types of non-lethal weapons (Adang, Wateren, and Steernberg 1999) to completion of nationwide introduction in 2003. Based on a literature study and visits to police forces in different countries, Adang et al. (1999) recommended that introduction of any new weapon should only take place on the basis of clear specifications and a clear policy, with a system of certification of officers (based on clearly formulated competences), sufficient and regular training, good documentation of use of the new weapon and its consequences, and be accompanied by evaluation research. Specifically with relation to OC, aftercare measures should be identified.

Following this exploratory phase, street trials with OC were held in four forces during a six-month period. Before the trials, a policy was developed (modelled after the International Association of Chiefs of Police OC policy) (IACP 1994). According to the policy, the use of OC is allowed to assist in the apprehension of a person who is ready to use a weapon with which one can stab or hit, to contain an individual trying to evade arrest, and in self-defense. OC was not to be used against groups, children under the age of 12, the elderly (above the age of 65), visibly pregnant women, or people with visible breathing problems. Also, OC should only be used a maximum of two times on the same suspect (in approximately one-second bursts), and not within a distance of one meter. According to the policy, the officer about to spray also had to warn the suspect, if possible. The policy indicated that OC was positioned on the same level as the baton in the use-of-force continuum.[1] After each use of OC, the suspect was to be provided with aftercare as soon as possible. To this end, all police vehicles in the participating forces were equipped with special decontamination towelettes and cleansing sprays. At selected police stations, eye showers were installed. The selection of stations was conducted in such a way that a sprayed suspect could rinse his eyes with tepid water within 15 minutes. If an individual sprayed with OC showed reactions deviating from the "normal" reaction to OC, officers were to seek medical assistance immediately.

Adang and Mensink (2000; 2001; 2004) evaluated the trials. They conducted a survey on the opinions of officers both before and after the trials and analysed the use of OC during the trials based on officer reports and interviews with sprayed suspects. They discussed placement of OC on the use-of-force continuum, aftercare issues, education and training, and logistical and organizational aspects. They made a number of recommendations for the nationwide introduction of OC. Account should be taken of the specific situation in the Netherlands, a country with 26 separate police forces but with a use-of-force policy and acquisition of weapons and equipment decided on at a national level. The establishment of a national project group under a national coordinator, with project coordinators in each police force, was crucial as it ensured good communication between national and regional levels.

Adang et al. (2005) reported on the nationwide introduction of OC. With more than 4,000 suspects sprayed during the trials and introduction (and even more officers as part of their training), they concluded that the introduction of OC took place without medical complications. They also concluded that a more realistic view on OC as a weapon had emerged among officers, that OC is not a magical bullet, and that sometimes it does not work and can even be counterproductive (e.g., when it causes suspects to become more aggressive). Adang et al. (2005) also identified several *best practices* that may contribute to a safe and responsible use of OC in line with the policy:

- street trials in a limited number of areas prior to nationwide introduction;
- certification as a precondition for equipment with OC;
- incorporation of OC training in a comprehensive situation-oriented education and training setting including tactical-communicative approaches to potentially dangerous situations;
- attention given to aftercare procedures, including provision of aftercare on the spot, eye showers at police stations reachable within 15 minutes, communication to hospitals and general practitioners, and involvement of doctors with the police forces;
- monitoring during the whole introduction period, which eased identification of issues and allowed for adjustments along the way; and
- clear communication to the public, contributing to preventive effects of OC introduction and acceptance of OC by the public.

Adang et al. (2005) also identified a number of important points to consider related to the introduction of OC. These included:

- the content of training, which should include practical exercises specifically aimed at avoiding self- and cross-contamination and instructions on how to act when an officer or fellow officer is affected by spray (therefore, some form of self-experience is required);

- logistical and organizational aspects that might require specific attention (and sometimes lead to delays);
- developing specifications for OC, for inert training spray, and for aftercare products;
- the procurement of a holder/holster for OC canisters for duty belt and uniform in use;
- the way in which OC is introduced in a police force—gradually, with officers carrying OC as soon as they are certified or all at once. Both options have advantages and disadvantages (e.g. there were several incidents where officers who were not yet certified were affected by OC and did not know what to do);
- use of OC around police animals—at the start of the introduction, no thought was given as to the implications of OC use around police dogs and police horses;
- ensuring that OC is used within the guidelines—in the Netherlands, the prohibition against using OC against groups and vulnerable individuals did not prove to be an issue. However, officers frequently used OC: 1) within one meter of a suspect; 2) more than two times on the same suspect; and 3) without giving a warning or trying to gain compliance without use of OC. Additionally, the evaluation drew attention to the use of OC against individuals in handcuffs or in police custody, "creative" use of OC (e.g., by spraying in the officer's hand and rubbing a suspect's face), and off-duty use of OC. Following recommendations during the trial and introductory period, more attention was paid to these aspects in education and training. In practice, OC was sometimes also used as a means to try and prevent a suicide attempt;
- the need to involve supervisory officers was initially underestimated—clarification of the issues mentioned above required involvement of supervising officers. In forces that involved supervisors from the start of the introduction, implementation was easier. In forces that organized regular meetings to discuss examples where OC was used, involvement of supervising officers in application of guidelines was enhanced; and
- limited availability of data—apart from the data gathered specifically for the evaluation study, little data were available on an ongoing basis and there was no culture within forces to analyse and discuss use-of-force data or to ensure that these data could be used for education and training purposes.

The above points are relevant to the introduction of any new weapon and would be relevant to other police forces around the world. Recommendations in a recent report on the use of ECDs by the Royal Canadian Mounted Police RCMP (Kennedy 2008) made some six years after introduction of these weapons are nearly identical to the lessons identified in the Netherlands following the introduction of OC. Indeed, there are many parallel issues between the introduction and use of OC and ECDs (Kaminski 2005).

The Canadian report also points to "usage creep" and lack of involvement of supervisors and recommends that ECDs are placed higher on the use-of-force continuum (recommendation 1); that aftercare procedures are improved (recommendations 2 and 3); that guidelines should be clarified (recommendation 4); that reporting is improved and information on use be analyzed (recommendations 5 and 6); and made available to benefit education and training (recommendations 8 and 9); and that national and divisional use-of-force coordinators should be appointed to deal with issues related to the use of ECDs (recommendation 7).

LONG-TERM CONSEQUENCES OF THE INTRODUCTION OF OC

On the basis of experiences in other countries, it was expected that introduction of OC would have several beneficial consequences, such as less violence against police, fewer injuries to suspects and officers, and fewer complaints about police use of force. Kaminski, Edwards and Johnson (1998) already indicated the limitations of studies using simple "before and after" comparisons (e.g., the one group pretest–posttest design) that limit the conclusions that can be drawn from much of the research. Their more sophisticated analysis indicated that the introduction of OC significantly reduced violence against police as a result of what they term the "Velcro effect" (the availability of OC). The data available on the Dutch introduction do not allow similar conclusions to be drawn due to the fact that there was no reliable registration of violence against police or police injuries as a consequence of violence. Most studies, however, found decreases in injuries following the introduction of OC (Adkins 2003; Bowling and Gaines 2000; Gauvin 1994; Morabito and Doerner 1997; Zwanzinger 1998; see Lumb and Friday [1997] for an exception). Regarding police use of force, Adang et al. (2005) indicated the self-reported frequency increased and that OC became the weapon of choice, without an associated decline in the use of other weapons. This finding is consistent with those of Adkins (2003); Gauvin (1994); Lumb and Friday (1997); Rogers and Johnson (2000); and Zwanzinger (1998). The Dutch data suggested that OC substituted for other, previously underreported, use-of-force options, especially physical force, batons, and dogs. In addition, it appears that OC is partly used as a replacement for verbal communication. Although there are anecdotal reports where officers did not have to resort to using their firearm because of the availability of OC, on the whole use of the firearm has not declined in the Netherlands after introduction of OC.

Use of OC appears to be associated with fewer injuries to suspects compared to use of other weapons. As a criterion, Adang et al. (2005) used whether or not officers reported suspects required medical care following arrest (as opposed to asking officers whether suspects were "injured"). Officers indicated suspects required medical attention in three percent of arrests (n = 3,006 suspects sprayed). Substitute prosecutors (who deal with suspects at the police station) indicated seven percent of suspects they saw required medical attention (n = 1,955 suspects seen by substitute officers). The difference between these two figures is easily explained by the fact that officers often do not know what the condition of the suspect is after they have brought him to the police station. The figures for OC compare favorably with those reported by Timmer and Beijers (1998), who investigated police use-of-force reports filed by Dutch police forces during 1996–1997. They report that 14% of 115 suspects on whom physical force was used required medical care, 10% of 59 suspects on whom a baton was used, 45% of 92 suspects on whom dogs were used, and 38% of 33 suspects at whom aimed shots were fired (not all "aimed" shots actually hit the suspect). Kennedy (2008) reported that 28% of suspects on which ECDs were used were medically examined afterwards (n = 4,234 usage reports).

Regarding complaints against police, there was no absolute or relative decline in complaints about police use of force following adoption of OC. Complaints about use of OC were rare, especially in light of the frequent use of OC. In the literature, Bowling and Gaines (2000), Gauvin (1994), and Rogers and Johnson (2000; also see Rappert 2002) report significant declines in complaints about police use of force after the introduction of OC. Adkins (2003), however, reported a clear increase in complaints about excessive use of force by police following the introduction of OC, though it was not known whether the increase was due to OC or other factors.

CONCLUSION

With the introduction of OC (as with the introduction of any new weapon) three issues consistently surfaced: 1) the safety of the weapon involved; 2) the "proper" and proportional use of the weapon and its position on the use-of-force continuum; and 3) the effectiveness of the weapon. As far as safety is concerned, OC causes intense pain during a limited time period and results in an infringement of the personal integrity of a person. The pain becomes more intense when OC spray comes into contact with an open wound. The effects of pepper-spray can last longer than is usually supposed (e.g., several hours and sometimes a day or longer). Lasting injuries do not typically occur, but the possibility cannot be ruled out that in rare instances OC may contribute to the death of a suspect (Petty 2004). Of course, adherence to use guidelines, not using OC against vulnerable individuals, proper training and proper aftercare procedures are needed to prevent this from happening, but the more often OC is used, the greater the risk of a fatality.

There is little doubt that OC is useful in situations where suspects have some sort of impact weapon or are violent. Depending on the number of suspects versus the number of officers, the relative strength of the suspect, known history of violence by the suspect, increased risk because of known HIV infection of the suspect, and other factors, OC may also be the best alternative in situations where suspects show signs of becoming violent. In these types of situations, the availability of OC allows officers to maintain a safe distance from a suspect until they are incapacitated. However, emphasizing the safety and effectiveness of OC, while at the same time ignoring or downplaying its physical and psychological impacts and disregarding risks other than lasting injury to the suspect, might stimulate disproportionate and indiscriminate use of OC. Even if one concurs (as we do) with Smith and Alpert (2000) that OC is a relatively safe and effective use of force alternative, it does not follow that OC should be the preferred option in situations where suspects are verbally resistant. Doing so seems unreasonable and could even be perceived as a form of abuse. Applying a very painful stimulus (OC) to a nonviolent, uncooperative suspect will often be considered disproportionate, given the fact that there are usually less extreme options available.

A policy that allows the use of OC in these circumstances may well lead to unnecessary deployment, at the expense of other, less painful techniques. This is of greater concern in situations where aftercare procedures are not initiated immediately, but are only implemented after a suspect has been transported to a police station, as is the case in many police forces in the United States (Broadstock 2002). Based on the physical impact of OC on suspects and the results of the street trials, we recommend a policy where it is stated explicitly that OC is not to be used as a replacement for hands-on physical control techniques. This recommendation is also based on the consideration that easy reliance on OC (at the expense of other options) is also potentially dangerous to officers given the fact that OC is not always effective (Adang et al. 2006; Kaminski, Edwards and Johnson 1999). In our view, the solution to safe and responsible police intervention should not be sought solely in the technology of less-than-lethal weaponry, but also in improving tactical and technical skills of police officers dealing with potentially dangerous situations. In addition, an over-eager and instrumental easy-to-use and trouble-saving application of OC, just because it seems so effective, could lead to alienation and hostility between a police force and the population it serves.

Police Use of the TASER in the United States: Research, Controversies, and Recommendations

Michael D. White and Justin Ready

ABSTRACT

OVER THE LAST decade the TASER has become an increasingly popular less-lethal force alternative among police agencies across the United States. Serious questions have been raised, however, concerning the weapon's use and effectiveness, as well as its potential to cause serious injury or death. Moreover, the ongoing debate surrounding police use of the TASER has been widely publicized, drawing national media attention and public scrutiny. Recent examples include the *Amnesty International* report (2004) which called for a moratorium on police use of the TASER, and the University of Florida incident during a Senator John Kerry speaking engagement (2007). This chapter summarizes the development of the TASER within the larger context of police use of force and highlights the primary controversies surrounding the device: when and against whom should the TASER be used?; how effective is the TASER?; and does use of the device pose an increased risk of death for suspects? The authors discuss the latest empirical research on all three areas of controversy, and the chapter concludes with recommendations for future research, as well as for police policy, training, and practice.

INTRODUCTION

Over the past decade, conducted energy devices (CEDs) have been widely adopted by law enforcement agencies across the United States. *TASER International*, the manufacturer of the TASER, estimates that more than 10,000

Michael D. White, Arizona State University
Justin Ready, Arizona State University

law enforcement agencies in the United States have purchased its weapons as a less-than-lethal force alternative, with approximately 10% of all police officers in the country carrying the device (Hamilton 2005). Despite its increasing popularity, questions have been raised concerning the TASER's use and effectiveness, as well as its potential to cause physiological harm. In response to these concerns, *Amnesty International* (2004) published a report in 2004 describing 74 cases in which a suspect died after being subjected to the TASER (e.g., TASER-proximate death). The report concluded with a call for a moratorium on their use.[1] More recently, the National Institute of Justice embarked on a more extensive study of deaths following electro-muscular disruption in which they acknowledge more than 300 cases of Americans dying after the TASER was used against them. Not surprising, the ongoing discourse on police use of the TASER has been widely publicized, with more than 400 news stories in the New York Times and LexisNexis detailing police TASER incidents in 2005 and 2006.[2]

THE CONTEXT: POLICE AND THE LEGITIMATE USE OF FORCE

The Nature and Prevalence of Police Use of Force

Police officers have the legal authority to use force in a wide range of situations, including physical force, the use of less-than-lethal weapons (e.g., baton, pepper spray, or the TASER), and as a last resort, the use of a firearm (Walker and Katz 2002). Egon Bittner (1970) argues that the capacity to threaten or use physical force is the core function of the police, which defines their role and shapes how they interact with suspects and citizens. Despite its critical role in law enforcement, research indicates that police use of force is a statistically rare event in the United States, occurring in about one percent of all police-citizen encounters (BJS 1999).[3] Nonetheless, because of the sheer volume of police-citizen encounters in a given year (approximately 43 million), an estimated 421,000 use-of-force incidents occur each year; or more than 1,000 events per day.

The application of physical force can have devastating consequences, not only for the suspect and the officer (see the chapter by Klinger in this volume), but also for the police department, the community and their relationship (Geller and Scott 1992). James Fyfe (1988) notes that use of force incidents have led to civil disorder and riots, the firing of police executives, millions of dollars in litigation, criminal prosecutions, and strained police-community relations. Examples of the consequences of police use of force include the Los Angeles riots following the acquittal of the four officers who beat Rodney King, and strained community relations in New York City following the shootings of Amadou Diallo in 1999 and Sean Bell in 2006 (Skolnick and Fyfe 1993; White and Klinger 2009).

The Force Continuum and Less-than-Lethal Force Alternatives

Importantly, there are constitutionally-derived mandates that govern police use of force which require that officers use only the minimum force necessary to accomplish their objective. Any force beyond the minimum required is considered excessive—the "reasonableness standard" established in *Graham v. Connor* (1989), 490 US 386. Police agencies closely monitor the use of force and provide policy guidance and training to officers through a "force continuum," which specifies the verbal and physical actions an officer can take in response to different levels of suspect resistance.[4]

Because of these policy mandates and the potential consequences of use of force (especially deadly force), police agencies have sought to expand their alternatives to the firearm. Accordingly, technological advances have led to the development of a range of alternatives such as oleoresin capsicum (OC) spray, kinetic impact weapons, foams, ballistic rounds and, most recently, conducted energy devices (CEDs) such as the TASER (see the chapter by Summers and Kuhns in this volume). Less-than-lethal weapons are intended to provide officers with a wider range of options when a situation requires the application of force but has not escalated to the point where lethal force is necessary or justified.

During the 1990s, OC spray (e.g., pepper spray) became increasingly popular among police agencies in the United States. This trend serves as a backdrop for the current examination of CEDs because many of the same issues and concerns have been raised (e.g., appropriate use, effectiveness, and physiological impact; Smith and Alpert 2000). A number of studies have examined police use of OC spray, concluding that it has a high rate of success in terms of incapacitation, results in fewer officer injuries, and reduces reliance on other types of force (Gauvin 1995; Kaminski, Edwards and Johnson 1998; Lumb and Friday 1997; Nowicki 1993).

THE TASER

The most popular CED is the TASER, manufactured by *TASER International* (most commonly the M26 or the X26 models).[5] The TASER fires two small probes at a rate of 180 feet per second and, on striking the subject, delivers a 50,000-volt shock over a five-second cycle (Vilke and Chan 2007).

> CEDs work by incapacitating volitional control of the body. These weapons create intense involuntary contractions of skeletal muscle, causing subjects to lose the ability to directly control the actions of their voluntary muscles. CEDs directly stimulate motor nerve and muscle tissue, overriding the central nervous system control and causing incapacitation regardless of the subject's mental focus, training, size, or drug intoxication state. This effect terminates as soon as the electrical

discharge is halted. Immediately after the TASER shock, subjects are usually able to perform at their physical baseline (Vilke and Chan 2007, 349).

The advantages of the TASER over other less-than-lethal alternatives include its relatively short duration of recovery time, its reliability at greater distances than sprays, its compact size and utility, and its perceived effectiveness.[6] Despite these advantages, controversies surrounding the device have emerged in a number of areas, and these issues have been exacerbated by the TASER's rapid growth in policing and researchers' failure to keep pace with the diffusion of this technology. The major issues—and the latest empirical research regarding each—are described below, but first a brief discussion concerning the availability of data is provided.

Brief Note on Available Data

Researchers' ability to inform the debate surrounding the physical impact and effectiveness of the TASER has been complicated by the limited available data. Preferably, researchers would draw on a national archive of incident-level data detailing police-citizen encounters involving the TASER. Unfortunately, no such archive exists. Researchers have been forced to rely on a range of disparate data sources to investigate questions about the TASER. These data sources have informed a handful of empirical studies (see White and Ready 2007; 2008; Smith et al. 2007); internal police reports; CED industry reports and data (e.g., *TASER International*'s website); human and civil rights group reports (e.g., *Amnesty International*); news media; and civil litigation against police department. The utility of many of these data sources is limited by questions concerning objectivity, availability, and accuracy and completeness of reporting.[7] Given these concerns, we limit our review primarily to independent, empirical research.

TASER CONTROVERSIES: WHAT WE KNOW

The Policy Controversy: When and against Whom

The first area involves *police policy*; more specifically, when and against whom is it appropriate to use the TASER? Police departments have varied considerably in terms of where they place the TASER on the force continuum, particularly with regard to suspects who are passively or verbally resisting police efforts. Questions have also been raised concerning their appropriate use against vulnerable persons, such as children and the elderly. *Amnesty International* (2007) has called attention to incidents involving repeated deployments against a single person and raised concerns regarding use of the device in the "drive stun" mode—where the TASER is placed directly on the individual's body without the use of probes. The drive-stun mode causes significant pain in the area of the body where the device is placed, but it has minimal effect on the central nervous system (e.g., it functions more as a pain-compliance technique).

A U.S. Government Accountability Office report (2005) found that placement of the TASER on the force continuum varied considerably across police agencies. For example, the Sacramento Police Department allowed for use of the TASER during dangerous situations, such as when a suspect is combative. Alternatively, the Orange County Sheriff's Department allowed use of the TASER when a suspect was passively resisting the verbal commands of an officer. Both the International Association of Chiefs of Police (IACP 2005) and the Police Executive Research Forum (PERF 2005) issued model policies to offer guidance to agencies in their deployment of CEDs. These guidelines state that CEDs should only be used against those who are actively resisting, that they not be used against children or the elderly except in emergency situations, and that each deployment be closely supervised and documented.

Unfortunately, there has been little empirical research examining when and under what circumstances police use the TASER.[8] Michael White and Justin Ready (2007; 2010) have examined TASER use by officers in the New York City Police Department (NYPD). Their descriptive analysis of 375 TASER incidents from 2002–2005 showed that:

- most suspects were male (89%), African American (52%) or Hispanic (27%), and in their 30s (mean age was 35);
- only 13% of suspects were under the influence of alcohol or drugs, but 93% were identified as exhibiting signs of mental illness[9];
- nearly all suspects (95%) had engaged in violent behavior (such as physically assaulting an officer or citizen);
- 40% of the suspects were armed, and among the armed suspects, the majority possessed a knife or cutting instrument (84% of armed suspects; 32% of all cases);
- 90% of the officers using the TASER in the NYPD were assigned to the Emergency Service Unit (ESU);
- back-up officers and supervisors were present in more than 90% of cases;
- 89% of suspects were incapacitated by the TASER, typically within five seconds;
- the TASER was deployed more than once by an officer in about one-fifth of the incidents (and rarely more than twice);
- officers used the device in the drive-stun mode in 48 incidents;
- in one-quarter of the cases, officers also used another less-than-lethal device; and
- only 24% of the subjects were not arrested on criminal charges, although nearly all were transported to a hospital for physical and/or psychological evaluation.

White and Ready (2010) concluded that the NYPD experienced positive outcomes while avoiding some of the current controversies because their policies and procedures mirror those outlined by PERF and IACP.

Ready, White and Fisher (2008) analyzed the content of all New York Times and LexisNexis news reports describing police use of the TASER from January 2002 through December 2005 (n = 353). They reported that: suspects were mostly male (more than 90%); a fairly small proportion of the suspects were under 18 or over 60 years old (16%); one-fifth of suspects were under the influence of drugs or alcohol (19%) and one-quarter were emotionally disturbed (26%); about one-third of the TASER incidents involved an armed suspect (36%; mostly a knife or cutting instrument); the TASER was used in response to active physical resistance or a physical assault in more than 85% of the news stories; and the weapon was used repeatedly by an officer during the same incident in about one-third of the news reports (Ready, White and Fisher 2008).

Although a large body of literature demonstrates that the news media's portrayal of crime and criminal justice issues—including the police—is often inaccurate (Chermak 1995; Manning 1997), the consistency in findings across the NYPD and news media data is noteworthy, suggesting that these data may offer a reasonably accurate picture of some typical incidents in which police officers use the TASER.[10]

The Effectiveness Controversy

The second area of contention involves *effectiveness*; how often the device works as intended. Research examining the effectiveness of the TASER has focused on two general questions: 1) how often the device terminates suspect resistance; and 2) whether use of the device reduces the prevalence of suspect and officer injuries. A number of departments have released reports on the effectiveness of the device. The Madison (WI) Police Department found that the device performed effectively during 77% of all deployments from July 2003 through January 2005. Similarly, the Seattle Police Department (SPD) found that use of the TASER ended suspect resistance in 85% of incidents in which it was used (SPD Special Report 2002).[11] In their study of the NYPD, White and Ready (2007; 2010) reported that the weapon immediately stopped suspects' resistance in 89% of cases, but that a sizeable minority of suspects (about 20%) began resisting again at a later point in the encounter—highlighting the temporary impact of the device. White and Ready (2010) also found the TASER was most frequently ineffective when one or both probes missed the target (or did not penetrate the suspect's skin), the suspect weighed more than 200 pounds, the suspect was intoxicated (by drugs, alcohol, or both), and if the officer and suspect were in close proximity (three feet or less).

Several police agencies have reported reductions in injuries sustained during police-citizen encounters after issuing the TASER to their line personnel.

Police departments in Los Angeles, Austin (TX), Putnam County (FL), and Cincinnati (OH) reported reductions in injuries to both suspects and officers after adopting the TASER (Jenkinson, Neeson and Bleetman 2006; *TASER International* 2006). Michael Smith and colleagues (2007) examined use-of-force data from the Miami-Dade Police Department and Richland County (SC) Sheriff's Department (MDPD and RCSD, respectively) and found that use of CEDs was associated with fewer suspect and officer injuries in the MDPD but not the RCSD, indicating that "not every agency's experience will be the same regarding CED use and injuries" (Smith et al. 2007, 439).

The Physiological Impact Controversy

The third controversy surrounding the TASER involves *physiological impact*; does the weapon lead to an increased risk of death? In 2001, *Amnesty International* began raising concerns regarding the physiological risks of the TASER, and as noted earlier, their 2004 report called for a moratorium on use of the device. Concern over the health risks associated with the TASER has led to a wealth of recent research including review of coroner reports in death cases, literature reviews of available research, and bio-medical laboratory research on animals and healthy human volunteers. Gary Ordog and colleagues (1987) examined 218 emergency room cases involving suspects subjected to the TASER; three suspects died, and all three had high levels of PCP in their systems (see also Kornblum and Reddy 1991). Jared Strote and colleagues (2006) examined autopsy reports in 28 TASER-proximate death cases and reported that the TASER was not listed as a direct cause of death in any of the cases.

A number of studies have examined the physiological impact of the TASER on animals (e.g., pigs and dogs) and healthy human volunteers, focusing specifically on cardiac rhythm disturbances such as ventricular fibrillation (McDaniel, Stratbucker and Smith 2000; McDaniel et al. 2005; Roy and Podgorski 1989; Stratbucker, Roeder and Nerheim 2003). Others have monitored healthy human volunteers following TASER deployment and found no evidence of changes in heart rhythm or functioning (Ho et al. 2006; Levine et al. 2005). In their review of this research, Gary Vilke and Theodore Chan (2007, 353) concluded:

> The potential for life-threatening cardiac dysrhythmias or cardiac muscle damage to occur as a result of the electrical discharge from current TASER devices appears to be low based on the available studies. However, there may be theoretical risks to patients with pacemakers or underlying cardiac disease, and the effect of recurrent or prolonged TASER discharges remains unclear.

Vilke and Chan (2007, 353) also noted that existing research has yet to fully investigate "non-cardiac effects" of the TASER, including the device's impact on metabolism—such as potassium, sodium, and pH levels in the blood—and respiration, including carbon dioxide elimination and respiratory rate.

The implications of the medical research with animals and healthy human volunteers are limited by fundamental differences between the research subjects and those most likely to experience the TASER in real world settings.[12] In October 2007, the Wake Forest University Medical Center concluded a study involving physician review of 1,000 real-world TASER incidents, thereby overcoming the limitations of laboratory research with animals and human volunteers. The Wake Forest study found that 99.7% of suspects had minor or no injuries.[13] William Bozeman, the study's lead investigator stated "The injury rate is low and most injuries appear to be minor. These results support the safety of the devices" (Wake Forest University Baptist Medical Center 2007). In 2007, the National Institute of Justice (NIJ) convened a steering group to study "deaths following electro muscular disruption," and in a special report published in June 2008, they concluded that "there is no conclusive medical evidence within the state of current research that indicates a high risk of serious injury or death from the direct effects of CED exposure" (NIJ 2008, 3).

Summary and Discussion

This chapter explored the primary controversies surrounding police use of the TASER and offered a snapshot of the current state of empirical research in each area. Unfortunately, a scarcity of independent data addresses the use and effectiveness considerations, but the NYPD studies suggest that agencies can successfully deploy the TASER—avoiding problems with misuse and abuse— by implementing procedures and policies in accordance with PERF and IACP recommendations. It is also worth noting that the NYPD adopted the weapon in a limited capacity, opting to equip only the Emergency Services Unit (ESU) and supervisors. Alternatively, a sizeable and growing body of research examines the physiological impact controversy, and the latest research shows that the TASER does not appear to be directly associated with an increased risk of injury or death (NIJ 2008).

Further Research

Given the emerging controversies, the dearth of independent empirical research on police use of the TASER in a natural setting is disconcerting, and much work remains to be done before researchers and practitioners can definitively respond to the questions that have been raised. The next section describes the primary areas that, in our opinion, should be the focus of future research on the TASER.

Physiological Impact

A fair amount of research has explored the physiological impact of the device, and the research has consistently shown that the vast majority of TASER deployments will result in little or no injury to suspects. Nevertheless, nearly 300 individuals have died after being subjected to the TASER, and our understanding of why fatalities occur, or what factors might increase the likelihood of death, is still inadequate. Vilke and Chan (2007) note that research has not fully explored the impact of the TASER on body metabolism and respiration, nor has it sufficiently explored the physiological impact of multiple or prolonged TASER deployments. In short, the discussion of bodily harm has moved beyond fundamental questions such as how often deaths occur and whether a causal link exists, to more complicated questions about why deaths do occur in a small number of cases.

Regrettably, little is known about whether the characteristics of TASER incidents ending in death differ in notable ways from non-fatal cases, and perhaps more importantly, whether identifiable risk factors increase the likelihood of death. A major obstacle to investigating these questions involves limitations in the available data. Previous investigations have relied on data sources where no variation exists in the outcome of interest: did the TASER deployment result in a suspect death? For example, in research involving TASER-related death cases exclusively, such as Strote et al. (2006), the *Amnesty International* (2004) report, and the recent NIJ study (2008), the outcome of interest (death) always occurs. Alternatively, in the biomedical laboratory studies with human volunteers, White and Ready's NYPD studies (2007; 2010), and the Wake Forest study (2007), the outcome of interest never (or almost never) occurs. The low base rate of TASER-related deaths occurring in any one police jurisdiction precludes the use of police reports for predictive models.

In short, no single database to our knowledge includes details relating to both fatal and non-fatal TASER incidents. The creation of such a database—properly weighted to adjust for the scarcity of death cases—would allow researchers to examine the incident-level circumstances, as well as the characteristics of suspects and officers across encounters. Researchers could then use multivariate techniques to determine whether identifiable risk factors are present—such as repeated deployments or drug use—which are associated with an increased probability of death. Indeed, if identifiable predictors of suspect death do exist, these findings may be used to inform policy and practice to reduce the likelihood of fatal outcomes.

Use and Effectiveness

Available data on use of the TASER by police is insufficient and basic answers to questions about how often the weapon is used, against whom, under what circumstances, and with what effect remain unclear. Potential data sources that capture incident-level characteristics of fatal and non-fatal TASER events occurring across the United States would allow researchers to characterize typical TASER deployments, and offer insights on how the device could be more efficiently and effectively used.[14] In the interim, researchers and practitioners are encouraged to work together to conduct studies on use of the TASER. As the body of empirical literature grows, researchers can then piece together a mosaic of studies on single and multiple departments to improve our knowledge base. Moreover, the Department of Justice (through NIJ) had funded several national-level research studies on the TASER—including the recent study of deaths and survey research spearheaded by Lorie Fridell and Geoffrey Alpert—and we are hopeful that government agencies will continue to support those and other initiatives.

The Question of Race

A substantial body of literature has documented racial disparities in police use of force (e.g., BJS 2005; Reiss 1971; Robin 1963; Terrill and Reisig 2003). While this research on police use of force would suggest that the TASER may be used disproportionately against minority suspects, few inquiries into this question have been carried out. In February 2004, however, the *Seattle Post Intelligencer* reported that 45% of the people subjected to the TASER by the police were black, while census data indicate that blacks make up less than 10% of the city's population (Castro 2004). In December 2006, *The Houston Chronicle* published an article stating that the Houston police have used the TASER "indiscriminately" against black suspects (Villafranca 2006). Michael White and Jessica Saunders (2010) explored six different data sources on the TASER and reported a virtual absence of any discussion of race and police use of the device.[15] They speculate that the physiological impact question may have overshadowed questions about race, but that "these articles may signal that questions relating to racial bias and the TASER are on the horizon for police departments in the U.S." (White and Saunders 2010, 29). Their analysis shows, however, that limited available data exist to effectively respond to those concerns over racial bias. Future research on the TASER would benefit from exploring these questions.

The TASER in Other Settings

Although the body of knowledge on police use of the TASER is limited, we know even less about TASER use in other settings, including the fields of corrections and private security.[16] All of the controversies outlined in this chapter apply equally well to these other settings, and the potential for abuse may be even greater because of the custodial nature of corrections and the traditional shortcomings for training in private security. Currently no empirical studies, reports, or data on TASER use in these other settings have been carried out, and researchers are encouraged to fill these gaps. Also, *TASER International* has begun marketing its products to private citizens for personal protection and self-defense (e.g., the C2 model). Researchers might also focus on TASER use by private citizens, as the potential for misuse and abuse is significant.

The TASER and Other Forms of Force

There is also a need for research that examines the impact of TASER adoption on overall levels of use of force by police, as well as specific types. What happens after a department issues the TASER to its line personnel? Does use of the TASER by police have any impact on levels of deadly force? Although most police departments do not recommend use of the TASER in situations where deadly force is justified, the device may serve to de-escalate police citizen encounters before lethal force becomes necessary. Also, after TASER adoption, do overall levels of use of force increase, decrease, or remain the same? Perhaps police officers increasingly use the TASER instead of physical force or other less-than-lethal alternatives such as the baton or pepper spray. In that case, overall levels of force may remain stable while the type of force used changes significantly. Alternatively, *Amnesty International* has argued that many police departments "are using the TASER as a routine force option" (*New York Times* 2004), suggesting that police are now using the device in circumstances where no force (or a much lesser degree) would have been used before. In those circumstances, departments may actually witness an increase in overall use of force incidents. Given the consequences of use of force, departments should closely monitor use of the TASER and explore the impact of the device on officer decision-making in potentially violent police-citizen encounters.

Currently Available Less-than-Lethal Alternatives and Emerging Technologies for the Future

Diana L. Summers and Joseph B. Kuhns

ABSTRACT

CONTINUED PRESSURE ON police to maintain order and arrest offenders, while also considering the protection of human rights and life, requires continual review of use-of-force procedures and of the weapons made available to police. Innovations in less-than-lethal weaponry may allow police to strike a balance between these two sometimes competing goals. While the widespread adoption of stun guns and incapacitating sprays has helped increase officer and suspect safety, future advancements in other less-than-lethal weapons including ballistics, disorientation instruments and acoustic technologies may help ensure that offenders can be safely, yet securely, apprehended and that officers and bystanders can also remain safe in the process. This chapter provides a glimpse of some of the emerging technologies that might be used in lieu of deadly force and also offers some suggestions for testing, training, and adopting those technologies.

INTRODUCTION

As early as 1907, and in some cases even before this year, police, military, and policymakers sought to develop deadly force alternatives in the United States. When officers are presented with a dangerous situation involving disorderly citizens, the primary objective is to bring matters to a non-fatal conclusion through the use of less-than-lethal weapons. The National Security Research, Inc. (2003) states that less-than-lethal weapons "should never be considered a replacement for the legal use of lethal force; rather . . . officers

Diana L. Summers, Northeastern University
Joseph B. Kuhns, University of North Carolina at Charlotte

should use [less-than-lethal] weapons as an instrument of force continuum between show of force . . . and deadly force" (10). Brian Lawton (2007) observes that the most defining characteristic of the role of a police officer is their discretion to use force, and the force continuum allows officers to apply the appropriate amount of force that is necessary for each situation. Current and future technological developments and training assists officers and law enforcement leaders with improving this decision process, while protecting the rights and safety of the citizens that officers are sworn to protect.

Police and policymakers classified a wide range of instruments and weapons under the term "less-than-lethal" as policing methods evolved over the decades (Davison 2006). In 1907, the United States began the first training sessions for police service canines in New York and New Jersey as less-than-lethal options (Dorriety 2005; Hutson et al. 1997). Until 1952, only about 14 police service canine programs existed. This number soon increased rapidly as law enforcement entities across the country began to incorporate these canines. By 1989 the number of canines and handlers exceeded 7,000, and thus became an important less-than-lethal alternative for officers in the United States (Dorriety 2005).

The 1960s saw an increase in the development of less-than-lethal technologies as a response to the growing number of public protests and the need for greater, more effective crowd and riot control, while maintaining the highest degree of safety for citizens. These weapon technologies were in the early stages of development and mainly included forms of irritant chemical weapons, also referred to as riot control agents (RCAs). The objective of RCAs was to inflict temporary but substantial sensory irritation to the eyes and respiratory tract (Davison 2006). Some examples of RCAs were teargas grenades, teargas pen-guns, and chemical mace (which was later replaced with oleoresin capsicum) (White and Ready 2007).

Other common forms of less-than-lethal weapons utilized by police during the 1960s included batons and water cannons. Water cannons expanded into the realm of electrical weapons as developers patented the idea of using two jets of water with opposing charges to subdue suspects through temporary electrical shock (Davison 2006). This concept was later replaced with more modern forms of electric less-than-lethal weapons, such as the TASER (*TASER International* 2008). Projectile weapons were also under development in the late '60s and early '70s, including rubber and plastic bullets, wooden block projectiles, and the 'beanbag' gun, which is a canvas pouch filled with lead shot (Davison 2006).

The need to further develop existing less-than-lethal weapons and design new alternatives was further emphasized in 1985 amid concerns over the lack of testing and data collection on these weapons to determine safety and effectiveness. In this same year, the Supreme Court ruled in *Tennessee v. Garner* (1985), 471 U.S. 1 that the use of deadly force to apprehend a non-violent, unarmed fleeing suspect was unreasonable seizure under the Fourth Amendment. Following this decision, *Graham v. Connor* 490 U.S. 386, (1989) (which defined "objective reasonableness" as the standard by which officers must judge use-of-force situations) and the Rodney King incident, the government made public the dire need to find suitable force alternatives for police. In response, the late 1980s and 1990s was a time period of less aggressive policies toward suspect apprehension and emerging new less-than-lethal tactics and weapons (Kinnaird 2003).

Some scholars would argue that the less-than-lethal weapons utilized by police in the late 1980s and early 1990s did not change substantially from those used in the 1960s, despite the publicity and motivation to develop new weapons (Davison 2006). In part, this statement is factual. It is true that most law enforcement entities still use traditional less-than-lethal weapons, such as oleoresin capsicum, chemical irritants, rubber bullets, and electric stunning devices. However, it is also the case that new less-than-lethal weapons and tactics have been implemented in the field, and research and development surrounding future less-than-lethal weapons has continued (Homant and Kennedy 2000).

CURRENTLY AVAILABLE LESS-THAN-LETHAL WEAPONS

Conducted / Directed Energy Devices

During the late 1970s, researchers first introduced a less-than-lethal weapon for police that emitted electric pulses. This conducted energy device (CED), which later evolved into the TASER (an acronym for Thomas A. Swift Electric Rifle), induces involuntary muscle contractions that incapacitate individuals by propelling two small probes connected to the weapon by high-voltage wires at a distance of approximately 21 feet (National Institute of Justice 2007; White and Ready 2007). The probes can deliver up to 50,000 volts of electricity for five seconds and can penetrate up to two inches of clothing (Bleetman, Steyn and Lee 2004). In policing, the two most commonly used forms of the TASER are the M26 Advanced TASER and the TASER X26. The primary purpose of this weapon is not to inflict pain, but rather to incapacitate by causing a temporary loss of neuromuscular control, allowing officers to safely restrain the suspect (White and Ready 2007). The TASER and other CEDS, such as Stinger Handheld Projectile Stun Guns, have become important less-than-lethal weapons for police in the United States. CEDS have advantages over other less-than-lethal alternatives, including reliability and accuracy at greater distances, size, the relatively short duration of recovery time, no impediment by wind like chemical sprays, and limited risk to officers or bystanders (Amnesty International 2004; White and Ready 2008; see the chapter by White and Ready in this volume).

Chemical Irritants

Many chemical irritants used by law enforcement today are similar to those carried by police in the 1960s and 1970s. These include oleoresin capsicum

(OC) spray (derived from the capsicum pepper plant, strengths ranging from one to ten percent concentration levels), teargas, and stink/smoke bombs. Other chemical sprays have been derived from a cayenne pepper base. These irritants cause inflammation and temporary but intense irritation at the point of contact, which is generally the facial region (Chan et al. 2000; see the chapter by Adang and Kaminski in this volume). Again, the primary objective is to temporarily incapacitate the individual until police are able to properly apprehend them in the safest way possible.

To address large, violent crowds during a protest or riot, products such as the Pyrotechnic Grenade #2 CS were designed. The #2 CS is a 21.9-ounce canister with a pelletized chemical agent and a fly-off fuse. When thrown by hand or launched from a weapon, the chemical irritant discharges from one opening on the bottom of the canister and four openings on the top. There are also 16- and 17-ounce versions of the Pyrotechnic Grenade, each with various pelletized chemical agents and operated in the same fashion (National Security Research, Inc. 2003). These less-than-lethal products allow police to disperse disorderly crowds, keeping a potentially uncontrollable situation from further escalating.

Police Service Canines

Use of police service canines to assist in tracking, locating and restraining suspects is another widely available less-than-lethal alternative. Canines are also trained to sniff out contraband and explosives, find missing persons, and assist in crowd control (Denham and Mallon 1999; Hutson et al. 1997). There are a handful of breeds trained by police, but the most popular is the German Shepard. These canines are utilized by over 2,000 U.S. law enforcement agencies, and are prized for their keen senses of smell and hearing, agility, temperament, and intelligence (Hutson et al. 1997). There are a number of training techniques practiced by canines and police handlers, such as the "bite and hold," "find and bark," and the newly implemented "bark and hold" (Hutson et al. 1997; Mesloh 2006). The "bite and hold" is the traditional technique and most commonly used when training police service dogs. The canine apprehends the suspect by biting and does not release until the handler arrives. The "bark and hold" method was suggested by the Department of Justice in 2001 as a way of protecting the canine from suspects who learned to prepare themselves for an attack. The "bark and hold" method is accomplished by the canine locating and barking, but will not engage the suspect unless he or she attempts to flee (Mesloh 2006). The "find and bark" technique is similar to the "bark and hold," with the only difference being the canine will circle the individual while barking aggressively until the handler can safely apprehend the suspect (Hutson et al. 1997). It is important to note that all three techniques used by canines and their handlers are conducted with constant voice commands and visual monitoring to ensure the canines react to each situation as they were trained.

Impact Munitions

The term "impact munitions" encompasses a wide variety of projectiles and ballistics that work by striking the individual with adequate force to cause compliance, but with low probability of causing serious injury (Hubbs and Klinger 2004; Kenny, Heal and Grossman 2001). As was the case with chemical irritants, a handful of less-than-lethal impact munitions are still in use today as was the case decades ago. These include rubber and plastic bullets and beanbag projectiles (Davison 2006). However, significant advancements have been made to this group of less-than-lethal weapons.

Originally, Special Weapons and Tactics (SWAT) teams mainly utilized impact munitions (Hubbs and Klinger 2004). Since the 1990s, however, law enforcement agencies have begun to equip patrol officers with impact munitions as a deadly force alternative. The ARWEN (Anti-Riot Weapon-Engield)-37 and the Sage SL-6 are examples of weapons available for riot control. Each weapon is capable of firing five and six rounds, respectively, of plastic batons into a crowd in order to cause dispersion (Hubbs and Klinger 2004; National Security Research, Inc. 2003). The SA-4 PepperBall System, designed by PepperBall Technologies, Inc. (2008), is an impact munitions device that launches up to four projectiles containing around four grams of extremely hot pepper powder that explode into a cloud on impact. This weapon is accurate at distances of up to 30 feet. In extreme temperatures, the pepper agent is replaced with an impact round containing an anti-freezing liquid (PepperBall Technologies, Inc. 2008).

Beanbag rounds have been modified slightly since their first appearance decades earlier. Currently law enforcement is employing the use of a 37 MM beanbag round inside a cartridge of smokeless propellant. The projectile is typically a two-by-two inch fabric bag containing lead shot and fired from a twelve-gauge shotgun. It is designed to deliver kinetic energy across a broad surface without penetrating the target (Grange, Kozak and Gonzalez 2002). Beanbag rounds are intended to incapacitate a suspect temporarily, allowing the officer to apprehend and control while reducing the threat of lethal harm to either party. This less-than-lethal weapon is also useful for crowd-control purposes, animal-control situations, and to knock out windows (National Security Research, Inc 2003).

THE FUTURE OF LESS-THAN-LETHAL WEAPONS DEVELOPMENT

While the less-than-lethal weapons currently deployed by police have increased the number of deadly force alternatives, police and policymakers are continually seeking to develop new weapons and alternatives to increase suspect and officer safety. The development of future less-than-lethal weapons takes generally a minimum of three to five years (Pilant 1993), but will significantly contribute to the mission of reducing deadly force.

Acoustic Devices

One group of less-than-lethal weapons currently under development is acoustic devices. One such device is the Long Range Acoustic Device™ (LRAD) designed by the American Technology Corporation. The LRAD is capable of issuing a verbal warning before emitting a "deterrent tone" that affects the behavior of those in range of the device (American Technology Corporation 2008). Previous models of acoustic devices consumed high levels of power and were incredibly bulky and heavy, greatly restricting the area of placement. The LRAD, by contrast, utilizes customized, efficient capacitive transducers and requires conservative amounts of power. The deterrent tone emitted from the LRAD can be accurately directed, reducing the risk of excessive audio level exposure for operators or nearby bystanders. The LRAD is small, light, and compact, allowing the device to be placed in multiple environments (American Technology Corporation 2008). LRADs are beneficial in situations requiring effective crowd control, clearing out buildings, or preventing entry into a structure.

Devices such as the LRAD rely on increasing sound pressure levels to cause temporary discomfort and pain in order to incapacitate targets. Challenges with this process include producing the strong, directed tones over distances above 50 meters (Altmann 2001). Acoustic devices are therefore most effective at short range and inside or around buildings where sound waves can reverberate. Some examples of sound sources from acoustic devices currently in development are high-powered, low-frequency acoustic beams; very–low-frequency "acoustic bullets" emitted from antenna dishes; infrasound from banks of large speakers and high-power amplifiers; and baseball-sized acoustic pulses set to less-than-lethal levels of sound pressure levels (Altmann 2001). The effects caused by short-term exposure to these sound sources are discomfort similar to standing near an air horn or loud speakers, disorientation, blunt-object impact, and intolerable sensations. A less-than-lethal acoustic weapon for helicopter deployment is also being developed, along with acoustic sirens to be installed on vehicles (such as police cruisers in the future) and an acoustic beam weapon for building denial purposes (Altmann 2001). Military personnel currently utilize these weapons, but with further development the LRAD and similar devices may be an available option for law enforcement officers.

Directed Energy Devices

The Active Denial System, a less-than-lethal directed energy device (DED), has been recently developed by the U.S. Department of Defense for use in law enforcement and corrections. The Active Denial System emits electromagnetic radiation at 95 GHz, stimulating nerve endings and causing discomfort but not permanent injury. The individual experiences heightened discomfort, causing them to cease their current actions. Once the individual moves away from the beam or the device is turned off, the symptoms dissipate quickly (National Institute of Justice 2007). This allows police to use the device at greater distances without physical contact with the suspect. The product is not currently widely used by law enforcement officials, but the National Institute of Justice has developed small prototypes for use by police (National Institute of Justice 2007).

Disorientation Devices

The National Institute of Justice describes less-than-lethal disorientation devices as "equipment [that] temporarily incapacitates people while causing little harm" (2007). The majority of these devices are still under development. One example of a disorientation device is the Flash-Bang round. Designed to be fired from a twelve-gauge shotgun approximately five meters above a rioting or disorderly crowd, the Flash-Bang round distracts large numbers of people with an intense flash of light (National Institute of Justice 2004a). When the Flash-Bang round explodes, "flake aluminum is ejected and ignited" to create the dazzling flash of light equivalent to looking directly at the sun for sixty milliseconds (Lewis 2003, 117). No permanent damage is incurred from the Flash-Bang round and it is effective up to a 100-yard range. Developers have designed two forms of the flash-bang round. One version allows the operator to manually set the distance desired for the round to burst, while the other version has a radar-controlled burst capability (Lewis 2003). The radar-controlled burst capability will allow for even greater control and accuracy of the weapon, further lessening the chances of unintentional effects.

The Diversionary Flash-Bang Stun Hand Grenade designed by Universal Propulsion is another less-than-lethal disorientation weapon (National Institute of Justice 2004a). This device is almost 5 inches long with a weight of just over 14 ounces and is designed to be thrown into a room. A loud bang and intense flash temporarily disorients any occupants inside, allowing officers or military personnel to enter and apprehend suspects without the use of lethal force (National Institute of Justice 2004a).

These less-than-lethal weapons provide only a glimpse of the emerging technologies currently under development, all with the purpose of reducing the need for deadly force. Many of these weapons are still in developmental stages; and, following rigorous testing, may be added to the arsenal of current less-than-lethal options for patrol officers.

CONTROVERSY SURROUNDING LESS-THAN-LETHAL WEAPONS

Concerns over the implementation of less-than-lethal weapons have mounted as the popularity and rapid advances in technology have increased since the 1990s. As described before, the purpose of developing less-than-lethal weapons is to provide more alternatives in dangerous situations than just the use of deadly force. Use of these less-than-lethal weapons will save lives and reduce injuries to citizens, while increasing efficiency of police work and safety of officers. However, controversy continues to raise questions about the effects of less-than-lethal weapons on humans. Media reports of injuries caused from less-than-lethal weapons during police encounters makes police use of force seem common and every day, when in fact the opposite is true. A report by the U.S. Department of Justice found that only 2.1% of all arrests nationwide involved the use of any weapons by police (Garrett 2005). While the vast majority of police encounters exclude weapons, police and policy-makers want to ensure that when a situation does require force, the officers have a myriad of less-than-lethal weapons available.

The use of chemical irritants, in particular oleoresin capsicum (OC) spray, has generated controversy from the media due to alleged connections between its application and severe complications or respiratory failure (Chan et al. 2000; Denham and Mallon 1999; National Institute of Justice 2003). Common complaints from individuals recently in contact with OC spray include burning, pain, temporary blindness, and corneal abrasions caused by rubbing the eyes (Brown, Takeuchi and Challoner 2000; Denham and Mallon 1999). Researchers have tested the effects of OC spray to determine if the spray indeed resulted in any respiratory compromise or other severe complications. In one study, researchers tested the use of the spray on individuals in the sitting position and a restraint (prone) position. A total of 34 subjects participated in over 136 trials, during which researchers monitored all vital signs and pulmonary functions. No evidence was found that exposure to OC spray resulted in any pulmonary dysfunction, hypoventilation, or increased risk for respiratory arrest or death when the individual was in either position (Chan et al. 2000).

Another body of research conducted in North Carolina examined the effectiveness and safety of OC spray use by officers. The number of officer and suspect injuries was measured before and after OC spray was introduced in 1995. The two-year long study assessed whether the introduction of OC spray affected injuries to officers from assaults, injuries to suspects from use of force, and the number of excessive force complaints against officers (National Institute of Justice 2003). The results of the study illustrated that the number of complaints of excessive force declined, as well as the number of injuries to both suspects and officers, following the introduction of OC spray in 1995. These findings from the research studies on use of OC spray support its utilization by law enforcement to diffuse violent situations and maintain suspect safety.

Injury patterns resulting from canine bites, and the fact that they are an independent separate being, have raised concerns with utilizing the dogs as deadly force alternatives (Hutson et al. 1997). Additional concerns have been raised about the level of training the canines receive. In 1988 the U.S.

Supreme Court ruled that police service canines "do not constitute deadly force, and therefore the force used [by the canine] was not unreasonable" (Dorriety 2005, 93). The Court upheld the ruling in 1988 in similar cases in 1989 (*Graham v. Connor*) and 1994 (*Matthews v. Jones*), explaining that there was no substantial risk of death from canines, and it would serve little purpose for police if the dogs were unable to produce "dangerous and threatening traits" (Dorriety 2005, 93).

Other controversial less-than-lethal devices include CEDs, such as the TASER and stun gun (Amnesty International 2004; National Institute of Justice 2008a; 2008b). Serious injuries of suspects have been reported and the Justice Department is aware of over 300 deaths associated with electro-muscular-disruption (effects of CEDs). This has led some scholars to argue that these weapons fit too closely to deadly force in the use-of-force continuum (Grange, Kozak and Gonzalez 2002). In response, an expert panel of medical professionals conducted a study to determine the impact of use of CEDs, finding that many of the deaths following a CED discharge were the result of prolonged exposure or repeated use and secondary effects following use (such as using the device on a person in water, resulting in drowning) (National Institute of Justice 2008a). The panel found no conclusive medical evidence indicating a high risk of death or injury from direct effects of CEDs, and advised law enforcement officials not to refrain from utilizing these weapons "provided the devices are used in accordance with accepted national guidelines" (National Institute of Justice 2008a, 3).

Finally, "at-risk" individuals are those who are at a greater risk for injury caused from less-than-lethal weapons. Factors such as drug use, alcohol consumption, smoking, and other harmful behaviors increase the potential for health complications due to the application of less-than-lethal weapons. Pre-existing health conditions (such as asthma and heart arrhythmia), which are unknown to the officer, also enhance the probability for unforeseen difficulties (National Institute of Justice 2008a). Because each arrest situation is unique, law enforcement continues to rely on the officer's training and experience to determine what level of force is necessary to maintain public order and reduce the likelihood of injuries or death.

SUGGESTIONS FOR FUTURE TESTING, TRAINING, AND ADOPTION

When officers find themselves in a situation where use of deadly force is legally unjustified, they must turn to less-than-lethal alternatives to diffuse volatile situations. These weapons, given the great importance placed on them to protect the safety and welfare of citizens, require further testing to ensure the effectiveness of their purpose. The Weapons and Equipment Research Institute at Florida Gulf Coast University has conducted extensive less-than-lethal weapons testing since 2004 (Mesloh et al. 2008). Researchers at institutions such as this assess potential risks and redesign less-than-lethal weapons to produce only the intended effects of incapacitation and develop plans to address any gaps in technology that need to be filled. One important goal of these research institutions is to design a less-than-lethal weapon that would be simple for police to operate, but complex enough to discourage use by non-police personnel (Kinnaird 2003).

Such extensive testing must not be limited to a research or manufacturing setting, but must also be conducted with the officers in the field who utilize these weapons. To minimize the potential for officer misuse or abuse of the weapons, greater attention must be paid to training courses given to officers. A study conducted by the National Institute of Justice (2004b) surveyed 239 rural law enforcement agencies regarding their technology use and related training needs. A "no-competence" rating was reported for the majority of agencies in regards to less-than-lethal weapons, illustrating the urgent need to focus training efforts (National Institute of Justice 2004b). By satisfying training needs across law enforcement agencies, incidents of officers mishandling less-than-lethal weapons resulting in serious injury or death of suspects will be greatly reduced.

One major obstacle faced by the adoption of less-than-lethal weapons by law enforcement in the United States (and other countries with decentralized and/or uncoordinated police agencies) is fragmentation. Fragmentation, where new technology and weapons are obtained on an agency-by-agency basis, is mostly due to the fact that no two police departments in the United States operate in the same manner (Foster 2005). Each agency has a limited budget to purchase equipment and provide training. A large police department may have sufficient resources to train and equip officers with new less-than-lethal technologies, whereas rural law enforcement agencies struggle to fund such innovations, much less train their officers adequately.

Because society has entrusted police officers with protecting the safety of citizens and maintaining order, officers must, at all costs, protect the welfare of citizens by causing no more harm than is justifiable or unavoidable (Jussila 2001). The current and future less-than-lethal weapons offers officers an alternative to using lethal force, and allows for methods of apprehending individuals when lethal force is not permissible. The weapons described above are the products of technological advancements that must be considered with an open mind. Misuse of less-than-lethal weapons is not a fault of the weapon, but rather of the individual controlling the weapon. Through adequate officer training and reliable regulations on the weapons, the true potential for less-than-lethal alternatives can be achieved.

Conclusion: A Journey Through the World of Police Use of Force

Edward R. Maguire

INTRODUCTION

On May 3, 1986, Hong Kong Police investigating a burglary at the Tin Sin Sightseeing Company discovered two Chinese males loitering in the alley behind the building. When one of the men ran away, a 23-year-old police constable chased after him and fired three shots during the pursuit. All three shots missed the man and he was arrested at the conclusion of the chase. A police administrator reviewing the incident concluded that no disciplinary action against the constable was warranted for shooting at the man, because the constable was acting on the knowledge that a serious crime (the burglary) had been committed.[1]

On December 30, 2003, Sergeant Colin Russell and Constable Joe Many Fingers of the Blood Tribe Police Service in Alberta, Canada responded to a call requesting the removal of an intoxicated male who was frightening his daughter and elderly mother. The suspect had a lengthy criminal record and a propensity for violence. When the police arrived he armed himself with a concealed knife. When the officers tried to arrest him, he attempted to stab them with the knife. Sergeant Russell sustained knife wounds to his head and back, while Constable Many Fingers was able to evade the offender's attempts to stab him. The officers succeeded in subduing the offender and arresting him. Both officers were issued a commendation for bravery from the First Nations Chiefs of Police Association for the heroism and selflessness they displayed during this incident.[2]

These two incidents illustrate the wide variety of opinion over time and place about what constitutes acceptable police use of force. In the first case, the suspect may have committed a property crime but presented no direct or imminent threat to the officer, yet the officer shot at him anyway. In the

Edward R. Maguire, American University

second, the suspect presented a clear threat, and the officers would have been justified in shooting him, yet they showed great restraint in choosing not to shoot in spite of the danger they faced.

Use of force varies widely across officers, situations, organizations, and political systems at multiple levels. Social science research on police use of force has attempted to understand and explain some of these differences (Alpert and Dunham 2004; Worden 1995). But the vast majority of this research has been conducted in developed western democracies, primarily the United States, Britain, Canada, and Australia. This research has focused intently on understanding why some police officers use force more than others; why some situations are more likely to result in police use of force than others; and why some police agencies or communities have greater rates of force used by police than others. Little research, however, has examined police use of force in developing nations, and even less research has compared police use of force across nations.[3] Because most research focuses on one nation at a time, scholarship on the police use of force tends to rely on a narrow range of variation.

The great contribution of this volume is to widen the range of observed variation in police use of force, so that scholars might be able to take a step back and ask some bigger questions. After all, if theories that purport to explain police use of force are robust, shouldn't they be able to explain police use of force across its full range of variation throughout the globe? This volume takes readers on a whirlwind tour of police use of force in many nations, from the heavily armed police death squads of Brazil; to the unarmed police of Norway, England, Scotland, and Wales; from the repressive *mano dura* policies adopted by police in Latin America; to the summary executions carried out by police in India; from the police in Sweden, where officers are taught to shoot at a suspect's legs; to the police in the United States, where officers are taught to shoot at the "center of mass." The purpose of this volume is primarily descriptive: to present the results of research conducted around the world on police use of force. But its implications are more far reaching. By shining light on the incredible level of variation in police use of force around the world, this volume begs the question about why such variation exists. It therefore represents a remarkable opportunity for theorizing about the sources of these differences. Whether you are an undergraduate college student, an experienced police practitioner, a policymaker interested in police use-of-force policy, or a professional researcher, this book challenges you to answer a deceptively simple question: Why does the nature and extent of police use of force vary so tremendously across nations? For such a simple question, the answers are very complex.

VARIATIONS IN STANDARDS

One of the most compelling patterns that is repeated throughout this volume is the great variety in standards about what constitutes acceptable use of force by police. In this section we explore some of these variations in standards. In the next section we explore just a handful of possible explanations for why these differences exist.

Level of Armament

Most, but not all, of the nations represented in this volume issue firearms to police officers to carry during the course of their duties. According to Myhrer and Strype (in this volume), police in Norway are not allowed to be armed "during ordinary duty unless specially authorized by the Chief of Police." They carry firearms "stored in locked and sealed containers" and must receive authorization from the Chief of Police (in all but the most extraordinary circumstances) to break the seal and remove the firearms. Otherwise the police are only authorized to be armed in certain types of assignments or situations. The authors hypothesize that "the time delay inherent in asking for and receiving arming authorization calls for alternative police tactics, such as freezing the dangerous situation. It also seems reasonable to assume that the time delay also provides more optimal conditions for making informed and rational decisions about how to solve critical situations."

Waddington and Wright (in this volume) point out that while most police officers in England, Scotland, and Wales are still unarmed, the police use of firearms in Britain has become more common, "suggesting that the relationship between police and citizen has undergone significant shifts." Knutsson and Norée (in this volume) report that the Danish police were only issued firearms in 1965 "after a tragic episode in which four officers were killed in one incident." Thus the decision about whether to arm the police, or how heavily or thoroughly to arm them, appears dynamic and likely depends, to some extent, on the degree of perceived threat.

Questions about level of armament do not only apply to the use of firearms; several of the authors in this volume raise compelling issues associated with the adoption of less-than-lethal techniques and technologies. Terrill and Paoline, for instance, emphasize that standards about the use of conducted energy devices like the TASER are uneven among police agencies in the United States. The TASER is placed in different locations on use-of-force continua: in some agencies it is placed just above verbal commands and in others it is placed just below deadly force. Agencies have also adopted different standards with regard to the level of citizen resistance sufficient to warrant the use of the TASER. Police in many nations argue that if given the TASER, they will use *lower* levels of deadly force. For instance, Australian police officials have argued that several police shootings of mentally ill people could have been prevented if the officers had been armed with TASERs (see Baker in this volume). At the same time, credible concerns have been raised about the number of deaths caused by police use of TASERs. Concerns have also been raised about the side effects and police misuse of chemical agents like oleoresin capsicum (OC) (see Kaminski and Adang, in this volume) and CS (see Buttle, in this volume). Many other forms of force used by police have similarly generated public debate, including the police use of chokeholds, batons, and dogs. Throughout the world, there exists significant variation in the forms of force the police are authorized to use and the nature and extent of actual use by police officers on the street.

Warning Suspects Before Firing and Firing Warning Shots

There also appears to be wide variation in the extent to which police are expected to warn a suspect before commencing fire. For instance, according to Wong (in this volume), Hong Kong Police standing orders require a constable to give a verbal warning to a suspect before shooting. Northern Ireland's policy also requires police to issue a verbal warning of their intent to shoot, unless doing so would endanger life or is clearly inappropriate. That same policy discourages the use of warning shots because they pose serious risks (Police Service of Northern Ireland).

According to Knutsson and Norée (in this volume), "in the Danish, Norwegian, and Swedish rules, it is explicitly stated that warning shots should be fired before effective fire is commenced. The concept of using warning shots does not, however, exist in the Finnish regulations." Knutsson's study of Swedish police found that in cases in which firearms were used against a person, "warning shots were discharged in fifty-four percent of the events, a combination of warning and effective fire in fifteen percent of the cases, and effective fire in thirty-one percent." Contrast these examples with police in the United States, who are expressly trained *not* to fire warning shots. For instance, the policy of the Seattle Police Department is premised on the notion that officers must make a decision to use deadly force in a split second and they may only have one brief opportunity to open fire: "the national standard among police agencies is not to fire warning shots. The Seattle Police Department complies with that standard. . . . Making (likely to be ineffective) shots in the air that have the added potential of harming others may not be the best use of that one opportunity" (Seattle Police Department). The model use of force policy established by the International Association of Chiefs of Police represents a moderate position between those that require or encourage the use of warning shots and those that prohibit them. It states that "warning shots may be fired if an officer is authorized to use deadly force and only if the officer reasonably believes a warning shot can be fired safely in light of all circumstances of the encounter" (International Association of Chiefs of Police 2005).

Implicit in the arguments against the use of warning shots are two hypotheses.[4] First, firing warning shots may place officers and bystanders in danger by giving suspects additional time to fire their own weapons or to execute an aggressive act. Second, warning shots fired by police may injure or kill other people. We are unaware of any rigorous empirical research that tests either hypothesis. One impressionistic review of cases in which warning shots were fired concluded that the shots were effective in convincing suspects to surrender in most cases (Mulroy and Santiago 1998). At the same time, the media has documented many instances of bystander injury and death resulting from the use of warning shots. Also, warning shots are sometimes fired into the air. Because what goes up must come down, research shows that firing weapons into the air can cause serious injuries and death (Ordog et al. 1994). Finally, research shows that bullet ricochets also present significant risks (Burke and Rowe 1992). Given the worldwide variation in the use of warning shots and the gravity of the topic, systematic research to evaluate the strengths and weaknesses of using warning shots would be timely.

Shooting to Injure versus Shooting to Kill

There also appears to be some variation in the extent to which officers attempt to minimize harm to the suspect after making the decision to shoot. For instance, according to Myhrer and Strype (in this volume), the Norwegian police must use their gun in "a proper and proportionate way . . . the gun should be fired in such a way that the damage caused is as little as possible." Officers must assess the effects of each shot before taking additional shots. At the same time, "almost no situations escalate to the point at which the police need to fire guns." Knutsson's (in this volume) study of the Swedish police found it "extremely rare that shots were fired with the intent to kill . . . to get the desired effect with the least amount of force, Swedish officers are taught and trained to initially aim at the suspect's legs . . . in pressing situations of self-defense, officers may of course aim and shoot at the chest." Once again, the *harm minimization* strategies used by Scandinavian police differ considerably from standard doctrine in the United States, as exemplified in the following statement by the Seattle Police Department:

> In Seattle as in other law enforcement agencies, officers are trained that the most certain and effective way to stop armed and dangerous assailants is to aim for their "center of mass." Movies and television programs make it seem that shooting at a person's arm or leg is easily done. In reality, such a shot is both improbable and risky. Deadly force incidents evolve in seconds, often presenting officers with limited opportunities to intervene. In light of this, officers are trained to take the high percentage shot, which is center of mass. (Seattle Police Department)

According to Wong (in this volume), police policy in Hong Kong is similar: "All officers should be aware that it is part of their training to open fire at center body mass and not at extremities."

The logic underlying deadly force policies requiring officers to aim at center of mass is implicitly supported in the evidence provided by Morrison (in this volume). He points out that bullet "hit rates" for American police departments range from 15% to 60%. Put differently, "most police bullets miss their target because hit rates rarely exceed thirty percent." These findings suggest that shooting policies encouraging officers to fire warning shots and/or to aim for the legs may endanger officers (or bystanders) by wasting precious moments in split-second situations. Although American police agencies do not have explicit across-the-board "shoot to kill" policies, any policy that instructs officers to shoot at center of mass is likely to result in increased fatalities, given the concentration of vital organs located in that region of the body. At the same time, policies encouraging officers to shoot at the limbs may place the officer (or bystanders) at greater risk for injury or death. Thus the decision about which policy to adopt may essentially involve making a judgment about the value of the suspect's life and the value of the police officer's life. Deadly force policy requires careful consideration of actuarial notions far more common in military circles, like "acceptable casualties" and "reasonable risk" among personnel (Williams 2000). We are unfamiliar with any systematic research on shoot-to-wound versus shoot-to-kill policies (or point-of-aim policies) throughout the world, but clearly such research would be beneficial.

Level of Force

Even within the realm of non-lethal force, there appear to be tremendous variations in the level of force viewed as acceptable by the public, the courts, police officials, and scholars. Consider the following quote from one of the leading police executives in the United States, William Bratton, former commissioner in New York City and former chief in Los Angeles:[5] "It is important to define 'police brutality.' We defined brutality as unnecessary behavior that caused broken bones, stitches, and internal injuries. But those were not the numbers that had gone up significantly. What had risen were reports of police inappropriately pushing, shoving, sometimes only touching citizens. We were taking back the streets and it wasn't easy work" (Bratton 1998, 291). Bratton's comments imply two controversial viewpoints. First, when police use inappropriate force that fails to cause serious injuries, their actions do not constitute police brutality. Second, when "taking back the streets," it is okay to use inappropriate levels of force, as long as no serious injuries result. In other words, the ends justify the means.

Harvard professor Mark Moore offers a different perspective on the use of force by police. He reminds us that "state authority is one of the most important assets we citizens grant to the police" (2003, 21). Because authority in all its manifestations, including the capacity to use force, are "assets" granted to the police to enable them to carry out their work, . . . it is important to think quantitatively in terms of *how much* authority police are using as well as whether they are using it properly or not. Ideally, a police department

would make minimum use of force and authority in accomplishing its purposes. . . . We have to be sure that there is some *proportionality* in the way
they use force and authority—that they do not use much more force and
authority than seems necessary to deal with given criminal events or larger
crime problems. (Moore 2003, 22)

Bratton boldly asserts a point of view to which many citizens, police, and
government officials throughout the world—particularly in communities
plagued by violent crime—quietly subscribe. This perspective is based on a
premise that police are more effective when they *take the fight* to the criminals; some collateral damage may result from this approach, but that is the
cost of living in a safe community. Moore (2003) suggests that police should
adopt considerably more restraint in the use of force; that one way for police
to think about efficiency is to achieve a given crime control benefit without
resorting to excessive or unreasonable force. Over time and place, police
agencies tend to vacillate between these two perspectives on the appropriate
level of force.

EXPLAINING VARIATIONS IN STANDARDS

Our brief journey through the world of police use of force has thus far
focused on some of the differences between nations. We now examine a handful of potential explanations for these differences. Space limits preclude a
more comprehensive review of theoretical explanations, so this section provides just a brief glimpse.

One of the primary reasons for differences in use of force standards and
policies over time and place may be the influence of key events. Unfortunately, in the realm of police use of force, such key events are often tragic
and tend to occur within the public eye under intense media scrutiny. Organizational researchers refer to sudden, unanticipated, and influential events that
have a dramatic effect on organizations as "environmental jolts" (Mayer
1982). Often, key events serve as a sort of environmental jolt or a wake-up
call that shocks the system and promotes change in the policy or practice of
police use of force. For instance, according to Knutsson and Norée (in this
volume), the Danish police were issued firearms in 1965 "after a tragic episode in which four officers were killed in one incident."

Three noteworthy incidents served as a potent environmental jolt for
police agencies in the United States. On April 11, 1986, FBI agents in Miami
attempted to stop a vehicle driven by two heavily armed bank robbery suspects with previous military experience. In the ensuing shootout, two FBI
agents were killed and five others were wounded; both suspects were killed
as well (Federal Bureau of Investigation 1986). Because one of the suspects
continued firing at the agents even after he had been shot several times, the
incident raised questions about whether the FBI's handguns were sufficient.

Moreover, some of the agents had difficulty reloading their revolvers during the shootout. As a result, the FBI switched to semiautomatic weapons with greater capacity and more stopping power. The incident also led many local police agencies to switch from revolvers to semiautomatic handguns (Malcolm 1990).

On February 15, 1997, two heavily-armed bank robbery suspects wearing body armor engaged in a shootout with Los Angeles police in North Hollywood. Officers were so heavily outgunned by suspects that they went into a gun store to appropriate more powerful weapons and ammunition. The two suspects were eventually killed by police, but 15 people, including 10 police officers, were injured in the shootout. As a result of the incident, Los Angeles police were authorized to begin carrying .45 caliber semiautomatic pistols to replace their revolvers and smaller caliber (9mm) semiautomatics. In addition, supervisors were authorized to begin carrying AR-15 assault rifles (CNN 1997). Once again, many American police agencies learned from the incident that their weaponry was insufficient to stop heavily armed suspects. For instance, a Washington, DC police commander, in justifying his department's controversial decision to acquire hundreds of AR-15 rifles, cited the Los Angeles shootout as the "one incident in America that got every single police department to look at their weapons. . ." (Klein 2008).

Another tragic event had different implications for use of force by American police: the April 20, 1999 shootings at Columbine High School in Jefferson County, Colorado. Before Columbine, conventional police tactical doctrine in "active shooter" situations was for patrol officers to secure the perimeter and wait for a SWAT (or similar tactical) unit to make entry. The Columbine shootings led police in the United States to question this approach. If police officers had made entry sooner, they may have been able to save some lives. The United States has seen a dramatic shift in tactical doctrine for managing active shooter incidents since Columbine. Police are now trained that the first police officers to respond to an active shooter incident should make entry (most such events occur within buildings, often workplaces or schools) and neutralize the shooters, either by forcing surrender or using deadly force. A variety of specific tactical methodologies have been proposed for how to make entry, but they all operate on the same basic principle: "make a controlled and effective entry to stop the violence immediately" (Wood 2001, 80).

All three of these tragic incidents were featured prominently in the American media and had a fundamental influence on the way police think about the use of deadly force in the United States. Across the nation, police agencies have replaced revolvers with semiautomatic pistols with greater capacity and often with larger-caliber bullets; they have also armed themselves with more high-powered weapons, including automatic weapons. Both moves are likely to save police lives, but at the same time, research suggests that more deaths are likely to result from improvements in armament (Carr et al. 2008; Reedy and Koper 2003; Richmond et al. 2004). Police have also altered their basic tactical approaches to active shooter situations. Similar key incidents in other nations have had similar effects, resulting in increases in police armament or the adoption of more aggressive tactics (*Police Journal* 2007; *Herald Sun* 2008). Given the many avenues through which law enforcement policy tends to diffuse outward from the United States, these changes are likely to have global implications (Newburn 2002).

Key events, however, are not the only factor influencing police use of force. The nature of the population being policed may also have a strong impact on use of force patterns. For instance, Waddington and Wright (in this volume) point out an historical curiosity: while most of the United Kingdom has unarmed police, Northern Ireland has always had an armed police service. They emphasize that

> the same coterie of officials under the leadership of the same politician, with much the same vision and facing much the same political opposition, gave birth to two diametrically opposed models of policing. . . . The reasons for policing taking such dramatically divergent paths either side of the Irish Sea, lay in *who* was being policed: on the mainland, the civil population was composed of "free-born Englishmen" for whom full citizenship beckoned; whereas, the majority of the population of the colony of Ireland was composed of a rebellious peasantry to be repressed. (167)

If Waddington and Wright are correct, the nature and tone of policing may depend on the characteristics of the population: if there is an underclass to control or repress, use of force will be greater. This hypothesis is consistent with social conflict theory, which asserts that the majority will seek to control the minority through the enactment of laws and through the actions of state agencies like the police. One study found, for instance, that even after controlling for other factors like crime and rioting, inequality still has an effect on the amount of deadly force used by police, a finding that is also consistent with conflict theory (Jacobs and Britt 1979). This explanation for variations in use of force by police resonates much more loudly when we move beyond the handful of developed nations where most police research takes place. A genuine understanding of police use of force means studying it in the places where it is used most: in the world's slums, squatter communities, and shantytowns.

Another obvious explanation for differences in use of force between nations may be differences in culture. Wong (in this volume) concludes that there is a cultural difference between the east and west with regard to use of force. People in China view fleeing from the police as a more serious offense than people from other countries and therefore would be likely to support the police use of force against fleeing suspects. Similarly, while some people may view extrajudicial killings by police as abhorrent, evidence suggests that residents in some nations support the idea of police summarily executing known criminals or terrorists (Peters 2006). One study found that "widespread fear of criminals leads many Brazilians to support death squads and police brutality against crime suspects" (Brooke 1990, 3). Another study found that a majority of British respondents supported a police shoot-to-kill policy for suspected terrorists (YouGov.com).[6] Cultural tolerance for police use of force may have a potent effect on international variations in the use of force. Unfortunately there is very little research to test this hypothesis.

Another reason for differences in use of force policies may simply be that some nations (or some agencies) make different value judgments about the risks they are willing to take in endangering the lives of police officers, members of the public and criminal offenders. For instance, one U.S. police officer has written that in active shooter situations, "the proper value system for effective public safety is in the following order: 1. Protection of the officer's life. 2. Protection of the lives of fellow officers. 3. Protection of the lives of victims and witnesses on-scene. 4. Protection of the rights of the suspect" (Williams 2000, 172). When nations choose not to arm their officers, when they choose to arm them insufficiently relative to the threats they face, or when they adopt tactics that place officers unnecessarily in harm's way, they are clearly making different value judgments about these priorities. Effective use of force policy means balancing threats to police and civilians against the rights of the suspect.

ACHIEVING A BALANCE IN POLICE USE OF FORCE

Legitimacy is the foundation of law and legal authority. Improper or excessive use of force by police can jeopardize the perceived legitimacy of the police. Legitimacy is "a quality possessed by an authority, a law, or an institution that leads others to feel obligated to obey its decisions and directives voluntarily" (Tyler and Huo 2002, 102). The notion of voluntary compliance is the defining characteristic of legitimacy. If the majority of people chose not to comply voluntarily with the law or legal authorities, formal social control institutions would become overwhelmed. Legitimacy engenders compliance without invoking the significant social and economic costs of achieving social control through formal institutions like police or courts. According to sociologist Morris Zelditch (2006): "if a regime is legitimate, even the disaffected, no matter how much they dislike the regime, tend, for a time at least, to willingly comply with it. . . ." (325). On the other hand, when people are subject to laws or rules they view as illegitimate, they are more likely to rebel or become defiant (Sherman 1993). A rich tradition of research on "procedural justice" shows that when people believe they have been treated unfairly by legal authorities like police and judges, they are less likely to obey the law (Tyler 2006). Thus it is in the best interest of legal authorities, including police, to sustain public perceptions of their legitimacy.

Legitimacy is the foundation of the law in all cultures, though in different cultures legitimacy may be derived from different sources. Modern liberal democracies, for instance, derive their legitimacy from the free and fair election of representatives by the people. These democratically-elected officials pass laws and enact bureaucratic policies and procedures that (in theory) are consistent with those laws. Many Islamic nations derive their legitimacy from their adherence to Shari'a (Islamic law); deviations from the religious principles embodied in Shari'a and the Quran are considered violations of the law (Jerichow 1998). In China, the world's most populous nation, traditional cultural values encourage citizens to view individual liberty as secondary to the collective good of the people. Deference to authority is valued. China continues to defy the predictions of democratic theorists by generating interpersonal trust and popular regime support at levels much greater than among the democratic nations in the region (Nathan 2007; Tang 2005). The point is that legitimacy does not have a single universal source; the foundations of legitimacy vary by culture, history, and tradition. Although the sources of legitimacy may vary, the notion that legitimacy underlies the effectiveness of the law and its enforcement is universal.

Inappropriate use of force by the police represents a significant threat to the legitimacy of the state. In the 1960s, a turbulent time in American history, riots engulfed many American cities, often touched off as a result of police use of force perceived by minority citizens as illegitimate. Police actions were so often the catalyst triggering riots that one sociologist termed them *police riots* (Stark 1972). The United States is certainly not alone in suffering collective violence after incidents of police use of force. Riots erupted throughout Greece in December 2008 after police in Athens shot and killed an unarmed 15-year old boy (Carassava 2008). Police in Montreal shot three unarmed youths in August 2008, killing one of them and sparking riots that injured several police officers and a paramedic (*USA Today* 2008). As David Bayley has written, "every country has a Rodney King" (Bayley 1995, 261). These incidents share a common thread: people rebelling against the perception that the state's use of violence is excessive and inappropriate.

Social scientists from a number of disciplines have found evidence for the "brutalization hypothesis"—the idea that the state's use of violence may legitimize or encourage the use of violence by the populace (Shepherd 2005). Police in many nations justify the police use of violence against criminals based on a belief that it will reduce crime. If the brutalization hypothesis is valid, then inappropriate use of force by police may not just trigger short-term forms of rebellion like protests and riots, it might increase violent crime over the long-term by facilitating the use of violence and weakening the legitimacy of the law and legal authority. As Glebbeek (in this volume) argues, the tough policing or *mano dura* strategy implemented in El Salvador, Guatemala, Nicaragua, and Costa Rica "feeds the culture of violence that has existed in many Central American countries since the end of the civil wars."

Many years ago, Herbert Packer (1968) argued that through time and place, legal systems vacillate between concerns with "due process" on one end of the continuum and "crime control" on the other. The due process model values individual liberties and is primarily concerned with principles like fairness and equality. The crime control model values safety and order and is primarily concerned with controlling crime. The two models exist in constant tension with one another. As crime (however it is defined) increases, concern with due process wanes. As the state begins to adopt practices to control crime that infringe on individual liberties and a fundamental sense of fairness, concern with due process increases. In an era in which many nations are grappling with the threat of terrorism, debates about the proper balance between liberty and security make Packer look prescient (Gould 2002).

The notion that police use of force is dynamic, wavering back and forth between liberty and security, between due-process and crime control, is often invoked within the context of western liberal democracies. Yet these observations apply to other contexts that most westerners would view as well beyond their narrow frames of reference. Consider, for instance, the policing of morality in Islamic states. Under a previous reform administration led by Reza Shah, police in Iran once "roamed the streets to snatch scarves from the heads of women" who were observing traditional Islamic dress codes (Mackey 1996, 183). Less than half a century later, "Reza Shah's police, who beat women for wearing the chador [an Iranian style of veil], had been replaced by Khomeini's police, who beat women for not wearing the veil" (Mackey 1996, 298; see also Howland 1997). Standards about what constitutes excessive force wax and wane, shifting in response to political, historical, and cultural dynamics.

Nowhere do the philosophical arguments about liberty and security become more real than in the debate over summary executions by police officers. I recently interviewed a police officer in a developing nation with a serious violent crime problem. He admitted to carrying out extrajudicial killings of known violent offenders. He described the process by which the instructions were relayed to him as well as the methods used to carry out the killings. He shared his frustrations of arresting serious violent offenders who are repeatedly released by the courts because witnesses are too afraid to testify. He shared the helplessness he felt when people who had received death threats came to him and asked for his assistance and he was unable to help them. We might assume from our high moral ground that summary executions by police are wrong. This officer made a compelling argument that the extrajudicial killings he carried out were less harmful than allowing known violent offenders to continue hurting and killing other people.

These are the compelling issues that arise when looking at police use of force from a global perspective, as Kuhns and Knutsson and their slate of authors have done in this volume. Published research on police use of force tends to be parochial and ethnocentric. American police and scholars sometimes dominate the debate, with the British not far behind. But there is great variation in use of force, from Jakarta to Jamaica, from Chicago to Shanghai, and the world over. Researchers relish in variation, both describing and explaining it. This volume illustrates the great variety in use of force policy and practice around the world. Let it serve as a rallying call for police researchers to expand their horizons and begin examining this variety, both for the sake of enhancing the content validity of their industry, and to be of more use to governments and NGOs pondering the weighty questions raised about police use of force.

Notes

CHAPTER 1

1. This issue is particularly pressing given the fragmented structure of policing in the United States, as there are thousands of police agencies, all of which are permitted to establish their own force policy as they see fit. At best, individual states are able to regulate policies for agencies within their jurisdiction (e.g., New Jersey). Moreover, entities such as the International Association of Chiefs of Police (IACP) do put forth "model policies" but these are simply advisory and are not binding. This may not be the case in countries with a unified or singular police agency, as national standards can be established much more readily.

2. While we restrict our discussion to various "news" media outlets (e.g., television, newspapers, and Internet), we acknowledge that public perceptions can also be shaped internationally by popular culture depictions of police use of force via television and movie dramas (e.g., *Hill Street Blues*, *NYPD Blue*, *Dirty Harry*, etc.), as well as literary work about the police (see, for example, Joseph Wambaugh's classic novels).

3. Graham, suffering from the onset of a diabetic seizure, was driven by a friend (Berry) to a convenience store to buy orange juice. Upon entering the store and witnessing a line of customers, Graham and Berry quickly left the store and began driving to a friend's house. Police officer Connor witnessed this suspicious behavior and conducted a traffic stop. Despite claims from Berry as to Graham's diabetic state, he was physically detained until a check was conducted with store employees to ensure no wrongdoing had occurred. Graham filed suit alleging excessive force. The District Court and Court of Appeals ruled against Graham, but the Supreme Court granted *certiorari* finding (9-0) that the lower courts did not apply the appropriate standard (e.g., Fourth Amendment objective reasonableness). The case was remanded to District Court, which subsequently ruled in Graham's favor.

4. Tom McEwen notes that force policies incorporating a continuum approach "... are much more likely than other policies to address the fundamental issue of physical force (open hand control, fists, use of body, etc.)" (1997, 50).

5. For example, 75% of those surveyed reported it is unacceptable for police officers to use more force than legally permissible.

CHAPTER 6

1. India is a federation of 28 states and 9 union territories.

2. Dacoity is defined under section 391 of the Indian Penal Code as robbery committed conjointly by five or more persons.

3. Gossman (2002) describes types of "death squads" that operate in various parts of India, differentiating between out-of-uniform police officers who formed death squads in Punjab; security forces operating in Kashmir and in Assam; and special police squads operating in Naxal-infested areas such as Bihar, Chattisgarh, Andhra Pradesh, parts of Orissa, Maharashtra, Madhya Pradesh, and are spreading to Uttar Pradesh.

4. The total strength of the Mumbai police force in 2006 was approximately 41,000 officers, responsible for the safety and security of 14 million people. Women officers at all ranks amount to roughly 2.5% of the total strength and like policing worldwide, Mumbai police is a male-dominated organization. Eighty-six police stations, grouped into thirty-nine divisions and twelve policing zones manage day-to-day operational policing in Mumbai.

5. Private communication with the office of the DCP (Deputy Commissioner of Police) Crime Branch.

6. Officers have been divided into four categories: Sub-Inspectors and Inspectors; Lower Middle Management; Upper Middle Management; and Senior Management.

7. Indications that there are corrupt and unethical reasons why some officers are more prone to "doing" *encounters* were evident in many interviews.

8. This allegation was refuted by other officers, who explained that officers acted on the information of informants and sources, certain officers had links or contacts in certain gangs, which meant that their "operations" were limited to taking action against those particular gang members only.

9. Needless to add, there was no proof of any particular case of this kind, but there certainly were hints of murkiness of this kind in the narratives of more than a few officers.

10. Some state police forces follow a policy of one *encounter*–one rank promotion.

CHAPTER 7

1. In El Salvador the police reform was stipulated in the Chapultepec Peace Accords, signed 16 January 1992 and in Guatemala in the Accord on Strengthening Civil Power and the Role of the Armed Forces within a Democratic Society (AFPC), signed in September 1996 as part of the Comprehensive Peace Accord that was signed on 26 December 1996.

2. See for more information on the El Salvadorian police reform: Call 1999; Perez 2003; Stanley 2000; Stanley and Call 1997; Stanley, Vickers and Spence 1996; Williams and Walter 1997; WOLA 1995.

3. See for an extensive elaboration on the Costa Rican Police force the doctoral thesis of Quirine Eijkman (2007).

4. It is difficult to find reliable homicide data that can be used for a comparison between countries. In a publication of Geneva Declaration (2008) the following sub regional aggregates are given: the world average for 2004 is 7.6 homicides per 100,000 population. In Central America homicides range from 20 to 30 homicides per 100,000 (as this is an average of five countries in Central America, including Costa Rica, this average is low). In West and Central Europe the average is lower than three homicides per 100,000 and for North America it is between five and ten homicides per 100,000 (Geneva Declaration 2008, 71).

CHAPTER 8

1. "Criminal homicide occurs when a person purposely, knowingly, recklessly or negligently causes the death of another. Murder and manslaughter are both examples of criminal homicide." (NOLO.com).

2. While in recent years the gap between rich and poor has somewhat decreased, Brazil has a *Gini* coefficient of 0.53 ('zero' means perfect equality, and 'one' means complete inequality). The U.S. *Gini* is 0.41; China's 0.47; India's 0.31 (Dyer 2008).

3. Fabio Soares defines informal sector workers as those "whose contract is not registered in his/her work-card (*carteira de trabalho*)...." Registration entitles them to several wage and non wage benefits such as 30 days of paid holiday per year, contribution for social security, right to request unemployment benefit in case of dismissal, monetary compensation if dismissed without a fair cause, maternity and paternity paid leave and so on. Because Soares' informal sector estimate does not include domestic workers, the actual size of the informal sector is a great deal larger than given.

4. Rank-and-file Militarized Police have almost no opportunities for significant career mobility (e.g., attaining Officer rank); earn low salaries (in 2007, Rio de Janeiro rank-and-file earned 594 USD monthly); and operate within a rigidly controlled work structure. Labor strikes are not allowed (but now occur). An entry level Rio de Janeiro Civil Police Investigator earned on average in 2007, 497 USD (*Caso de Policia*), hierarchy is less rigid in the Civil Police organization and worker strikes are allowed.

5. Many poor urban communities in Brazil have "community policing" systems, however, as Husain's (2007) research has demonstrated for Rio de Janeiro, community policing can be neither established in the first place nor maintained without regular incursions of Rio's most militarized force, the BOPE (Batalao de Operacoes Policias Especias).

6. For a more long-range picture of homicide in Brazil see the Centers for Disease Control (2004).

7. Of course, criminologists know many of the reasons that homicides might escape documentation in rural areas, or why rural homicides might not—even if recorded—be sent to official record keepers in urban areas. All of the standard explanations for differences in crime recording, record keeping, and statistical reporting between rural and urban areas are operational in Brazil. However, there is still good reason to believe that in Brazil, real homicide rates are higher in urban than in rural areas.

8. Homicide rates for the states of Rio de Janeiro (56.4 per 100,000), Pernambuco (54.4) and Espirito Santo (51.3) are relatively similar; Recife (pop. 1.5 million), in Brazil's northeastern Pernambuco State, has Brazil's highest urban murder rate (90.9)—over two times that of Rio de Janeiro City (40.7) (Alston 2008, 9), despite

Rio's being notorious for high homicide rates. And while São Paulo State's 2005 homicide rate was 15/100,000 (Goertzel and Kahn 2007), São Paulo City's 2005 rate was 36.9/100,000 (Souza and Sa 2005), falling in 2007 to 11.6/100,000 due to a legislated gun ban, restrictions on late-night drinking establishments, and what officials call greater "success in fighting violence" (Downie 2008).

9. In a related finding, the risk of homicide for children and youth (between 5 and 20 years old) in Rio de Janeiro doubles if their (largely female-headed) family's income is under 135 USD a month. The addition of 108 USD to a family's monthly income (to 270 USD) is associated with a reduction in youth homicide risk (Valladares and Preteceille 2003b).

10. Research by Mitchell and Wood (1999), based on a victimization supplement in Brazil's 1988 Census (IBGE), explains that blacks in Brazil were more likely to be assaulted by policemen than whites, even after controlling for region, urban status, age, education and income. In particular, the "odds of a black person being assaulted ... by a policeman were 2.4 times higher than those of whites" (Cano).

11. Between 1993 and 2007, the proportion of households in Brazil located in *favelas* or in similarly disadvantaged neighborhoods, increased (from 3.2% to 3.6%), representing two million households and at least eight million people. Sixty-six percent of *favela* households are headed by a black male or female (Zenker 2008).

12. As this chapter illustrates, some of the best data on police use of force comes from researchers at the State University of Rio de Janeiro's Laboratory for the Analysis of Violence, with Ignacio Cano, professor of research methodology, producing excellent studies of police violence for Rio de Janeiro. Two equally impressive institutions and researchers in São Paulo, each with a history of documenting police violence in Brazil, are: University of São Paulo's Nucleus for the study of Violence (NEV), whose director, sociologist, Sergio Adorno and his NEV associate Nancy Cardia, have produced sophisticated research on police violence (1997). Another São Paulo human rights entity, *Justica Global*, a non-governmental organization in São Paulo headed by Sandra Carvalho, conducts research and produces impressive reports in English and Portuguese on police violence. Two new scholars of police violence, Saima Husain and Mercedes S. Hinton, have each carried out and published their research on police violence in Rio de Janeiro.

13. There are several reasons for this. Research demonstrates that Brazilians do not to accord much legitimacy to police. For example, in 1997, one in four São Paulo randomly interviewed residents claimed they feared the police more than common criminals; another third of those sampled asserted that police and common criminals are equally dangerous (Reuters 1997; see also Huggins, 2000a). At the same time, between a quarter and forty percent of respondents in the ten Brazilian state capitals believed that police should have the right to stop and frisk persons suspected of illegality, although only between 8% and 27% of those sampled granted police the right to shoot even an armed suspect (Cardia 1999). In a 2002 study, a "Rio de Janeiro survey found that forty-seven percent of respondents supported the killing of murderers and thieves by police" (in Alston 2008, 19). National victimization surveys (in Valladares and Preteceille 2003a, 19) demonstrate that among Brazilian victims of physical violence, 61% do not report the assault to police, explaining that either they suspected police involvement or doubted police resolve or ability to investigate the crime.

14. One Secretary of Public Security for Rio de Janeiro gave "bonuses" to police who killed "criminals" (see Hinton 2006; Husain 2007).

15. This statement, representing a police worldview, became the title of Saima Husain's (2007) careful study of police and human rights in Rio de Janeiro.

16. Militarized police "misconduct" is investigated by a military official and passed on to a military tribunal if evidence suggests misconduct. However, in the case of alleged "intentional homicide of civilians committed by on-duty military police … jurisdiction pass[es] to the mainstream justice system, with the eventual possibility of a civilian jury trial. [At the same time,] Military investigators retain responsibility for the initial inquiries that determine whether the homicide was 'intentional,' … [which is] a very effective filter allowing police to claim that deaths occurred whilst the victim was 'resisting arrest'" (McCaulay 2002).

17. While the various measures of an execution are rooted in Brazilian research practice, certain designations of these measures are mine: "immobilization/'over-kill' ratio;" "citizen/police death ratio;" "*representational* lethality index;" "homicidal profiling."

18. Rio de Janeiro police are "responsible for nearly eighteen percent of the total killings and kill three people every day. Extrajudicial executions are committed by police who murder rather than arrest criminal suspects, and also during large-scale confrontational 'war' style policing, in which excessive use of force results in the deaths of suspected criminals and bystanders." (Alston 2008, 9–10).

19. Washington is said to have the highest per capita police murder rate of citizens in the United States (Leen et al. 1998).

20. These figures are derived by adding three year's citizen killings by police for Washington, DC and three years for New York City and then dividing this number by the number of years. This gave 10 killings annually for Washington, DC and 20 for New York City.

CHAPTER 11

1. Among several other assignments, Sven Silverudd has been chief shooting instructor at the Swedish National Police Academy. The database is described in detail in Johannes Knutsson and Jon Strype (2002).

2. The lawful authority for the police to use force, including by means of firearms, is stated in the Police Act of 1984. The specific regulation for firearms is given in the government's Decree on Use of Firearms in the Police Service 1969, and in the National Police Board's Instructions and Common Advices on the Use of Firearms 2001. Rules for self-defense are given in the Penal Code. Norée (2004; 2005) has criticized the Decree for being outdated and badly constructed, making it hard to apply.

3. The National Police Board is headed by the National Police Commissioner who is appointed by the government. Among other things, the NPB is responsible for the development of new methods and technological support. It is also—through the National Police Academy—responsible for the training of police officers.

4. This means that for Sweden, the "split-second syndrome" is of relevance (Fyfe 1993). Critical incidents occur in seconds and require immediate resolution with little or almost no time for assessing the situation. For Norway, the transactional phase model where incidents are analyzed according to a developmental process involving social transactions is more adequate (Binder and Scharf 1980). Five phases can be

identified (anticipation, entry and initial contact, dialogue and information exchange, final decision, and aftermath).

CHAPTER 12

1. When we speak of the Nordic countries we refer to all the countries apart from Iceland, which is not included in this study.

2. Regard must also be made to the international conventions that the Nordic countries have signed. Of greatest practical importance is the European Convention on Human Rights. The adherence to the convention may in last instance be tried by the European Court of Justice.

3. The Danish Police Act is from 2004, the Finnish and Norwegian Police Acts are from 1995, and the Swedish Police Act is from 1984.

4. In Denmark the Decree of the National Police Commissioner Concerning Police Use of Firearms from 1998, is in use. In Finland the Ministry of the Interior's Decree on Police Use of Forcible Means from 2004 is in effect. In Norway the Justice of Department's Instructions of Arms for the Police from 1989 is practiced. And in Sweden, with the oldest regulations, the government's Decree on Use of Firearms in the Police Service from 1969 still is in use, besides the National Police Board's Instructions and Common Advices on the Use of Firearms in the Service of the Police, from 2001.

5. See Skolnick and Fyfe for discussion on the continuum of force (1993).

6. We are only focusing on firearms and do not discuss batons, pepper spray, and other means of force that are available to the police.

7. In case of an emergency a police officer may take the decision on their own initiative.

8. The national SWAT teams in the Nordic countries have access to other types of firearms, among them marksmen rifles. We are only discussing the general use of firearms.

9. The data originates from Rigspolitiet (Denmark), the Finish Police Academy, Politidirektoratet (Norway) and for Sweden from former Superintendent Sven Silverudd who has collected the data from the Swedish National Police Board and from Swedish Police Districts.

10. The differences are not statistically significant.

11. The value is not statistically significant compared to Norway, but is significantly different when compared with both to Denmark and Sweden.

12. The inadequate regulation means that Swedish police officers unnecessarily end up in "split second syndrome" situations, something that should be avoided (Fyfe 1993).

13. Denmark has had some years with a number of civilians who were shot to death. It may be due to chance factors (Politiets vienscenter, 2007), but if it is not, it has to be seriously considered.

CHAPTER 17

1. At the beginning of the trials, the policy indicated OC should be considered to be positioned close to the firearm and after impact weapons, but this was changed halfway through the trials.

CHAPTER 18

1. "TASER-proximate" death is the term the authors use to describe an incident where the suspect was struck with a TASER, subsequently died, but there is no definitive evidence to identify the TASER as the cause of death. By the end of 2007, *Amnesty International* estimated that the number of TASER-proximate deaths exceeded 300 (Amnesty International, 2007).

2. The public nature of the TASER controversy is perhaps best illustrated by the now-famous *YouTube* video of a Senator John Kerry speaking engagement in which a University of Florida student says "don't taze me, bro" to police officers right before he is struck with the device.

3. This estimate becomes much greater if handcuffing and verbal commands are included as use of force.

4. As the subject's resistance or aggression increases, the officer may utilize greater degrees of force and is allowed to remain one level above the suspect as the interaction progresses (e.g., an officer is permitted to use a less-lethal weapon such as a TASER in response to physical resistance by a suspect).

5. There are competitors to TASER, including Stinger Systems and Law Enforcement Associates, but *TASER International* dominates the market with approximately 95% of stun device sales in the United States. Stinger Systems has sold just 12,000 stun devices since 2000. Law Enforcement Associates introduced their stun gun only recently, in March 2005.

6. For example, the effects of OC spray are often felt for several hours, and their range of effectiveness is much shorter (which increases the likelihood of other officers being sprayed). Bean bag guns and similar impact munitions are often fired from a specialized shotgun which is larger and more cumbersome than a CED.

7. See White and Saunders (2010) for a more complete discussion of available data on police use of the TASER.

8. We can get a general idea of the circumstances in which police use the TASER by examining internal police department reports, CED industry reports and data, and civil and human rights group reports, but there are obvious concerns over the objectivity of these sources. As a result, we focus solely on empirical studies conducted by independent researchers.

9. These are not clinical judgments. Rather, they are conclusions drawn by the officers on-scene based on available evidence.

10. The one exception to this statement regarding consistency across data sources involves suspects who are emotionally disturbed. The NYPD uses the TASER primarily in incidents involving emotionally disturbed individuals (indeed it is outlined in their policy and procedures), while other departments across the country have broader deployment patterns (as reflected in the media reports).

11. Field report analyses produced by *TASER International* (2002) have placed the TASER's effectiveness at similar levels, ranging from 83% to 94%.

12. That is, individuals struck by the TASER in police-citizen encounters are likely to be neither healthy nor voluntary; they are much more likely to be under the influence of drugs or alcohol, to have pre-existing physical and mental conditions, and to physically resist after TASER deployment—all of which may be associated with an increased risk of serious physiological side effects.

13. Two suspects died, but neither death occurred as a result of the TASER.

14. For nearly 30 years there have been similar calls for a national archive of officer-involved shootings, but, to date, those calls have been unheeded.

15. White and Saunders (2010) examined all of the data sources outlined in an earlier section of this chapter: 1) official police department data examined in independent studies (most notably the New York Police Department, 2002–2007); 2) Internal police reports that are publicly available; 3) CED industry data (*TASER International*), 4) civil and human rights group reports and data (*Amnesty International* and the *American Civil Liberties Union*); 5) media data (searches on *LexisNexis* and *New York Times Select* for all newspaper articles on the TASER from 2002–2006); and 6) civil litigation against officers and departments for improper use of CEDs.

16. We also know little about the military's use of the TASER, though this setting is less relevant because the rules and regulations governing the military are different—particularly in times of war.

CHAPTER 20

1. The description of this incident was paraphrased from Wong's study of police use of force in Hong Kong (in this volume).

2. The description of this incident was drawn from communication with Constable (now Sergeant) Many Fingers, and from the text of the commendations for bravery issued to these two officers by the First Nations Chiefs of Police Association (FNCPA). I am grateful to the FNCPA for their permission to use this material.

3. For a rare exception, see Chevigny (1995).

4. A third possibility is that warning shots may encourage other officers to fire based on a mistaken belief that the initial officer has already made the decision to shoot the suspect. Recent research evidence casts doubt on the popular notion of "contagious" fire by police officers (White and Klinger 2009). However, the study does not examine contagious fire that results from firing warning shots.

5. Note that at the time this quote was written, Bratton was Commissioner of the New York Police Department.

6. Presents the results of a public opinion poll of 1,671 adults in Britain from July 22–24, 2005.

Appendix

Summary Statistics by Country

Country	Total Midyear Population 2008	Government	Overall # of Crimes (2007)	Overall # of Crimes Per 100,000 (2007)	Method of Policing	# of Officers per 100,000 (2002)	Armed/ Unarmed Policing	# of Police Departments	Pop. Density (sq. km)*	Unemployment Rates (2007)
United States	303,824,646	Constitution-Based Federal Republic	22,503,636	7,472.82	Federal, State, Local	326.37	Armed	11,368 Departments	30.92	4.6
Brazil	196,342,587	Federal Republic	6,707,955 (2003)	3646.42 (2003)	Federal, State, Local		Armed	27 Civil Police Regions	23.07	9.3
United Kingdom	60,943,912	Constitutional Monarchy	5,894,014	9,697.89	Federal, State, Local	270.49 (2007)	Unarmed except in NIR	10 regions, 52 Departments	248.93	5.3
Guatemala	13,002,206	Constitutional Democratic Republic			National?		Armed?		119.41	3.2**
China	1,330,044,605	Communist State			National	12.78***	Armed	31 Local Security Bureaus	138.59	4.0
Hong Kong	7,018,636	Limited Democracy	80,796	1,157.47	National via China?	390.91 (2008)	Armed	23 Districts	6,427.32	4.0
India	1,147,995,898	Federal Republic	5,102,460 (2006)	458.97 (2006)	Federal, State, Local	98.22 (2006)	Armed	12,591 Police Stations	349.19	7.2
Poland	38,500,696	Republic	1,153,000	2,993.39	National	258.98	Armed	16 Voivodeships	123.13	12.8
Norway	4,644,457	Constitutional Monarchy	318,199	6,875.63	National	174.18 (2005)	Unarmed	27 Districts	14.34	2.5
Sweden	9,045,389	Constitutional Monarchy	1,234,784 (2002)	13,790.04 (2002)	National	180.96	Armed	21 Police Authorities	20.10	6.1
Denmark	5,484,723	Constitutional Monarchy	491,026 (2002)	9,135.89 (2002)	National	192.09	Armed	12 Districts	127.27	2.8

Finland	Republic	5,244,749	814,141	15,541.61	National	160.09	Armed	90 Districts	15.51	6.9
Netherlands	Constitutional Monarchy	16,645,313	1,422,863 (2002)	8,825.14 (2002)	National	212.35	Armed	26 Regional Forces	400.84	4.6
Australia	Federal Parliamentary Democracy	21,007,310	31,302	150.86	Federal, State, Local	304.19	Armed	8 Jurisdictions	2.73	4.4

* based on 2008 population data.

** 2005 estimate.

*** Approximation (website stated over 170,000 trained officers).

Sources: Central Intelligence Agency World Factbook; United States Census Bureau, International Data Base; 8th Survey United Nations Office of Drugs and Crime; http://www.policiacivil.rj.gov.br/; http://www.dpf.gov.br/; http://www.ssb.no/english/; http://www.afp.gov.au/_data/assets/pdf_file/87998/ACTPolicingAR08.pdf; http://www.police.wa.gov.au/ContactUs/Australianjurisdictions/tabid/1352/Default.aspx; http://www.police.uk/forces.htm; http://www.homeoffice.gov.uk/rds/ia/atlas.html; http://www.homeoffice.gov.uk/rds/pdfs08/hosb0208.pdf; http://www.gov.hk/en/about/abouthk/factsheets/docs/police.pdf; http://www.police.gov.hk/hkp-home/english/statistics/compare06.htm; http://www.aic.gov.au/conferences/occasional/xiancui.html; http://english.gov.cn/2005-10/02/content_74192.htm; http://india.gov.in/citizen/police_st_ut.php; http://india.gov.in/citizen/police.php; http://ncrb.nic.in/cii2006/home.htm; http://www.police.nl/PoliceGB/police_arms.htm; http://www.stat.fi/tup/suoluk/suoluk_oikeusolot_en.html; http://www.intermin.fi/poliisi/home.nsf/pages/index_eng. Dates of Access: November–December 2008.

References

ACLU of Southern California. 1993. "Pepper Spray: A Magic Bullet Under Scrutiny." Los Angeles: American Civil Liberties Union of Southern California.

Adams, K. 1996. "Measuring the Prevalence of Police Abuse of Force." In *Police Violence: Critical Issues in Policing: Contemporary Readings*, ed. R. G. Dunham and G. P. Alpert, 531–546. Prospect Heights, IL: Waveland Press.

Adang, O. M. J. and J. Mensink. 2000. *Eindrapportage Onderzoek Invoering Pepper Spray bij de Nederlandse Politie.* LSOP, Apeldoorn.

Adang, O. M. J. and J. Mensink 2001. *"Spray!" Een Nieuw Geweldmiddel Voor de Nederlandse Politie.* Elsevier bedrijfsinformatie, 's-Gravenhage.

Adang, O. M. J. and J. Mensink. 2004. "Pepper Spray: An Unreasonable Response to Suspect Verbal Resistance." *Policing: An International Journal of Police Strategies and Management* 27: 206–219.

Adang, O. M. J., J. Mensink, and C. Esman. 2005. *Spray met Visie, Visie op Spray. Afsluitende Onderzoeksrapportage van het "Pepperspray Project."* Apeldoorn, Politieacademie.

Adang, O. M. J., R. J. Kaminski, M. Q. Howell, and J. Mensink. 2006. "Assessing the Performance of Pepper Spray in Use-of-force Encounters: The Dutch Experience." *Policing: An International Journal of Police Strategies and Management* 29(2): 282–305.

Adang, O. M. J., Wateren, R. v.d., and P. J. S. Steernberg. 1999. *Netten, Stokken en Sprays. Nieuwe Wapens voor de Nederlandse Politie?* Elsevier bedrijfsinformatie, 's-Gravenhage.

Adkins, L. D. 2003. "Oleoresin Capsicum: An Analysis of the Implementation of Pepper Spray into the Law Enforcement Use of Force Continuum in a Selected Police Department." Master's thesis, East Tennessee State University.

Ahnan, Ron. "The Politics of Police Violence in Democratic Brazil." *Latin American Politics and Society,* Spring 2007, via BNET, http://findarticles.com/p/articles/mi_qa4000/is_200704/ai_n19197283/pg_1?tag=artBody;col1.

Alas, J. M. C. and J. R. Argueta. 2007. *Cultura Política de la Democracia en Honduras: 2006.* San Salvador: Proyecto de Opinión Pública de América Latina (LAPOP).

Alpert, G. and R. Dunham. 2004. *Understanding Police Use of force: Officers, Suspects, and Reciprocity.* Cambridge, UK: Cambridge University Press.

Alpert, G. and W. C. Smith. 1994. "How Reasonable is the Reasonable Man? Police and Excessive Force." *The Journal of Criminal Law and Criminology* 85 (2): 481–501.

Alston, Philip. 2008. "Mission to Brazil." United Nations Human Rights Council, http://www2.ohchr.org/english/issues/executions/docs/A_HRC_11_2_Add_2_English.pdf.

Altmann, J. 2001. "Acoustic Weapons—A Prospective Assessment." *Science & Global Security* 9: 165–234.

Alvarez, A. 1992. "Trends and Patterns of Justifiable Homicide: A Comparative Analysis." *Violence and Victims* 7 (4): 347–56.

American Technology Corporation. 2008. "Long Range Acoustic Device," American Technology Corporation, http://www.atcsd.com/site/content/view/37/47/

Åminne, C-G. and J. Lounaskorpi. 2005. Polisens Bruk av Skjutvapen–Det Finska Exemplet. In *Polisens Bruk av Skjutvapen i Norden,* ed./J. Knutsson. Oslo: Politihøgskolen.

Amnesty International. 2009. "April 1. China: Preliminary Briefing to the UN Committee against Torture." Amnesty International, http://www.amnesty.org.

Amnesty International. 1988. *United Kingdom: Northern Ireland: Killings by Security Forces and "Supergrass" Trials.* London: Amnesty International.

Amnesty International. 2004. *Excessive and Lethal Force? Amnesty International's Concerns about Deaths and Ill Treatment Involving Police Use of Tasers.* London: Amnesty International (AI Index: AMR 51/139/2004).

Amnesty International. 2005. *Brazil: 'They Come in Shooting': Policing Socially Excluded Communities.* London: Amnesty International.

Amnesty International. 2007. *Amnesty International's Concerns about TASER Use.* Statement to the U.S. Justice Department inquiry into deaths in custody. New York: Amnesty International.

Anderson, D. M. and D. Killingray. 1991. *Policing the Empire: Government, Authority and Control, 1830–1940.* Manchester, UK: Manchester University Press.

Anderson, D. M. and D. Killingray. 1992. *Policing and Decolonisation: Politics, Nationalism and the Police, 1917–65.* Manchester, UK: Manchester University Press.

Arraigada, I. and L. Godoy. 1999. *Seguridad Ciudadana y Violencia en América Latina: Diagnóstico y Políticas en los Años Noventa.* Santiago de Chile: United Nations, CEPAL.

Asian Political News. 2005. "China's Official Media Says 3 Died in Police Crackdown on Village." *Asian Political News,* December 19. http://findarticles.com/p/articles/mi_m0WDQ/is_2005_Dec_19/ai_n15957394/pg_1.

Asmal, K. 1985. *Shoot to Kill? International Lawyers' Inquiry into the Lethal Use of Firearms by the Security Forces in Northern Ireland.* Dublin: Mercier Press.

Associated Press. 1977. "Pepper Spray Ban Being Urged after Death of Suspect Weapon Too Often Aimed at Blacks, Winston-Salem NAACP Leader Says," November 4.

Association of Chief Police Officers. 1996. "Aerosol Incapacitants: Guidelines for Use." *ACPO Self Defence, Arrest and Restraint Committee.* London Home Office.

Association of Chief Police Officers. 1999. "CS Incapacitant Spray: Notes for Guidance on Police Use." *ACPO Self Defence, Arrest and Restraint Committee.* London: Home Office.

Australian. 2008a. "Police Training Slammed as Shoot Scene Becomes Shrine," December 15.

Australian. 2008b. "Shot Man 'Agitated:' Police," January 3.

Bailey, D. and J. Garofalo. 1989. "The Management of Violence by Police Patrol Officers." *Criminology* 27 (1): 1–25.

Baker, D. 2005. *Batons and Blockades: Policing Industrial Disputes in Australasia.* Melbourne: Circa.

Bao You Municipality. "Bao You Municipality, Public Security Bureau, Jiu-yuan Sub-bureau, proposal for Special Campaign on Control of Use of Service Guns," http://www.btjy.gov.cn/zfxxgk.files/gdw/jtnr/gafj/03/007-0300000-2008005%E5%85%AC%E5%8A%A1%E7%94%A8%E6%9E%AA%E7%AE%A1%E7%90%86%E4%BD%BF%E7%94%A8%E4%B8%93%E9%A1%B9%E6%95%B4%E6%B2%BB%E8%A1%8C%E5%8A%A8%E5%B7%A5%E4%BD%9C%E6%96%B9E6%A1%88.doc.

Barradas, Rita Barata, M. C. S. de Almeida Ribeiro, and J. C. de Moraes. 1999. "Social Inequalities and Homicide in Adolescents and Young Adults in S. Paulo, 1995." *Revista Brasileira de Epidemiologia* 2 (1–2): 50–59.

Bayley, D. 1995. "Police Brutality Abroad." In *And Justice for All: Understanding and Controlling Police Abuse of Force,* ed. W. A. Geller and H. Toch, 261–76. Washington, DC: Police Executive Research Forum.

Bayley, David and C. Shearing. 2001. *The New Structure of Policing.* Washington, DC: U.S. Department of Justice.

Becker, H. 1963. *Outsiders: Study in the Sociology of Deviance.* London: Free Press of Glencoe.

Belur, J. 2007. "Police Use of Deadly Force: Analysing Police 'Encounters' in Mumbai." PhD diss., London School of Economics.

Berggren, N-O. and J. Munck. 2003. Polislagen – en kommentar. 4. uppl. Stockholm: Norstedts juridik.

Bittner, E. 1970. *The Functions of Police in Modern Society.* Washington, DC: U.S. Government Printing Office.

Bleetman, A., R. Steyn, and C. Lee. 2004. "Introduction of the Taser into British Policing. Implications for UK Emergency Departments: An Overview of Electronic Weaponry." *Emergency Medicine Journal* 21: 136–140.

Bobb, M. J., M. H. Epstein, N. H. Miller, and M. A. Abascal. 1996. *Five Years Later: A Report to the Los Angeles Police Commission on the Los Angeles Police Department's Implementation of Independent Commission Recommendations.* Report to the Los Angeles Police Commission, Los Angeles, CA.

Bolesta, Stanisław. 1972. "The Legal Position of the Citizens Militia in the System of Bodies of the Polish People's Republic." In *Internal Security of the Republic of Poland in a Systemic Approach and from the Point of View of the Tasks of Public Administration,* 118–121. Warsaw.

Bonar, R. 1994. *Oleoresin Capsicum Spray, Technical Memorandum 19-94E.* Ottawa: Canadian Police Research Centre.

Bonifacio, P. 1991. *The Psychological Effects of Police Work: A Psychodynamic Approach.* London: Plenum Press.

Bowling, J. M. and M. Gaines. 2000. *An Evaluation of Oleoresin Capsicum (O.C.) Use by Law Enforcement Agencies: Impact on Injuries to Officers and Suspects.* Washington, DC: National Institute of Justice.

Bratton, W. 1998. *Turnaround: How America's Top Cop Reversed the Crime Epidemic.* New York: Random House.

Broadstock, M. 2002. "What is the Safety of "Pepper Spray" Use by Law Enforcement on Mental Health Service Staff? NZHTA Tech brief series 1(2)," http://nzhta.chmeds.ac.nz/Pepper_Spray.PDF.

Brooke, J. 1990. "Brazil Police Accused of Torture and Killing in Rights Report." *New York Times,* June 19.

Brouwer, G. 2005. *Review of Fatal Police Shootings by Victoria Police.* Melbourne: Office of Police Integrity.

Brown, J. 1997. *Comments on the Use of Capsaicin Spray.* Ottawa: Royal Canadian Mounted Police.

Brown, L., D. Takeuchi, and K. Challoner. 2000. "Corneal Abrasions Associated with Pepper Spray Exposure." *American Journal of Emergency Medicine* 18 (3): 271–272.

Brown v. Mississippi, 297 U.S. 278 (1936).

Browning, C. 1993. *Ordinary Men: Reserve Police Battalion 101 and the Final Solution in Poland.* New York: HarperCollins.

Bunker, R. J. 2005a. *Training Key # 581: Suicide (Homicide) Bombers Part I. El Segundo, California: Counter-OPFOR Program.* National Law Enforcement and Corrections Technology Centre-West: National Institute of Justice.

Bunker, R. J. 2005b. *Training Key # 582: Suicide (Homicide) Bombers Part II. El Segundo, California: Counter-OPFOR Program.* National Law Enforcement and Corrections Technology Centre-West: National Institute of Justice.

Bureau of Justice Statistics. 1999. *Contacts Between Police and the Public: Findings from the 1999 National Survey.* Washington, DC: U.S. Department of Justice.

Bureau of Justice Statistics. 2003. *Law Enforcement Management and Administrative Statistics (LEMAS): 2003 Sample Survey of Law Enforcement Agencies [computer file].* ICPSR04411-v1. Washington, DC: U.S. Dept. of Commerce, Bureau of the Census [producer], 2006. Ann Arbor, MI: Inter-university Consortium for Political and Social Research [distributor], 2006-05-10.

Bureau of Justice Statistics. 2005. *Contacts Between Police and the Public: Findings from the 2002 National Survey.* Washington, DC: U.S. Department of Justice.

Burke, T. and W. Rowe. 1992. "Bullet Ricochet: A Comprehensive Review." *Journal of Forensic Sciences* 37 (5): 1254–1260.

Buttle, J. W. 2003. " 'What's Good For Them, Is Good For Us:' Outside Influences on the Adoption of an Incapacitant Spray By the British Police." *International Journal of Police Science Management* 5 (2): 98–161.

Buttle, J. W. 2006. "Unravelling the 'Velcro Effect:' Is Deterring Assaults against the Police Indicative of a More Aggressive Style of Policing?" *International Journal of Police Science Management* 8 (2): 133–142.

Buttle, J. W. 2007. "A Constructive Critique of the Officer Safety Programme Used in England and Wales." *Policing and Society* 17 (2): 164–181.

Buvinic, Mayra, A. Morrison, and M. Shifter. "Violence in Latin America and the Caribbean: A Framework for Action," Inter-American Development Bank. http://www.iadb.org/sds/publication/publication_515_e.htm.

Caldeira, Teresa. 2000. *City of Walls: Crime, Segregation, and Citizenship in São Paulo.* Berkeley, CA: University of California Press.

Call, C. 1999. "From Soldiers to Cops: 'War Transitions' and the Demilitarization of Policing in Latin America and the Caribbean." PhD. diss., Stanford University.

Campbell, J. 1992. "A Comparative Analysis of the Effects of Post-Shooting Trauma on the Special Agents of the Federal Bureau of Investigation." PhD diss., Michigan State University.

Cannon, Lou. 2000. "One Bad Cop." *New York Times Magazine*, October 1.

Cano, Ignácio, "Racial Bias in Lethal Police Action in Brazil," Ignácio Cano, http://lpp-uerj.net/olped/documentos/ppcor/0061.pdf.

Cano, Ignácio. 1997. *The Use of Lethal Force by Police in Rio de Janeiro.* Rio de Janeiro: Boletim do ISER.

Cano, Ignácio and N. Santos. 2001. *Violencia Letal, Renda e Desigualdade Social no Brasil.* Rio de Janeiro: Letras 7.

Cano, Ignácio. 2003. "Summary Executions in Brazil: The Use of Force by State Agents." In *Justica Global*, ed. Sandra Carvalho, 11–67. São Paulo: Justica Global.

Cao, Liquin. 2002. *Curbing Police Brutality: What Works? A Reanalysis of Citizen Complaints at the Organizational Level.* Washington, DC: U.S. Department of Justice.

Carassava, A. 2008. "Youth Riots in Greece Enter a Second Day." *New York Times*, December 8.

Cardia, Nancy. 1999. *Primeira Pesquisa Sôbre Atitudes, Normas Culturais e Valores em Relação a Violência em 10 Capitais Brasileiras.* Brasília: Ministério da Justiça. Secretária de Estado dos Direitos Humanos.

Carr, B., C. Schwab, C. Branas, M. Killen, and D. Wiebe. 2008. "Outcomes Related to the Number and Anatomic Placement of Gunshot Wounds." *Journal of Trauma: Injury Infection and Critical Care* 64 (1): 197–203.

Caso de Policia, "Salários da Policía Civil e Militar do Rio," Caso de Policia, http://www.casodepolicia.com/2007/08/10/salarios-da-policia-civil-e-militar-do-rio/.

Castro, H. 2004. "Less Lethal Weapons Still Pack a Big Punch. New Police Guns Not as Deadly, But Require Lots of Extra Training. *Seattle Post Intelligencer,* February 2.

Centers for Disease Control and Prevention. 2004. "Homicide Trends and Characteristics: Brazil, 1980–2002." *Morbidity and Mortality Weekly Report* 53 (8): 169–171.

Chan, J. 1997. *Changing Police Culture: Policing in a Multicultural Society.* Cambridge, UK: Cambridge University Press.

Chan, L. 1996. "Police Discretion: Application of Deadly Force." Master's thesis, Hong Kong University.

Chan, T. C., G. M. Vilke, J. Clausen, R. Clark, P. Schmidt, T. Snowden, and T. Neuman. 2001. *Pepper Spray's Effects on a Suspect's Ability to Breathe.* Washington, DC: National Institute of Justice, U.S. Department of Justice.

Chan, T., G. Vilke, J. Clausen, R. Clark, P. Schmidt, T. Snowden, and T. Neuman. 2000. "Impact of Oleoresin Capsicum Spray on Respiratory Function in Human Subjects in the Sitting and Prone Maximal Restraint Positions," Final Report. Washington, DC: Department of Justice Study.

Chapman, S. 1967. "Police Policy on the Use of Firearms." *Police Chief* 34: 16–37.

Chatterton, M. 1979. "The Supervision of Patrol Work under the Fixed Points System." In *The British Police,* ed. S. Holdaway, 83–91. London: Edward Arnold.

Cheek-Milby, Kathleen. 1995. *A Legislature Comes of Age.* Hong Kong: Oxford University Press.

Chermak, S. 1995. "Image Control: How Police Affect the Presentation of Crime News." *American Journal of Police* 14 (2): 21–43.

Chevigny, P. 1995. *Edge of the knife: Police violence in the Americas.* New York: The New Press.

Chevigny, Paul. 1996. *Edge of the Knife: Police Violence in the Americas.* New York: The New Press.

Chinchilla, L. 2003. "Experiences with Citizen Participation in Crime Prevention in Central America." In *Crime and Violence in Latin America: Citizen Security, Democracy, and the State,* ed. J. S. Tulchin, H. Frühling, and H. Golding, 205–233. Washington, DC: Woodrow Wilson Center Press.

CNN. 1997. "Police Commission Beefs up LAPD Firepower," March 19.

Coady, T., S. James, and S. Miller. 2000. "Introduction." In *Violence and Police Culture,* ed. T. Coady, S. James, S. Miller, and M. O'Keefe, 1–13. Melbourne: Melbourne University Press.

Cohen, S. 2001. *States of Denial: Knowing about Atrocities and Suffering.* Cambridge, UK: Polity Press.

Colitt, Raymond. "'I'm Saving to Buy a Gun'." *IOL*, April 16, 2007, via www.iol.co.za, http://www.iol.co.za/index.php?set_id=1&click_id=3&art_id=nw2007041609324 3620C129636.

Comerford, J. 2006. *Lockout: An Eyewitness Account of Australia's Most Violent Conflict.* Sydney: CFMEU Mining and Energy.

Conroy, J. 2000. *Unspeakable Acts, Ordinary People: The Dynamics of Torture.* New York: Knopf.

Conroy, J. 2003. "Deaf to the Screams." *The Chicago Reader*, August 23.

Costanzo, M., E. Gerrity, and M. B. Lykes. 2006. "Psychologists and the Use of Torture in Interrogations." *Analyses of Social Issues and Public Policy* 6: 1–14.

Costanzo, M. and R. A. Leo. 2007. "Research Findings and Expert Testimony on Police Interrogations and Confessions to Crimes." In *Expert Psychological Testimony for the Courts*, ed. M. Costanzo, D. Krauss, and K. Pezdek, 69–98. Mahwah, NJ: Erlbaum.

Costanzo, M. A. & Gerrity, E. 2009. "The Effects and Effectiveness of Using Torture as an Interrogation Device: Using Research to Inform the Policy Debate." *Social Issues and Policy Review* 3: 179–210.

Constitution of the People's Republic of China. 1982.

Criminal Law Act 1967, UK.

Criminal Law of the People's Republic of China. 1997. Adopted by the Second Session of the Fifth National People's Congress on July 1, 1979 and amended by the Fifth Session of the Eighth National People's Congress on March 14, 1997.

Critchley, T. A. 1970. *The Conquest of Violence.* London: Constable.

Critchley, T. A. 1978. *A History of Police in England and Wales.* London: Constable.

Cullell, J. V. and L. R. Bixby. 2006. *The Political Culture of Democracy in Costa Rica: 2006.* San José, CR: Proyecto Opinión Publica de América Latina (LAPOP).

Cunningham, D. 2004. *Taiho-jutsu: Law and Order in the Age of the Samurai.* Boston: Tuttle Publishing.

Cutler, T. 1973. "Sunday, Bloody Sunday." In *Strikes: Studies in Twentieth Century Australian Social History*, ed. J. Iremonger, J. Merritt, and G. Osborne, 81–99. Sydney: Angus and Robertson.

Dalton, V. 1998. "Police Shootings 1990–97." *Trends and Issues in Crime and Criminal Justice* 89: 1–6.

Dammert, L. and M. Malone. 2006. "Does It Take a Village? Policing Strategies and Fear of Crime in Latin America." *Latin American Politics and Society* 48 (4): 27–51.

Dantas Mota, Lourenco. 2004. "Civil War in Brazil is No Figure of Speech." *Brazzil Magazine*, October 6.

Davison, N. 2006. *The Early History of "Non-Lethal" Weapons. Occasional Paper No. 1.* Bradford Non-Lethal Weapons Research Projects Department of Peace Studies. United Kingdom: University of Bradford.

Delattre, E. 2002. *Character and Cops: Ethics in Policing*, 4th ed. Washington, DC: AEI Press.

Denham, W., and W. Mallon. 1999. "Injury Patterns Associated with Nonlethal Law Enforcement Techniques." *Top Emergency Medicine* 21: 30–38.

Derbeken, J. V. 1997. "Pepper Spray Ban Rejected by Judge." *San Francisco Chronicle*, November 15.

Dorriety, J. 2005. "Police Service Dogs in the Use-of-Force Continuum." *Criminal Justice Policy Review* 16: 88–98.

Doubet, M. 1977. *The Medical Implications of OC Sprays.* Millstadt, IL: PPCT Management Systems, Inc.

Downie, Andrew. 2008. "Effort to Mend a Violent Reputation." *Financial Times*, August 7.

Downs, Raymond L. 2007. "Less Lethal Weapons: A Technologist's Perspective." *Policing: An International Journal of Police Strategies and Management* 30:358–384.

Dreamscanbe Foundation. "Homicide Among Blacks in Brasil: Study Reveals that the Homicide Rate Among Blacks in Brasil is Comparable to Nations Undergoing Civil War," Dreamscanbe Foundation, http://www.dreamscanbe.org/3300? locale=en_US.

Drizin, S. A., and R. A. Leo. 2004. "The Problem of False Confessions in the Post-DNA World." *North Carolina Law Review* 82: 891–1007.

Durose, M., E. Schmitt, and P. Langan. 2005. *Contacts Between Police and the Public: Findings from the 2002 National Survey.* Washington, DC: U.S. Department of Justice.

Dyer, Geoff. 2008. "Brazil's Lesson for China: Do Not Ignore Inequality." *Financial Times*, March 3.

Eijkman, Quirine. 2007. We Are Here To Serve You!: Public Security, Police Reform And Human Rights Implementation in Costa Rica. Antwerpen/ Oxford: Intersentia.

Ellison, G. and J. Smyth. 2000. *The Crowned Harp: Policing Northern Ireland.* London: Pluto Press.

Emsley, C. 1983. *Policing and its Context.* London: Macmillan.

Emsley, C. 1996. *The English Police: A Political and Social History.* London: Longman.

Enorth.com. "Dragged Traffic Police for Two Kilos Before Absconding." *enorth.com,* February 2. 2006, http://news.enorth.com.cn/system/2006/02/14/001232249. shtml.

ERIC, IDESO, IDIES, IUDOP. 2004. *Maras y Pandillas en Centroamérica: Pandillas y Capital Social,* Volumen II. San Salvador: UCA Editores.

Ericson, R. 1982. *Reproducing Order: A Study of Police Patrol Work.* Toronto: University of Toronto Press.

Estado de São Paulo. 1997. "Risco de Morte no Morumbi e 18 Vezes Maior que Nos Jardins." December 11.

Fazhi Ribao. "Associate Professor Being Shot by Gun; Legal Expert is of the Opinion that the Regulations Should be More Detailed." *Fazhi Ribao,* November 15, 2007b, http://news.xinhuanet.com/legal/2007-11/15/content_7078010.htm.

Federal Bureau of Investigation. 1972. *Uniform Crime Report, 1971.* Washington, DC: Federal Bureau of Investigation.

Federal Bureau of Investigation. 1986. *Administrative Inquiry, Volume 1: Shooting Incident, Miami Florida, April 11, 1986.* Washington, DC: Federal Bureau of Investigation.

Federal Bureau of Investigation. 2008. *Uniform Crime Report, 2007.* Washington, DC: Federal Bureau of Investigation.

Federal Bureau of Investigation. 2008. *Law Enforcement Officers Killed and Assaulted, 2007.* Washington, DC: U.S. Department of Justice.

Findlay, M. 2004. *Introducing Policing: Challenges for Police and Australian Communities.* Melbourne: Oxford University Press.

Finnane, M. 1994. *Police and Government: Histories of Policing in Australia.* Melbourne: Oxford University Press.

FLACSO. 2007. *Report on the Security Sector in Latin America and the Caribbean.* Santiago: Facultad Latinoamericana de Ciencias Sociales, FLACSO Chile.

Folha de São Paulo. 1999a. "PM Fardado Mata 63% a Mais que em 98; Número de Policiais Mortos Crece 200%." October 20.

Folha de São Paulo. 1999b. "Morar sem Infra-estrutura Aumenta Risco de ser Morto." November 3.

Folha de São Paulo. 1998. "Vitoria e a Cidade Mais Perigosa para Jovens." December 10.

Fools Mountain Blog, "27: *BMY* Says: July 10th, 2008 at 4:01 am" in response to "Chinese Police Adopt New Form of Self-defense," Fools Mountain Blog, http://blog.foolsmountain.com/2008/07/09/chinese-police-new-self-defense/.

Foote, D. H. 1992. "The Benevolent Paternalism of Japanese Criminal Justice." *California Law Review* 80: 317–390.

Foster, R. E. 2005. *Police Technology.* Upper Saddle River, NJ: Pearson Prentice Hall.

Fridell, L. and A. Pate. 1993. "Death on Patrol: Killings of Police Officers." In *Critical Issues in Policing: Contemporary Readings*, ed. R. Dunham and G. Alpert, 568–596. Prospect Heights, IL: Waveland Press.

Fyfe, J. 1978. *Shots Fired: An Examination of New York City Police Firearms Discharges.* Ann Arbor, MI: University Microfilms International.

Fyfe, J. 1979. "Administrative Interventions on Police Shooting Discretion: An Empirical Examination." *Journal of Criminal Justice* 7: 309–323.

Fyfe, J. J. 1988. "Police Use of Deadly Force: Research and Reform." *Justice Quarterly* 5: 165–205.

Fyfe, J. J. 1989. "The Split-Second Syndrome and Other Determinants of Police Violence." In *Critical Issues in Policing,* edited by R. G. Dunham and G. P. Alpert, 476. Prospect Heights, IL: Waveland Press.

Fyfe, J. J. 1993. "The Split-Second Syndrome and Other Determinants of Police Violence." In *Critical Issues in Policing,* ed. R. G. Dunham and G. P. Alpert. Prospect Heights, IL: Waveland Press.

Fyfe, J. 1996. "Training to Reduce Police-Civilian Violence." In *Police Violence Understanding and Controlling Police Abuse of Force,* ed. W. A. Geller and H. Toch, 175. London: Yale University Press.

Fyfe, J. J. 1997. "The Split-Second Syndrome and Other Determinants of Police Violence." In *Understanding and Controlling Police Abuse of Force*, ed. W. A. Geller and H. Toch, 52–93. New Haven, CT: Yale University Press.

Fyfe, J. 1999. "Police Use of Deadly Force: Research and Reform." In *Policing Perspectives: An Anthology*, ed. L. Gaines and G. Cordner, 408–434. New York: Oxford University Press.

Garrett, R. 2005. "Dodging Arrows: When Adding Less-Lethal Technology, Pioneering Agencies can Protect Themselves through Education, Research and Training." *Law Enforcement Technology* 32: 18–28.

Gauvin, R. 1994. *Oleoresin Capsicum Spray: A Progress Report*. Portland, OR: Portland Police Department.

Gauvin, R. 1995. *Oleoresin Capsicum Spray: A Progress Report*. Portland, OR: Portland Police Department, Internal Affairs Unit.

Gawryszewsk, Vilma Pinheiro, and L. S. Costa. 2005. "Social Inequality and Homicide Rates in São Paulo City, Brazil." *Revista Saude Publica* 39 (2): 1–6.

Geller, W. 1985. "Officer Restraint in the Use of Deadly Force: The Next Frontier in Police Shooting Research." *Journal of Police Science and Administration* 13: 153–171.

Geller, W. and K. Karales. 1981. *Split-second Decisions: Shootings of and by Chicago Police*. Chicago: Chicago Law Enforcement Study Group.

Geller, W. A. and M. Scott 1992. *Deadly Force: What We Know. A Practitioner's Desk Reference on Police-Involved Shootings*. Washington, DC: Police Executive Research Forum.

Geller, W. and H. Toch. 1996. "Understanding and Controlling Police Abuse of Force." In *Police Violence: Understanding and Controlling Police Abuse of Force*, ed. W. A. Geller and H. Toch, 310. London: Yale University Press.

Geneva Declaration. 2008. *Global Burden of Armed Violence*. Geneva: Geneva Declaration Secretariat.

Gersons, B. 1989. "Patterns of PTSD Among Police Officers Following Shooting Incidents: A Two-Dimensional Model and Treatment Implications." *Journal of Traumatic Stress* 2: 247–257.

Glebbeek, M. 2003. *In the Crossfire of Democracy. Police Reform and Police Practice in Post-civil war Guatemala*. Amsterdam: Rozenberg Publishers.

Glebbeek, M. 2009. "Post-war Violence and Police Reform in Guatemala." In *Policing Insecurity: Police Reform, Security and Human Rights in Latin America*, ed. N. Uildriks, 79–94. Maryland: Lexington Books.

Global Justice. 2003. *Human Rights in Brazil. Global Justice Annual Report*. São Paulo: Justica Global.

Goertzel, Ted and T. Kahn. 2007. "Brazil: The Unsung Story of São Paulo's Dramatic Murder Rate Drop." *Brazil Magazine*, May 18.

Goetel, Mieczysław. 1996. *The Powers of a Police Officer: The Use of Means of Direct Force*. Szczytno.

Goldsmith, A. 2006. "Policing and Law Enforcement." In *Crime and Justice: A Guide to Criminology*, ed. A. Goldsmith, M. Israel, and K. Daly, 283–303. Sydney: Thomson Legal.

Gomez, J. L. R. 2005. *The Political Economy of Nicaragua's Institutional and Organisational Framework for Dealing with Youth Violence.* Working Paper 65. Crisis State Programme, Universidad Centroamericana at Managua.

Gossman, P. 2002. "India's Secret Armies." In *Death Squads in Global Perspective: Murder with Deniability*, ed. B. Campbell and A. Brenner, 261–286. New York: Palgrave Macmillan.

Gould, J. 2002. "Playing with Fire: The Civil Liberties Implications of September 11th." *Public Administration Review* 62: 74–79.

Gould, R. W. and M. J. Waldren. 1986. *London's Armed Police.* London: Arms and Armour.

Graduate Institute of International Studies. 2003. Small Arms Survey 2003: Development Denied. Oxford: Oxford University Press.

Graham v. Connor, 490 U.S. 386 (1989).

Granfield, O. J. and C. S. Petty. 1994. *Pepper Spray and In-Custody Deaths.* International Association of Chiefs of Police, Alexandria, VA.

Grange, J., R. Kozak, and J. Gonzalez. 2002. "Penetrating Injury from a Less-Lethal Bean Bag Gun." *Journal of Trauma, Injury, Infection, and Critical Care* 52: 576–578.

Gross, S. 1996. "The Risks of Death: Why Erroneous Convictions are Common in Capital Cases." *Buffalo Law Review* 44: 469–500.

Gross, S. R., K. Jacoby, D. J. Matheson, N. Montgomery, and S. Patel. 2005. "Exonerations in the United States, 1989 through 2003." *Journal of Criminal Law and Criminology* 95: 523–553.

Gudjonsson, G. H. 2003. *The Psychology of Interrogations and Confessions: A Handbook.* Chichester: John Wiley and Sons.

Guo, Qiao. 2007. "Dalian Police Committed Murder; Media Forbidden To Report." *Asia Weekly,* May 03, via Observechina. http://www.observechina.net/info/rtshow.asp?ID=43461&ad=5/3/2007.

Haldane, R. 1995. *The People's Force: A History of Victoria Police.* Carlton, AU: Melbourne University Press.

Hamilton, A. 2005. "From Zap to Zzzz." *Time,* www.time.com/time/magazine.

Harbury, J. K. 2005. *Truth, Torture, and the American Way.* Boston: Beacon Press.

Heilbronn, G. N. 1998. *Criminal Procedure in Hong Kong.* Hong Kong: Longman.

Henry, Vincent. 2004. *Death Work: Police, Trauma, and the Psychology of Survival.* Oxford and New York: Oxford University Press.

Hepburn, L., M. Miller, D. Azrael, and D. Hemenway. 2007. "The US Gun Stock: Results from the 2004 National Firearms Survey." *Injury Prevention* 13 (1): 15–19.

Herald-Sun. 2004. "Cops Meet on Pistols," July 13.

Herald-Sun. 2009. "Cops Keen to Test New Electronic Stun Gun," March 17.

Herald Sun. 2008. "Police Demand Semi-Automatic Pistols after City Gunfight," May 15.

Her Majesty's Inspectorate of Constabulary. 1997. Officer Safety: Minimising the Risk of Violence. *A Report by HMIC, Thematic Inspection.* London: Home Office.

Hersh, S. M. 2004. "Chain of Command." *The New Yorker*, May 17.

Hinton, Mercedes. 2006. *The State on the Streets: Police and Politics in Argentina and Brazil.* Boulder, CO and London, Lynne Rienner.

Ho, J. D., J. R. Miner, D. Lakireddy, R. Bultman, L. Laura, and W. G. Heegaard. 2006. "Cardiovascular and Physiologic Effects of Conducted Electrical Weapon Discharge in Resting Adults." *Academic Emergency Medicine* 6 (3): 239–243.

Holdaway, S. 1983. *Inside the British Police.* Oxford: Basil Blackwell.

Holmberg, L. 2004. *Politiets Brug af Skydevåben i Danmark 1985–2002.* Det juridiske fakultet, Københavns universitet. http://www.jm.dk/image.asp?page=image&

Homant, R. and D. Kennedy. 2000. "Effectiveness of Less than Lethal Force in Suicide-by-Cop Incidents." *Police Quarterly* 3: 153–171.

Home Office. 2005. *Police and Criminal Evidence Act 1984. Codes of Practice* (Rev. ed.) London: Stationary Office.

Hong Kong Human Rights Commission. 1993. *Hong Kong Human Rights Report 1993,* Hong Kong: Hong Kong Human Rights Commission.

Hong Kong Police. 2008. *Police General Order (PGO). PGO 29-03: Use of Police Firearms.*

Hong Kong SAR Government. 1999. "LCQ 8: Complaints received by CAPO." Press Release. April 21, 1999.

Hopkins, E. J. 1931. *Our Lawless Police: A Study of the Unlawful Enforcement of the Law.* New York: Viking Press.

Hoser, R. 1999. *Victoria Police Corruption.* Doncaster, AU: Katubi Publishing.

Howland, C. 1997. "The Challenge of Religious Fundamentalism to the Liberty and Equality Rights of Women: An Analysis under the United Nations Charter." *Columbia Journal of Transnational Law* 35: 271–377.

Hubbs, K. and D. Klinger. 2004. *Impact Munitions Data Base of Use and Effects.* Report made to the U.S. Department of Justice; National Institute of Justice.

Huggins, Martha K. 2008. Unpublished Paper by Author, "Expert Witness Asylum Report: Gay Petitioner," March 4.

Huggins, Martha K. 1991. *Vigilantism and the State in Modern Latin America.* New York: Praeger.

Huggins, Martha K. 1997. "From Bureaucratic Consolidation to Structural Devolution: Police Death Squads in Brazil." *Policing and Society* 7 (4): 207–234.

Huggins, Martha K. 1998. *Political Policing: The U.S. and Latin America.* Durham, NC: Duke University Press.

Huggins, Martha K. 2000a. "Modernity and Devolution: The Making of Police Death Squads in Modern Brazil." In *Death Squads in Global Perspective: Murder with Deniability,* ed. B. B. Campbell and A. D. Brenner, 203–228. New York: St. Martin's Press.

Huggins, Martha K. "Urban Violence and Police Privatization in Brazil: Blended Invisibility." *Social Justice: A Journal of Crime, Conflict, and World Order,* Summer 2000b, via BNET, http://findarticles.com/p/articles/mi_hb3427/is_2_27/ai_n28803271.

Huggins, Martha K. "Torture 101: Lessons from the Brazilian Case." *Journal of Third World Studies*, Fall 2005, via BNET, http://findarticles.com/p/articles/mi_qa3821/is_200510/ai_n15641242.

Huggins, Martha and J. MacTurk. 2000. Editorial Essay. "Armed and Dangerous: Where the Military and Police Can't Keep Order Private Security Takes Over," *Connection to the Americas,* Fall.

Huggins, Martha K., M. Haritos-Fatouro, and P. Zimbardo. 2002. *Violence Workers: Torturers and Murderers Reconstruct Brazilian Atrocities.* Berkeley, CA: University of California Press.

Huggins, Martha K. and M. Mesquita. 1999. "Civic Invisibility, Marginality, Moral Exclusion: The Murders of Street Youth in Brazil." In *Children on the Streets in the Americas: Globalization, Homelessness, and Education in the United States, Brazil and Cuba,* ed. R. Michelson, 257–270. London: Routledge.

Human Rights Watch. 2006. *Mexico: Lost in Translation.* New York: Author.

Hunt, J. and P. Manning. 1991. "The Social Context of Police Lying." *Symbolic Interaction* 14 (1): 1–20.

Husain, Saima. 2007. *In War Those Who Die Are not Innocent.* Amsterdam, NL: Rosenberg Publishers.

Hutson, H., D. Anglin, G. Pineda, C. Flynn, M. Russell, and J. McKeith. 1997. "Law Enforcement K-9 Dog Bites: Injuries, Complications, and Trends." *Annals of Emergency Medicine* 29: 637–642.

IACP. 1994. Pepper Aerosol Restraint Spray. Model policy 9/94.

IACP. 1995. *Pepper Spray Evaluation Project: Results of the Introduction of Oleoresin Capsicum (OC) into the Baltimore County, MD, Police Department.* Washington, DC: National Institute of Justice.

Ijames, S. 2005. "Personal Chemical Munitions: Are They Gone with the Electronic Wind?" PoliceOne.com. http://www.policeone.com/writers/columnists/Steve-Ijames/articles/121180-Personal-chemical-munitions-Are-they-gone-with-the-electronic-wind/.

Inbau, F. E., J. E. Reid, J. P. Buckley, and B. Jayne. 2001. *Criminal Interrogation and Confessions.* 4th ed. Gaithersburg, MD: Aspen.

Independent Police Complaints Commission (IPCC). "Number of Assault Allegations Endorsed by the IPCC by Nature of Injury and by Result of Investigation in the Years 1999–2001," IPCC. http://www.ipcc.gov.hk/en/pdf/Annex%201.pdf.

Innocence Project Report. 2007. *200 Exonerated: Too Many Wrongfully Convicted.* New York: Benjamin N. Cardozo School of Law, Yeshiva University.

International Association of Chiefs of Police. 2001. *Police Use of Force in America.* Gaithersburg, MD: International Association of Chiefs of Police.

International Association of Chiefs of Police (IACP). 2005. *Electro-muscular Disruption Technology (EMDT): A Nine-step Strategy for Effective Deployment.* Alexandria,VA: IACP

International Association of Chiefs of Police. 2005. *Model Policy: Use of Force.* Alexandria, VA: IACP National Law Enforcement Policy Center.

IPCC. 2007a. *Stockwell One: Investigation into the Shooting of Jean Charles de Menezes at Stockwell Underground Station on 22 July 2005.* London: Independent Police Complains Commission.

IPCC. 2007b. *Stockwell Two: An Investigation into Complaints about the Metropolitan Police Service's Handling of Public Statements Following the Shooting of Jean Charles de Menezes on 22 July 2005.* London: Independent Police Complaints Commission.

Jacobs, D. and D. Britt. 1979. "Inequality and Police Use of Deadly Force: An Empirical Assessment of a Conflict Hypothesis." *Social Problems* 26 (4): 403–412.

Jenkinson, E., C. Neeson, and A. Bleetman. 2006. "The Relative Risk of Police Use-of-force Options: Evaluating the Potential for Deployment of Electronic Weaponry." *Journal of Clinical Forensic Medicine* 13 (5): 229–241.

Jennings, A. 1988. "'Shoot to Kill': The Final Courts of Justice." In *Justice Under Fire: The Abuse of Civil Liberties in Northern Ireland*, ed. A. Jennings. London: Pluto Press.

Jerichow, A. 1998. *The Saudi File: People, Power, and Politics.* New York: St. Martin's Press.

Jin, Gao-Feng. 2006. "The Protection and Remedies for Victims of Crime and Abuse of Power in China." In *The Use and Application of the United Nations Declaration of Basic Principles of Justice for Victims of Crime and Abuse of Power–Twenty Years after Its Adoption*, Work Product of the 131st International Training Course: Resource Material Series No.70, pp. 145–156. United Nations: UNAFEI.

Johnson, D. 2002. *The Japanese Way of Justice: Prosecuting Crime in Japan.* Oxford: Oxford University Press.

Johnston, R. W. 1992. *The Long Blue Line.* Brisbane: Boolarong Press.

Joudo, J. and J. Curnow. 2008. *National Deaths in Custody Program Annual Report 2006.* Canberra: Australia Institute of Criminology.

Joyner, C. and C. Basile. 2007. "The Dynamic Resistance Response Model: A Modern Approach to the Use of Force." *FBI Bulletin* 76 (9): 15–20.

Jussila, J. 2001. "Future Police Operations and Non-Lethal Weapons." *Medicine, Conflict and Survival* 17: 248–259.

Kacieniewski, David. 1998. "Police's Use of Deadly Force in New York is Low for Nation." *New York Times*, January 2.

Kaminski, R. and M. Martin. 2000. "An Analysis of Police Officer Satisfaction With Defence and Control Tactics." *Policing: An International Journal of Police Strategies and Management* 23 (2): 123–153.

Kaminski, R. J. *Common Issues Regarding Oleoresin Capsicum and Tasers.* 2005. Kennedy School of Government, Harvard University, and Office of Justice Programs, U.S. Department of Justice on-line symposium on less-than-lethal force, January 18.

Kaminski, R. J., S. M. Edwards, and J. W. Johnson. 1998. "The Deterrent Effects of Oleoresin Capsicum on Assaults against Police: Testing the Velcro-effect Hypothesis." *Police Quarterly* 1 (2): 1–20.

Kaminski, R. J., S. M. Edwards, and J. W. Johnson. 1999. "Assessing the Incapacitative Effects of Pepper Spray During Resistive Encounters with the Police." *Policing: An International Journal of Police Strategies and Management* 22 (1): 7–29.

Kappeler, V., R. Sluder, and G. Alpert. 1998. *Forces of Deviance: Understanding the Dark Side of Policing.* Prospect Heights, IL: Waveland Press.

Karczmarczyk, Michał. 2007. *The Use of Means of Direct Force and Firearms in the Aspect of Personal Safety of Police Officers and Other Participants of Extraordinary Events.* Szczytno.

Karlsson, I. and S-Å. Christianson. 2003. "The phenomenology of traumatic Experiences in Police Work." *Policing: An International Journal of Police Strategies and Management* 20 (3): 419–438.

Kasinsky, R. G. 1995. "Patrolling the Facts: Media, Cops, and Crime." In *Media, Process, and the Social Construction of Crime*, ed. G. Barak, 203–234. New York: Garland.

Kassin, S. and G. H. Gudjonsson. 2004. "The Psychology of Confessions: A Review of the Literature and Issues." *Psychological Science in the Public Interest* 5: 33–67.

Kassin, S. M., R. A. Leo, C. A. Meissner, K. D. Richman, L. H. Colwell, A. M. Leach, and D. La Fon. 2007."Police Interviewing and Interrogation: A Self-report Survey of Police Practices and Beliefs." *Law and Human Behavior* 31: 381–400.

Keenan, J. 1997. "Safe Distance." *Police Review*, December 1.

Kennedy, P. E. 2008. RCMP Use of the Conducted Energy Weapon (CEW) Final Report Including Recommendations for Immediate Implementation. Commission for Public Complaints Against the Royal Canadian Mounted Police.

Kenny, J., S. Heal, and M. Grossman. 2001. The Attribute-Based Evaluation (ABE) of Less-Than-Lethal, Extended-Range, Impact Munitions. The Applied Research Laboratory and Pennsylvania State University, Los Angeles Sheriff's Department.

Kinnaird, B. 2003. *Use of Force: Expert Guidance for Decisive Force Response.* New York: Looseleaf Law Publications, Inc.

Klein, A. 2008. "D.C. Police to Carry Semiautomatic Rifles on Patrols." *Washington Post*, May 17.

Klinger, D. 2001a. "Suicidal Intent in Victim-Precipitated Homicide: Insights From the Study of Suicide-by-Cop." *Homicide Studies* 5 (3): 206–226.

Klinger, D. 2001b. *Police Responses to Officer-Involved Shootings.* Final Report to National Institute of Justice. Grant #97-IJ-CX-0029.

Klinger, D. 2004. *Into the Kill Zone: A Cop's Eye View of Deadly Force.* San Francisco: Jossey-Bass.

Klockars, C. 1991. "The Dirty Harry Problem." In *Thinking About Police: Contemporary Readings.* 2nd edition, ed. C. Klockars and S. Mastrofski, 428–439. New York: McGraw-Hill.

Klockars, C. 1996. "A Theory of Excessive Force and Its Control." In *Police Violence: Understanding and Controlling Police Abuse of Force*, ed. W. A. Geller and H. Toch, 1–22. London: Yale University Press.

Knutsson, J. ed. 2005. *Polisens Bruk av Skjutvapen i Norden*. Oslo: Politihøgskolen.

Knutsson, J. 2006. "Polisers Bruk av Skjutvapen i Norge och Sverige." *Nordisk tidskrift for Kriminalvidenskab*. 93 årgang 1: 37–50.

Knutsson, J. and J. Strype. 2002. *Polisens Bruk av Skjutvapen [Police Use of Firearms]*. PHS Rapport 2002:1. Stockholm: Polishögskolan.

Knutsson, J and J. Strype. 2003. "Police Use of Firearms in Norway and Sweden: The Significance of Gun Availability." *Policing and Society* 13 (4): 429–439.

Kock, E. and B. Rix. 1996. "A Review of Police Trials of the CS Aerosol Incapacitant, Home Office Police Research Group," *Police Research Series Paper 21*. London: Home Office.

Koonings, K. and D. Kruijt, eds. 1999. *Societies of Fear: The Legacy of Civil War, violence and terror in Latin America*. London and New York: Zed Books.

Korda, Xelaju. 2006. *Aesthetics of (In)Security: Mentally Mapping Danger in Morumbi*. Tulane University: Stone Center for Latin American Studies.

Kornblum, R. and S. Reddy. 1991. "Effects of the Taser in Fatalities Involving Police Confrontation." *Journal of Forensic Science* 36 (2): 434–448.

Kroes, W. and J. Hurrell. 1975. *Job Stress and the Police Officer*. Washington, DC: U.S. Government Printing Office.

Kruijt, D. 2008. *Guerrillas: War and Peace in Central America*. London and New York: Zed Books.

Kureczka, A. 1996. "Critical Incident Stress in Law Enforcement." *FBI Law Enforcement Bulletin* 65 (2/3): 10–16.

Langan, P. A., L. A. Greenfeld, S. K. Smith, M. R. Durose, and D. J. Levin. 2001. *Police and the Public: Findings from the 1999 National Survey*. Washington, DC: Bureau of Justice Statistics, N.J., 184957.

Lara, F. B. 2006. La Policía Nacional: Antecedentes, Retos y Evolución. http://www.franciscobautista.com.

Lassiter, G. D. and A. L. Geers. 2004. "Evaluation of Confession Evidence: Effects of Presentation Format." In *Interrogations, Confessions, and Entrapment*, ed. G. D. Lassiter, 197–214. New York: Kluwer Press.

Lau, Siu–Kai, P. Wan, and K. Shum. 1999. *Hong Kong Politics: A Bibliography*. Hong Kong: Hong Kong Institute of Asia Pacific Studies, Chinese University of Hong Kong.

Law of the People's Republic of China on State Compensation. 1995. Adopted at the Seventh Meeting of the Standing Committee of the Eighth National People's Congress on May 12, 1994, promulgated by Order No. 23 of the President of the People's Republic of China on May 12, 1994, and effective as of January 1, 1995.

Law Reform Commission of Hong Kong. 1984. Report on Confession Statements and Their Admissibility in Criminal Proceedings [Topic 8], Dec. 14.

Law Reform Commission of Hong Kong. 1992. Report on Arrest [TOPIC 25] August.

Lawrence, R. 2000. *The Politics of Force: Media and the Construction of Police Brutality*. Berkeley, CA: University of California Press.

Lawton, B. 2007. "Levels of Nonlethal Force: An Examination of Individual, Situational, and Contextual Factors." *Journal of Research in Crime and Delinquency* 44: 163–184.

Leen, Jeff, J. Craven, D. Jackson, and S. Horwitz. 1998. "District Police Lead Nation in Shootings." *Washington Post,* November 15.

Leo, R. A. 1996. "Inside the Interrogation Room." *Journal of Criminal Law and Criminology* 86: 266–303.

Leo, R. A. 2001. "Questioning the Relevance of *Miranda* in the Twenty-first Century." *The Michigan Law Review* 99: 1000–1029.

Leo, R. A. 2002. *Miranda,* Confessions and Justice: Lessons for Japan? In *The Japanese Adversary System in Context: Controversies and Comparisons,* ed. M. Feeley and S. Miyazawa, 200–219. London: Palgrave.

Leo, R. A. 2008. *Police Interrogation and American Justice.* Cambridge, MA: Harvard University Press.

Leo, R., M. Costanzo, and N. Shaked-Schroer. 2009. "Psychological and cultural aspects of interrogation and false confessions: Using research to inform legal decision making." In *Psychological Expertise in Court: Psychology in the Courtroom,* (Vol. 2) ed. D. Krauss and J. Lieberman, 25–56. London: Ashgate.

Levine, S., C. Sloane, T. Chan, G. Vilke, and J. Dunford. 2005. "Cardiac Monitoring of Subjects Exposed to the Taser." *American Emergency Medicine* 13 (5): S47.

Lewis, B. 2003. "NIJ's Less-Than-Lethal Flash-Bang Round Project." *Corrections Today* 65: 117–119.

Lexadin. "Penal Code Part 3, Chapter XXVI," The World Law Guide: Legislation Poland, http://www.era.int/domains/corpus-juris/public_pdf/polish_penal_code3.pdf.

Lifton, Robert J. 2000. *The Nazi Doctors: Medical Killing and the Psychology of Genocide.* New York: Basic Books.

Loader, Ian. 1999. "Consumer Culture and the Commodification of Policing and Security." *Sociology* 33 (2): 373–392.

Loader, I. and A. Mulcahy. 2003. *Policing and the Condition of England: Memory, Politics and Culture.* Oxford: Oxford University Press.

Lu, H., and T. D. Miethe. 2003. "Confessions and Criminal Case Disposition in China." *Law and Society Review* 37: 549–578.

Lumb, R. C. and P. C. Friday. 1997. "Impact of Pepper Spray Availability on Police Officer Use of Force Decisions." *Policing: An International Journal of Police Strategies and Management* 20 (1): 173–185.

Lundman, Richard J. 1980. *Police Behavior.* Oxford: Oxford University Press.

Macías, R. C. and J. M. C. Alas. 2007. *The Political Culture of Democracy in El Salvador: 2006.* San Salvador: Proyecto de Opinión Pública de América Latina (LAPOP).

Mackey, S. 1996. *The Iranians: Persia, Islam, and the Soul of a Nation.* New York: Penguin Group.

Malcolm, A. 1990. "Many Police Forces Rearm to Counter Criminals' Guns." *New York Times,* September 4.

Małopolska Policja, "Journal of Laws: Police Act, dated April 6th, 1991," Małopolska Policja, http://www.malopolska.policja.gov.pl/eng/kgp/police_act.pdf. London: Longman.

Manning, P. 1997. "Media Loops." In *Popular Culture, Crime & Justice*, ed. F. Bailey and D. Hale, 25–39. Belmont, CA: Wadsworth.

Mao, Z. 1968. On the Correct Handling of Contradictions Among the People. In Select Works of Mao Tse-tung. *Vol. V. 384–421.* Beijing: Foreign Languages Press.

Mayer, A. 1982. "Adapting to Environmental Jolts." *Administrative Science Quarterly* 27 (4): 515–537.

McCaulay, Fiona. 2002. "Problems of Police Oversight in Brazil." Working Paper Series (CBS-33-02). University of Oxford Centre for Brazilian Studies at Oxford University.

McCulloch, J. 2001. *Blue Army: Paramilitary Policing in Australia.* Carlton: Melbourne University Press.

McDaniel, W. C., R. A. Stratbucker, M. Nerheim, and J. E. Brewer. 2005. "Cardiac Safety of Neuromuscular Incapacitating Defense Devices." *Pacing and Clinical Electrophysiology* 28: 284–287.

McDaniel, W. C., R. A. Stratbucker, and R. Smith. 2000. *Surface Application of TASER Stun Guns Does not Cause Ventricular Fibrillation in Canines.* Proceedings of the Annual International Conference of the IEEE EMBS. Chicago, IL.

McEwen, T. 1997. "Policies on Less-than-Lethal Force in Law Enforcement Agencies." *Policing: An International Journal of Police Strategy and Management* 20 (1): 39–59.

McKenna, M. 2009. "Pursuit of Shock Tactics." *The Australian,* January 13.

McKenzie, I. 2000. "Policing Force: Rules Hierarchies and Consequences." In *Core Issues in Policing*, ed. F. Leishman, B. Loveday, and S. Savage, 183.

McManus, G., J. Griffen, W. Witterroth, M. Boland, and P. Hines. 1970. *Police Training and Performance Study.* Washington, DC: U.S. Government Printing Office.

Meissner, C. A. and S. M. Kassin. 2004. "'You're Guilty, So Just Confess!' Cognitive and Conformational Biases in the Interrogation Room." In *Interrogations, Confessions, and Entrapment,* ed. G. D. Lassiter, 85–106. New York: Kluwer Academic.

Mesloh, C. 2006. "Barks or Bites? The Impact of Training on Police Canine Force Outcomes." *Police Practice and Research* 7: 323–335.

Mesloh, C., R. Wolf, M. Henych, and F. Thompson. 2008. "Less Lethal Weapons for Law Enforcement: A Performance-Based Analysis." *Law Enforcement Executive Forum* 8: 133–149.

Miller, J. 2000. *Shoot and Demonise: The Death of Roni Levi.* South Yarra, AU: Hardie Grant Books.

Miller, S. 2000. "Shootings by Police in Victoria: The Ethical Issues." In *Violence and Police Culture*, ed. T. Coady, S. James, S. Miller, and M. O'Keefe, 205–218. Melbourne: Melbourne University Press.

Miller, S. and J. Blackler. 2005. *Ethical Issues in Policing.* Aldershot, UK: Ashgate.

Milton, C., J. Halleck, J. Lardner, and G. Abrecht. 1977. *Police Use of Deadly force.* Washington, DC: Police Foundation.

Ministry of Public Security. "Ministry of Public Security issued 'Five Prohibitions' effective February 1 (with reporters questions)," *MPS Net,* January 1, 2003, http://www.chinaelections.org/NewsInfo.asp?NewsID=20599.

Ministry of Public Security. "Ministry of Public Security will soon Draft Regulations on the Obstruction of People's Police in the Carrying out of Duties." *enorth. com,* July 20, 2006, http://news.enorth.com.cn/system/2006/07/20/001363275. shtml.

MINUGUA. 2003. *Fourteenth Report on the Verification of Human Rights.* Guatemala: Misión de las Naciones Unidas en Guatemala (MINUGUA).

Miranda v. Arizona 384 U.S. 436 (1966).

Mitchell, Michael J., and C. H. Wood. 1999. "Ironies of Citizenship: Skin Color, Police Brutality, and the Challenge to Democracy in Brazil." *Social Forces* 77: 1001–1020.

Mo, Honge. 2006. "Police Should Only Shoot as Last Resort." *China Daily,* April 12. http://english.gov.cn/2006-04/12/content_251575.htm.

Moor, K. 2005. "Police Shootings Failed Own Tests." *Herald-Sun,* November 25.

Moore, M. 2003. *The "Bottom Line" of Policing: What Citizens should Value (and Measure) in Police Performance.* Washington, DC: Police Executive Research Forum.

Morabito, E. V., and B. Doerner. 1997. "Police Use of Less-than-lethal Force: Oleoresin Capsicum (OC) Spray." *Policing: An International Journal of Police Strategy and Management* 20 (4): 680–697.

Morrison, G. 2003. "Police and Correctional Department Firearm Training Frameworks in Washington State." *Police Quarterly* 6 (2): 192–221.

Morrison, G. 2006a. "Deadly Force Programs Among Larger U.S. Police Departments." *Police Quarterly* 9 (3): 331–361.

Morrison, G. 2006b. "Police Department and Instructor Perspectives on Pre-service Firearm and Deadly Force Training." *Policing: An International Journal of Police Strategies and Management* 29 (2): 226–245.

Morrison, G. 2008. "The FBI's Practical Pistol Course: Police Reform, Officer Safety, and Handgun Training in the Mid-20th Century." *Law Enforcement Executive Forum* 8 (1): 41–64.

Morrison, G., and B. Vila. 1998. "Police Handgun Qualification: Practical Measure or Aimless Activity?" *Policing: An International Journal of Police Strategies and Management* 21 (3): 510–533.

Moser, C. and C. McIlwaine. 2001. *Violence in a Post-Conflict Context. Urban Poor Perceptions from Guatemala.* Washington, DC: The World Bank.

Moser, Caroline and B. van Bronkhorst. 1999. "Youth Violence in Latin America and the Caribbean: Costs, Causes, and Interventions." LCR Sustainable Development Working Paper 3, Urban Peace Program Series, http://www.american.edu/councils/americas/Documents/GangViolence/moser_bronkhorst_violence_wb_paper.pdf.

Muir, W. K. Jr. 1977. *Police: Streetcorner Politicians*. Chicago: University of Chicago Press.

Mulroy, D. and J. Santiago. 1998. "Warning Shots Revisited." *Law and Order* 46 (4): 96–99.

NACLA. 2007. In Tegucigalpa, the Iron Fist Fails. *NACLA Report on the Americas* 40 (4): 26–29.

Næshagen, F. 2000. "Norway's Democratic and Conservative Tradition in Policing." *Scandinavian Journal of History* 25: 177–95.

Nathan, A. 2007. Political culture and diffuse regime support in Asia. *Global Barometer*. Working Paper 43, Asian Barometer Project, National Taiwan University.

National Commission on Law Observance and Enforcement. 1931. *Report on Lawlessness In Law-Enforcement*. Vol. 11. Washington, DC: U.S. Government Printing Office.

National Guidelines: Police Use of Lethal Force. 1994. Payneham (SA): National Police Research Unit, Report Series 123.

National Institute of Justice. 1999. *Use of Force by Police: Overview of National and Local Data*. Washington, DC: U.S. Department of Justice.

National Institute of Justice. 2003. *The Effectiveness and Safety of Pepper Spray*. Washington, DC: Department of Justice.

National Institute of Justice. 2004a. *Department of Defense Nonlethal Weapons and Equipment Review: Special Report*. Washington, DC: Department of Defense.

National Institute of Justice. 2004b. *Law Enforcement Technology–Are Small and Rural Agencies Equipped and Trained?* Washington, DC: Department of Justice.

National Institute of Justice. 2007. "Types of Less-Lethal Devices," National Institute of Justice, http://www.ojp.usdoj.gov/nij/topics/technology/less-lethal/types.htm.

National Institute of Justice. 2008a. *Study of Deaths Following Electro Muscular Disruption: Interim Report*. Washington, DC: Department of Justice.

National Institute of Justice. 2008b. "NIJ In-Custody Death Study: The Impact of Use of Conducted Energy Devices," National Institute of Justice, http://www.ojp.usdoj.gov/nij/topics/technology/less-lethal/incustody-deaths.htm.

National Security Research, Inc. 2003. *Department of Defense Non-Lethal Weapons and Equipment Review: A Research Guide for Civil Law Enforcement and Corrections*. Washington, DC: Department of Defense.

Newburn, T. 2002. "Atlantic Crossings: Policy Transfer and Crime Control in the USA and Britain." *Punishment and Society* 4 (2): 165–194.

New York Times. 2000. "Despite Diallo. Data Show Gun Restraint," February 4.

New York Times. 2004. "Claims over Tasers' Safety are Challenged," November 26.

Neyroud, P. 2003. "Policing and Ethics." In *Handbook of Policing*, ed. T. Newburn, 585. Cullumpton, Devon, UK: Willan Publishing.

Neyroud, P and Beckley, A. 2001. *Policing, Ethics and Human Rights*. Cullumpton, Devon, UK: Willan Publishing.

Nielson, E. 1981. *Salt Lake City Police Department Deadly Force Policy: Shooting and Post Shooting Reactions*. Salt Lake City, UT: Salt Lake City Police Department.

NOLO.com. "Criminal Homicide," nolo.com, http://www.nolo.com/definition.cfm/ Term/51AB22D3-86AB-4B55-8648BC28B45909C0/alpha/H/.

Norée, A. 2004. *Polisers Rätt att Skjuta*. Stockholm: Norstedts Juridik.

Norée, A. 2005. Svenska Polisers Rätt att Skjuta. In *Polisens bruk av skjutvapen i Norden*, ed. J. Knutsson. Oslo: Politihøgskolen.

Nowicki, E. 1993. "Oleoresin Capsicum: A Non-lethal Force Alternative." *Law Enforcement Technology* 20 (1): 24–27.

Nucleus for the Study of Violence. "Número de Homicidios e Taxa por 100 mil Habitantes, Segundo as Capitais–Brasil 1991–1997." Núcleo de Esutdos da Vioféncia, University of São Paulo, February 14, 1997.

Ofshe, R. J. and R. A. Leo. 1997." The Decision to Confess Falsely: Rational Choice and Irrational Action." *Denver University Law Review* 74: 979–1122.

Oliver, B. 2003. *Unity Is Strength: A History of the Australian Labour Party and the Trades and Labour Council in Western Australia 1899–1999*. Perth, AU: API Network.

O'Loughlin, N. and P. Billing. 2000. "Positive Police Culture: Correcting Perceptions." In *Violence and Police Culture*, ed. T. Coady, S. James, S. Miller, and M. O'Keefe, 63–84. Melbourne: Melbourne University Press.

O'Neill, Mark. 2007. "China's Bad Comrade Cops." *Asian Sentinel*, November 22. http://www.asiasentinel.com/index.php?Itemid=31&id=892&option=com_content&task=view.

Ordog, G., J. Wasserberger, T. Schlater, and S. Balasubramanium. 1987. "Electronic Gun (Taser) Injuries." *Annals of Emergency Medicine* 16 (1): 73–78.

Ordog, G., P. Dornhoffer, G. Ackroyd, J. Wasserberger, M. Bishop, W. Shoemaker, and S. Balasubramanium. 1994. "Spent Bullets and Their Injuries: The Result of Firing Weapons into the Sky." *Journal of Trauma: Injury Infection and Critical Care* 37 (6): 1003–1006.

Owen-Kostelnik, J., N. D. Reppucci, and J. R. Meyer. 2006. "Testimony and Interrogation of Minors: Assumptions about Maturity and Morality." *American Psychologist* 61: 286–304.

Packer, H. L. 1968. *The Limits of the Criminal Sanction*. Stanford, CA: Stanford University Press.

Palmer, S. H. 1988. *Police and Protest in England and Ireland, 1780–1850*. Cambridge, UK: Cambridge University Press.

Paoline, E. A. III and W. Terrill. 2007. "Police Education, Experience, and the Use of Force." *Criminal Justice & Behavior* 34 (2): 179–196.

Patton, M. 2002. *Qualitative Research and Evaluation Methods*. 3rd ed. Thousand Oaks, CA: Sage Publications.

People's Daily. 2007. "Three Chinese Police Officers Killed in Gunfight Near Border," *People's Daily,* March 27. http://search.people.com.cn/was40/people/GB/english_index.jsp?type=1&channel=.

People's Police Law of the People's Republic of China. 1995. Adopted at the 12th meeting of the Standing Committee of the Eighth National People's Congress on February 28, 1995, promulgated by order No. 40 of the President of the People's Republic of China on February 28, 1995.

PepperBall Technologies, Inc. 2008. "Less-Lethal Products," PepperBall Technologies, Inc., http://www.pepperball.com/le/products.aspx.os.

Perez, O. 2003. "Democratic Legitimacy and Public Insecurity: Crime and Democracy in El Salvador and Guatemala." *Political Science Quarterly* 118 (4): 627–644.

Perske, R. 2008. "False Confessions From 53 Persons With Intellectual Disabilities: The List Keeps Growing." *Intellectual and Developmental Disabilities* 46: 468–479.

Peters, D. 2006. "Public Acquiescence of Police Brutality and Extrajudicial Killings in São Paulo, Brazil." PhD diss., University of Nevada, Reno.

Petty, C. S. 2004. *Deaths in Police Confrontation when Oleoresin Capsicum Is Used.* Washington, DC: National Institute of Justice.

Phillips, S. W. 1994. *Oleoresin Capsicum in Buffalo, Technical Report 04-95.* Ottawa: Canadian Police Research Centre.

Pieprzny, Stanisław. 2003. *Organization and Functioning.* Policja. Kraków.

Pilant, L. 1993. *Less-than-Lethal Weapons: New Solutions for Law Enforcement.* Alexandria, VA: International Association of Chiefs of Police.

Podgórski, Mariusz. 2007. *Means of Direct Force and Firearms.* Piła.

Police Executive Research Forum (PERF). 2005. *PERF Conducted Energy Device Policy and Training Guidelines for Consideration.* Washington, DC: PERF Center on Force and Accountability.

Police Journal. 2007. "Learn from the Tragedy of the Slain Patrol Crew." October, 12–13.

Police Service of Northern Ireland. "Policy Directive 12/08: Police Use of Firearms," Police Service of Northern Ireland, http://www.psni.police.uk/policy_directive_1208_police_use_of_firearms.pdf.

Politiets videnscenter. 2007. *Politiets Anvendelse av Skydevåben. En Tværfaglig Analyse av Perioden 2002–2006.* Rigspolitiets trykkeri: Rigspolitiet.

Pomykała, M., and R. Kazimierz. 2005. *Management of the Protection of Public Security and Order in a State: Selected Legal and Organizational Aspects of the Operation of the Police.* Rzeszów.

P.R.C. 1980. "Provisions for the Use of Weapons and Police Instruments by the People's Police." Approved by the State Council on 5 July 1980, and promulgated by the Ministry of Public Security on 15 July 1980.

P.R.C. 1981. "Measures for the Control of Weapons of 1981." Approved by the State Council on 5 January 1981 and promulgated by the Ministry of Public Security.

P.R.C. 1996. "Law of the People's Republic of China on Control of Guns." Adopted at the 20th Meeting of the Standing Committee of the Eighth National People's Congress on July 5, 1996, promulgated by Order No. 72 of the President of the People's Republic of China.

Principios. "Jovens Assassinados no Rio de Janeiro sao de Maioria Negra," Vermelho, http://www.vermelho.org.br/diario/2006/0321/0321_negros_rj.asp.

Ramos, Sylvia, "Police Violence in Rio de Janeiro: From Beatings to the Use of Lethal Force," *Rede Social* de Judica e Direitos Humanos, http://www.social.org.br/relatorioingles2005/relatorio010.htm.

Ramseyer, J. M. and E. B. Rasmusen. 2001. "Why is the Japanese Conviction Rate So High?" *Journal of Legal Studies* 30: 53–88.

Rappert, B. 2002a. "Assessing Chemical Incapacitant Sprays." *International Journal of Police Science Management* 4 (2): 115–126.

Rappert, B. 2002b. "Constructions of Legitimate Force: The Case of CS Sprays." *The British Journal of Criminology* 42 (4): 689–708.

Ready, J., M. D. White, and C. F. Fisher. 2008. "Shock Value: A Comparative Analysis of News Reports and Official Police Records on TASER Deployments." *Policing: An International Journal of Police Strategies and Management* 31 (1): 148–170.

Reaves, B. and M. Hickman. 2004. *Law Enforcement Management and Administrative statistics, 2000: Data for Individual State and Local Agencies with 100 or More Officers.* Washington, DC: US Department of Justice, Bureau of Justice Statistics.

Redlich, A. D. 2004. "Mental Illness, Police Interrogations, and the Potential for False Confession." *Psychiatric Services* 55: 19–21.

Redlich, A. D. 2007. "Military vs. Police Interrogations: Similarities and Differences." *Peace and Conflict* 13: 423–428.

Redlich, A. D. and S. Drizin. 2007. "Police Interrogation of Youth." In *The Mental Health Needs of Young Offenders: Forging Paths through Reintegration and Rehabilitation,* ed. C. L. Kessler and L. Kraus, 61–78. Cambridge, UK: Cambridge University Press.

Reedy, D. and C. Koper. 2003. "Impact of Handgun Types on Gun Assault Outcomes: A Comparison of Gun Assaults Involving Semiautomatic Pistols and Revolvers." *Injury Prevention* 9: 151–155.

Reiner, R. 2000. *The Politics of the Police.* Oxford: Oxford University Press.

Reiss, A. J. Jr. 1971. *The Police and the Public.* New Haven, CT: Yale University Press.

Reuters World Service. 1997. "Brazil Worst for Police Violence in Americas." Rio de Janeiro, April 6.

Richmond, T., C. Branas, R. Cheney, and C. Schwab. 2004. "The Case for Enhanced Data Collection of Gun Type." *Journal of Trauma: Injury Infection and Critical Care* 57 (6): 1356–1360.

Robin, G. 1963. "Justifiable Homicide by Police Officers." *Journal of Criminal Law, Criminology and Police Science* 3: 225–231.

Rogers, T. and S. Johnson. 2000. "Less than Lethal: An Analysis of the Impact of Oleoresin Capsicum." *International Journal of Police Science and Management* 3 (1): 55–67.

Rostker, B., L. Hanser, W. Hix, C. Jensen, A. Morral, G. Ridgeway, and T. Schell. 2008. *Evaluation of the New York City Police Department Firearm Training and Firearm-discharge Review Process.* Santa Monica, CA: RAND Corporation.

Roy, O. and A. Podgorski. 1989. "Tests on a Shocking Device—The Stun Gun." *Medical and Biological Engineering and Computing* 27: 445–448.

Ruddick, J. A. 1993. *A Toxicological Review of Capsaicinoid (Oloresin of Capsicums)*. Technical Report 02-93, Canadian Police Research Center, Ottawa.

Russ, G. 2005. "Chinese Court Bars Evidence Obtained through Torture." *Jurist Legal News and Research*, April 14. http://jurist.law.pitt.edu/.

Russell, M. 2009. "Renewed Calls for Police to Get Stun Guns." *Sunday Age*, January 4.

Ryan, E. 2008. "Stunning Developments: Some Implications of Tasers in Australia." In *Proceedings of the 2nd Australian and New Zealand Critical Criminology Conference*, ed. C. Cuneen and M. Salter, 342–361. Sydney: Crime and Justice Network.

Ryder, C. 1989. *The RUC: A Force Under Fire*. London: Methuen.

Sarre, R. 1993. *Police Use of Firearms: Issues in Safety*. Adelaide: University of South Australia.

Sced, M. 2006. "Mental Illness in the Community: The Role of Police." *Australasian Centre for Policing Research Issues* 3: 1–12.

Schade, T., G. Bruns, and G. Morrison. 1989. "Armed Confrontations: Police Shooting Performance in Dangerous Encounters." *American Journal of Police* 8 (2): 31–48.

Scheper-Hughes, Nancy Hoffman, and D. Hoffman. 1994. "Kids Out of Place." *NACLA* 27 (6): 16–23.

Scherer, M. and M. Benjamin. 2003. "Standard Operating Procedure." *Salon*, October 25. http://www.salon.com.

Schneider, C. and P. Amar. 2003. "The Rise of Crime, Disorder and Authoritarian Policing. An Introductory Essay." *NACLA report on the Americas* 37 (2): 12–16.

Scobell, A. 2003. *China's Use of Military Force: Beyond the Great Wall and the Long March*. Cambridge, UK: Cambridge University Press.

Scott, M. and S. Lyman. 1968. "Accounts." *American Sociological Review* 33: 46–62.

Seattle Police Department, "SPD Special Report: Use of Force by Seattle Police Department Officers," Seattle Police Department, http://www.seattle.gov/police/publications/useforce/default.htm.

Seattle Police Department. 2004. "Seattle Police Department TASER Use and Deployment Fact Sheet," Seattle Police Department, http://www.taser.com/documents/seattlepduse.pdf.

Sellin, T. 1938. "Culture Conflict and Crime." *The Social Science Research Council Bulletin* 41: 63–70.

Seron, J. P., and J. Kovath. 2004. "Judging Police Misconduct: Street-Level versus Professional Policing." *Law & Society Review* 38 (4): 665–710. New York: Praeger.

Sharf, P., and A. Binder. 1983. *The Badge and the Bullet: Police Use of Deadly Force*.

She, Lingyun. 2003. The Status, Cause and Response to Obstruction of Police in the Execution of Duties. Law School of Huazhong University of Science and Technology, via http://www.hustlaw.cn/Acade/Print.asp?ArticleID=3722.

Shearing, C. and R. Ericson. 1991. "Culture as Figurative Action." *British Journal of Sociology* 42 (4): 481–506.

Shepherd, J. 2005. "Deterrence versus Brutalization: Capital Punishment's Differing Impacts among States." *Michigan Law Review* 104: 203–256.

Sherman, L. 1993. "Defiance, Deterrence, and Irrelevance: A Theory of the Criminal Sanction." *Journal of Research in Crime and Delinquency* 30 (4): 445–473.

Sherman, L. and E. Cohn. 1986. *Citizens Killed by Big City Police, 1970–1984.* Washington, DC: Crime Control Institute.

Silvester, J. 2008a. "Police Use of Capsicum Spray Soars." *The Age*, March 3.

Silvester, J. 2008b. "Shooting Reignites Debate on Police Tactics and use of Taser Stun Guns." *The Age,* December 13.

Silvester, J., A. Rule, and O. Davies. 1995. *The Silent War: Behind the Police Killings that Shook Australia.* Sydney: Floradale Productions.

Sinclair, G. 2006. *At the End of the Line: Colonial Policing and the Imperial Endgame 1945–80.* Manchester, UK: Manchester University Press.

Sjskw.com. "The Protection and Limitation of Police Right to Open Fire," sjskw.com. http://www.sjskw.com/Article_Print.asp?ArticleID=1016.

Skolnick, Jerome H. and J. J. Fyfe. 1993. *Above the Law: Police and the Excessive Use of Force.* New York: Praeger.

Smith, M. R. and G. P. Alpert. 2000. "Pepper Spray: A Safe and Reasonable Response to Suspect Verbal Resistance." *Policing: An International Journal of Police Strategies and Management* 23 (20): 233–245.

Smith, M. R., R. J. Kaminski, J. Rojek, G. P. Alpert, and J. Mathis. 2007. "The Impact of Conducted Energy Devices and Other Types of Force and Resistance on Police and Suspect Injuries." *Policing: An International Journal of Police Strategies and Management* 30 (3): 443–426.

Soares, Fabio Veras, "Some Stylized Facts of the Informal Sector in Brazil in the Last Two Decades," ANPEC. http://www.anpec.org.br/encontro2004/artigos/A04A142.pdf.

Soares, Filho, Adauto, M. F. M. de Souza, C. Gazal-Carvalho, D. C Malta, A. P. Alencar, M. M. A. de Silva, and O. L. de Morais Neto. 2007. "Análise da Mortalidade por Homicídios no Brasil." *Epidemiol. Serv. Saúde* 16 (1): 7–18.

Solomon, R. and J. Horn. 1986. "Post-shooting Traumatic Reactions: A Pilot Study." In *Psychological Services for Law Enforcement. Officers*, ed. J. Reese and H. Goldstein, 383–393. Washington, DC: U.S. Government Printing Office.

Southern Weekly Magazine. 2008. "Police is a High Psychological Risk Profession." *Southern Weekly Magazine*, November 26. http://x.copcn.com/space.php?uid=1000922&do=blog&id=8398937.

Souza, Vinicious and Maria Eugenia Sa. "Crime Rate Decreases in São Paulo and Bogotá," Worldpress.org, http://www.worldpress.org/Americas/2119.cfm.

Stanley, W. 1996. "International Tutelage and Domestic Political Will: Building a New Civilian Police Force in El Salvador." In *Policing Change, Changing Police: International Perspectives,* ed. O. Marenin, 37–77. New York: Garland.

Stanley, W. 2000. *Building New Police Forces in El Salvador and Guatemala: Learning and Counter-learning.* Paper prepared for the 22nd international congress of Latin American Studies Association, Miami, FL.

Stanley, W. and C. Call. 1997. "Building a New Civilian Police Force in El Salvador." In *Rebuilding Societies after Civil War: Critical Roles for International Assistance*, ed. K. Kumar, 107–133. Boulder: Lynne Rienner Publishers.

Stanley, W., G. Vickers, and J. Spence. 1996. *Protectors or Perpetrators? The Institutional Crises of the Salvadoran Civilian Police*. Cambridge, MA: Hemisphere Initiatives; Washington, DC: Washington Office on Latin America.

Stark, R. 1972. *Police Riots: Collective Violence and Law Enforcement*. Belmont, CA: Wadsworth.

Statistics Norway. "Crime Statistics 2004," Official statistics of Norway, http://www.ssb.no/emner/03/05/nos_kriminal/nos_d388/nos_d388.pdf.

Steffee, C. H., P. E. Lantz, L. M. Flannagan, R. L. Thompson, and D. R. Jason. 1995. "Oleoresin Capsicum (Pepper) Spray and 'In-custody Deaths.'" *The American Journal of Forensic Medicine and Pathology* 16 (3): 185–92.

Stetser, M. 2001. *The Use of Force in Police Control of Violence: Incidents Resulting in Assaults on Officers*. New York: LBF Scholarly Publishing.

Stratbucker, R., R. Roeder, and M. Nerheim. 2003. "Cardiac Safety of High Voltage Taser X26 Waveform." Proceedings of the 25th Annual International Conference of the IEEE EMBS, Cancun, Mexico, 3261–3262.

Stratton, J. G., D. Parker, and J. R. Snibbe. 1984. "Post-traumatic Stress: Study of Police Officers Involved in Shootings." *Psychological Reports* 55: 127–131.

Strote, J., R. Campbell, J. Pease, M. S. Hamman, and R. Hutson. 2006. "The Role of Tasers in Police Restraint-related Deaths." *Annals of Emergency Medicine* 46 (3): S85.

Strype, J. 2005. Arming and Use of Firearms in the Norwegian Police. In *Politiets Bruk avSkytevåpen in Norden [Police Use of Firearms in the Nordic Countries]*, ed. J. Knutsson, 93–106. Oslo: Politihøgskolen.

Strype, J. and J. Knutsson. 2002. *Politiets Bruk av Skytevåpen [Police Use of Firearms]*. Oslo: Politihøgskolen.

Sullivan, T. P. 2004. "The Police Experience: Recording Custodial Interrogations." *The Champion* 28: 24–27.

Sunday Age. 2008. "Police Firearms Protocol Called into Question," December 14.

Supreme People's Court of P.R.C. 1983. Provisions Regarding People's Police Legitimate Self-defense Conduct in the Line of Duty.

Tang, W. 2005. *Public Opinion and Political Change in China*. Palo Alto, CA: Stanford University Press.

TASER International. 2006. "TASER Non-lethal Weapons: Field Data as of July 2006," Taser International. http://www.taser.com/facts/documents/Injury_Reduction_Stats_2Q_2006.ppt.

TASER International, Inc. 2008. "Taser C2," TASER International. http://www.taser.com/PRODUCTS/CONSUMERS/Pages/C2.aspx.

Tennessee v. Garner 471 U.S. 1 (1985).

Terrill, W. and E. A. Paoline III. 2006. *"Police Use of Force Policy Types: Results from a National Agency Survey."* Paper presented at the American Society of Criminology, Los Angeles, CA.

Terrill, W. and E. A. Paoline III. 2008. *Preliminary Findings from the Assessing Police Use of Force Policy and Outcomes Study.* Paper presented at the National Institute of Justice Conference, Washington, DC.

Terrill, W. and M. D. Reisig. 2003. "Neighborhood Context and Police Use of Force." *Journal of Research in Crime and Delinquency* 40 (3): 291–321.

The Age. 1994. "Police Shootings: Coroner Hits Culture of Risk," June 21.

The Age. 2003. "Westgate Bridge Drama," September 17.

The Age. 2005. "Police Shootings: Sorting Rights and Wrongs," April 22.

The Age. 2008. "Police to Get Semi-Automatics," June 6.

The Police Association. 2007. "Special Report: Semi-Automatic Pistols, A Case for Change." *Victoria Police Association Journal* 73 (6): 14–16.

Timmer, J. and G. Beijers. 1998. Geweldsmeldingen 1996–1997 Centrum voor Politiewetenschappen VU, Amsterdam.

Ting, H. 1988. Use of Firearms in the Royal Hong Kong Police: An Examination of Pattern and Police Attitudes. M.S. diss., Hong Kong University.

Toch, H. 1995. "The Violence-Prone Police Officer" In *Police Violence: Understanding and Controlling Police Abuse of Force,* ed. W. Geller and H. Toch, 94–112. Washington, DC: Police Executive Research Forum.

Torres, Horaldo da Gama, E. Marques, M. P. Ferreira, and S. Bitar. 2002. "Poverty and Space: Patterns of Segregation in São Paulo." Paper presented in workshop on "Spatial Segregation and Urban Inequality in Latin America," University of Texas, Austin, November 15–16.

Townshend, C. 1992. "Policing Insurgency in Ireland, 1914–23." In *Policing and Decolonisation: Politics, Nationalism and the Police, 1917–65,* ed. D. M. Anderson and D. Killingray. Manchester, UK: Manchester University Press.

Tuch, S. A. and R. Weitzer. 1997. "Racial Differences in Attitudes Toward the Police." *Public Opinion Quarterly* 61: 643–63.

Tuckey, M. 2004. *National Guidelines for Incident Management, Conflict Resolution and Use of Force: 2004.* Adelaide: Australian Centre for Policing Research.

Tyler, T. R. 2006. *Why People Obey the Law.* Princeton, NJ: Princeton University Press.

Tyler, T. R. and Y. J. Huo. 2002. *Trust in the Law: Encouraging Public Cooperation with the Police and Courts.* New York: Russell Sage Foundation.

Uelman, G. 1973. Varieties of police policy: A study of police policy regarding the use of deadly force in Los Angeles County." Loyala-L.A. Law Review 6: 1–61.

UNAH. 2008. *Observatorio de Violencia. Mortalidad y Otros.* Edition 9, April 2008. Tegucigalpa: Universidad Nacional Autónoma de Honduras.

UNDP. 2005. *Overcoming Fear: Citizen (In)security and Human Development in Costa Rica.* National Human Development Report. San José, CR: United Nations Development Program.

UNDP. 2006. "Delincuencia, Inseguridad Ciudadana y Ciudadana Social." In *Informe sobre Desarrollo Humano, Honduras. Hacia la expansión de la ciudadaní,* 127–146. Tegucigalpa: United Nations Development Program.

USA Today. 2008. "Fatal Shooting by Police Sparks Montreal Riot," August 11.

U.S. Department of State. 1999. *Human Rights Reports*. Washington, DC: U.S. Government Printing Office.

U.S. Department of State. 2005a. "Japan: Country Reports on Human Rights Practices," U.S. Department of State, http://www.state.gov/g/drl/rls/hrrpt/2005/61610.htm.

U.S. Department of State. 2005b. "Mexico: Country Reports on Human Rights Practices," U.S. Department of State, http://www.state.gov/g/drl/rls/hrrpt/2005/62736.htm.

U.S. Department of State. 2008. "Brazil: Country Reports on Human Rights Practices." Washington, DC: GAO.

U.S. Government Accountability Office. 2005. *Taser Weapons: Use of Tasers by Selected Law Enforcement Agencies.* Washington, DC: Report to the Chairman, Subcommittee on National Security, Emerging Threats and International relations, Committee on Government Reform, House of Representatives.

Valladares, Licia and E. Preteceille. 2003a. "Sistema Urbano, Mercado de Trabalho e Violência no Brasil e no Rio de Janeiro." Relatório final do projeto "Latin American Urbanization in the Late Twentieth Century: a comparative study," Alejandro Portes and Brian Roberts research coordinators.

Valladares, Licia and E. Preteceille. 2003b. "Analise e Problemas Metodologicos no Estudo do Sistema Urbano, do Mercado de Trabalho e da Violencia Urbana: O Caso do Brasil." Research Project on Urbanization.

Victoria Police. 1997. Annual Report 1996–1997.

Victoria Police Gazette. April 28, 1997.

Vienna Convention on Diplomatic Relations, 18 April 1961.

Vila, B. and G. Morrison. 1994. "Biological Limits to Police Combat Handgun-shooting Accuracy." *American Journal of Police* 13 (1) 1–30.

Vilke, G. M., and T. C. Chan. 2007. "Less Lethal Technology: Medical Issues." *Policing: An International Journal of Police Strategies and Management* 30:341–357.

Wacks, R., editor. 1993. *Police Powers in Hong Kong.* Hong Kong: University of Hong Kong School of Law.

Waddington, P. A. J. 1990. "'Overkill' or 'Minimum Force'?" *Criminal Law Review* 695–707.

Waddington, P. A. J. 1991. *The Strong Arm of the Law.* Oxford, UK: Clarendon.

Waddington, P. A. J. 1999b. "Police (Canteen) Sub-Culture: An Appreciation." *British Journal of Criminology.* 39 (2): 287–309.

Waddington, P. A. J. 1999a. *Policing Citizens: Authority and Rights.* London: UCL Press.

Wake Forest University Baptist Medical Center. 2007. "Nationwide Independent Taser Study Results Suggest Devices Are Safe." Press release. October 18. http://www1.wfubmc.ed/news/articleID=2165.

Waldren, M. J. 2007. *Armed Police: The Police Use of Firearms Since 1945.* Stroud, Gloucestershire: Sutton.

Walker, S., and C. M. Katz. 2002. *The Police in America: An Introduction.* New York:

Walsh, Sharon. 1999. "Foreign Gun Firms Find Rich Market for Goods They Can't Sell at Home," *San Francisco Chronicle,* September 25.

Walters, B. 2005. "Accounting for Lethal Force." *The Age,* April 8.

Warren, C. 2002. "Qualitative Interviewing." In *Handbook of Interview Research,* ed. J. Gubrium and J. Holstein, 83–102. Thousand Oaks, CA: Sage Publications.

Washburn, G. 2007. "City Council Settles Burge Police Torture Cases." *Chicago Tribune,* July 13.

Watson, M. 2001. "When Police Officers Kill." *New Law Journal,* August 17.

Webster, D. 2004. "The Murder of Australian Police." *Australian Police Journal* 58 (3): 137–141.

Weisburd, D., R. Greenspan, H. Rosann, E. E. Hamilton, H. Williams, and K. A. Bryant. 2000. *Police Attitudes Toward Abuse of Authority: Findings from A National Study.* Washington, DC: National Institute of Justice Research in Brief.

Weiss-Laxer, Nomi. 2006. "Crafting Copacabana: Images of Security and Strategies of Exclusion in Brazil's Tourism Capital." Master's thesis, Tulane University.

White, M. 2001. "Controlling Police Decisions to Use Deadly Force: Reexamining the Importance of Administrative Policy." *Crime and Delinquency* 47 (1): 131–151.

White, M. 2002. "Identifying Situational Predictors of Police Shooting Using Multivariate Analysis." *Policing: An International Journal of Police Strategies and Management* 25 (4): 726–751.

White, M. 2003. "Examining the Impact of External Influences on Police Use of Deadly Force over Time." *Evaluation Review* 27 (1): 50–78.

White, M., and J. Ready. 2007. "The TASER as a Less Lethal Force Alternative: Findings on Use and Effectiveness in a Large Metropolitan Police Agency." *Police Quarterly* 10 (2): 170–191.

White, M., and J. Ready. 2008. "The Impact of the Taser on Suspect Resistance: Identifying the Predictors of Effectiveness." *Crime & Delinquency.* 56 (1): 70–102.

White, M. D., and D. Klinger. 2009. "'Contagious Fire?' An Empirical Assessment of the 'Problem' of Multi-shooter/multi-shot Deadly Force Incidents in Police Work." *Crime and Delinquency.* In press. Pre-published in OnlineFirst June 24, 2008 as DOI:10.1177/0011128708319581

White, M. D., and J. Saunders. 2010. "Race, Bias and Police Use of the TASER: Exploring the Available Evidence." In *Race, Ethnicity and Policing: The Issues, Methods, Research and Future,* ed. S. Rice and M. D. White. New York: New York University Press.

White, R., and S. Perrone. 2005. *Crime and Social Control.* Oxford: Oxford University Press.

Williams, D. 1994. *Evaluation of Pepper Spray for the Winnipeg Police Department, Technical Memorandum 11-94.* Ottawa: Canadian Police Research Centre.

Williams, G. 2000. "Acceptable Casualties versus Reasonable Risk." *Law and Order* 48 (10): 171–174.

Williams, P., and K. Walter. 1997. *Militarization and Demilitarization in El Salvador's Transition to Democracy.* Pittsburgh: University of Pittsburgh Press.

WOLA. 1995. "Demilitarizing Public Order. The International Community, Police Reform and Human Rights in Central America and Haiti." Washington, DC: Washington Office on Latin America.

WOLA. 2006a. "Police Reform and the Rule of Law in Central America." *A WOLA Special Report,* 8–14. Washington, DC: Washington Office on Latin America.

WOLA. 2006b. "Social Cleansing and Extra Judicial Execution: A Human Right Challenge. "*A WOLA Special Report,* 15–19. Washington, DC: Washington Office on Latin America.

Wong, K. C. 2000. "An Assault on Thuggery," *South China Morning Post,* January 3.

Wong, Kam C. 2009. *Chinese Policing: History and Reform.* New York: Peter Lang.

Wood, D. 2001. "QUAD: Response to Active Shooter Situations." *Law & Order* 49: 77–80.

Worden, R. 1995. "The Causes of Police Brutality: Theory and Evidence on Police Use of Force." In *And Justice for All Understanding and Controlling Police Abuse of Force,* ed. W. Geller and H. Toch, 31–60. Washington, DC: Police Executive Research Forum.

Worden, R. E. 1996. "The Causes of Police Brutality: Theory and Evidence on Police Use of Force." In *Police Violence: Understanding and Controlling Police Abuse of Force,* ed. W. A. Geller and H. Toch, 23–51. New Haven, CT: Yale University Press.

Yi, Shishan. 2008. "Public Security Bureau Chief Charged with 'Illegal Possession of Gun Ammunitions' Attract Debate." *Dang Fang Fa Yan,* July 1. http://www.dffy.com/sifashijian/al/200807/20080701063820.htm. http://www.chinadaily.com.cn/china/2006-04/06/content_561164.htm.

YouGov.com, "YouGov/Mirror/GMTV Survey Results," YouGov.com. http://www.yougov.co.uk/extranets/ygarchives/content/pdf/OMI050101074_1.pdf

Zelditch Jr., M. 2006. "Legitimacy Theory." In *Contemporary Social Psychological Theories,* ed. P. J. Burke, 324–352. Palo Alto, CA: Stanford University Press.

Zenker, Ana Luiza. "Negros São Maioria Nas Favelas, Segundo Estudo do Ipea." *Agencia Brasil,* December 16, 2008.

Zheng, Caixiong. 2004. "Police Shooting of Suspects Sparks Debate." *China Daily* April 6.

Zimbardo, P. 2007. *The Lucifer Effect: Understanding How Good People Turn Evil.* New York: Random House.

Zwanzinger, H. 1998. *Pfefferspray: Einsatzerfahrungen in Osterreich 1994 bis 1998.* Bundesministerium des Inneren, Wien.

Index

About the Editors and Contributors

OTTO ADANG is Chair, public order management at the Police Academy of the Netherlands and Visiting Professor at the University of Liverpool (UK). Since 1998, he has headed the research program "Managing Dangerous Situations," which focuses on police-public interactions in potentially violent or dangerous situations. He has worked on research and evaluation projects and consulted with police forces across Europe and published extensively on public order management, football hooliganism, and police use of force.

DAVID BAKER is Head, Criminal Justice, Monash University, Gippsland, Australia. Previously, he was a lecturer in Monash's Police Studies and Criminology departments and a Training Instructor at the Victoria Police Academy. He is the author of *Batons and Blockades: Policing Industrial Disputes in Australasia* (2005) and his other research publications relate to the policing of dissent, histories of policing, comparative policing, transnational policing, police use of force, and police unionism.

JYOTI BELUR is a Research Associate at the Jill Dando Institute of Crime Science, University College London. Before completing her Ph.D. on the Police Use of Deadly Force from the London School of Economics, she served as a senior officer of the Indian Police Service for over 7 years. Dr. Belur's research interests include police racism, domestic violence, police use of force, Islamic radicalization, organized crime, and policing terrorism.

JOHN W. BUTTLE is a Senior Lecturer for the Department of Social Sciences at Auckland University of Technology in New Zealand. He earned his

Ph.D. in Criminology from the University of Wales, Bangor. John has written on how the police are trained to use force in England and Wales with a specific focus on how nonlethal weapons such as CS spray are utilized. Currently, his research has focused on rural policing and police reform in the social context of New Zealand.

MARK COSTANZO is Professor of Psychology and co-director of the Center for Applied Psychological Research at Claremont McKenna College. He has published research on a variety of law-related topics including police interrogations, false confessions, jury decision making, sexual harassment, attorney argumentation, alternative dispute resolution, and the death penalty. His books include *Psychology Applied to Law* (2004) and *Just Revenge: Costs and Consequences of the Death Penalty* (1997). He frequently serves as an expert witness and is recipient of the Outstanding Teaching and Mentoring Award from the Society for the Psychological Study of Social Issues.

MARIE-LOUISE GLEBBEEK, Assistant Professor of Cultural Anthropology at the Utrecht University in the Netherlands, studies police reform in post-civil war Guatemala, which resulted in her published Ph.D. dissertation, *In the Crossfire of Democracy: Police Reform and Police Practice in Post-Civil War Guatemala* (2003; 2004), and in several articles, among the most recent, "Post-War Violence and Police Reform in Guatemala" (in *Policing Insecurity: Police Reform, Security, and Human Rights in Latin America,* edited by Niels Uildriks, 2009). Her latest co-edited book (with Martha K. Huggins), *Women Fielding Danger: Negotiating Ethnographic Identities in Field Research*, on the gendered, ethnic/national, class/caste, and ethical challenges to field research was published in 2009 (Rowman & Littlefield). Her current research focuses on violence, crime, and citizens' security in Central America.

MARTHA K. HUGGINS, Charles A. and Leo M. Favrot Professor of Human Relations in sociology at Tulane University, is a core faculty member of Tulane's Roger Thayer Stone Center for Latin American Studies. A scholar of Brazil for 34 years, Huggins has taught at three Brazilian universities, published seven books (two of these also published in Brazil), and numerous academic articles on South America's largest country. Among Huggins' books, two have each received two "distinguished book" prizes—*Political Policing: The United States and Latin America* (Duke University Press, 1998) and *Violence Workers: Torturers and Murderers Reconstruct Brazilian Atrocities* (with Haritos-Fatouros and Zimbardo, University of California Press, 2002). Her most recent book is *Women Fielding Danger: Negotiating Ethnographic Identities in Field Research* (2008, with Marie-Louise Glebbeek). Huggins is writing a book from oral histories of police who were first responders during the Katrina disaster in New Orleans.

ROBERT J. KAMINSKI is an Associate Professor in the Department of Criminology and Criminal Justice, University of South Carolina (USC). Before joining the faculty at USC, he held analyst positions with the National Institute of Justice, U.S. Department of Justice; the New York City Criminal Justice Agency; and the Hindelang Criminal Justice Research Center. Dr. Kaminski's research focuses on policing issues, primarily violence against the police, police use of force, and less-lethal technologies.

DAVID A. KLINGER is Senior Research Scientist at the Police Foundation and Associate Professor of Criminology and Criminal Justice at the University of Missouri-St. Louis. He received his Ph.D. in Sociology from the University of Washington in 1992. Before joining the Criminology and Criminal Justice faculty at UMSL, Professor Klinger was Assistant (1992–1998) and Associate (1998–1999) Professor of Sociology at the University of Houston. Professor Klinger has also worked as a patrol officer for the Los Angeles and Redmond (WA) Police Departments. In 1997 he was the recipient of the American Society of Criminology's inaugural Ruth Caven Young Scholar Award for outstanding early career contributions to the discipline of criminology. Professor Klinger's research interests include a broad array of issues in the field of crime and justice, with an emphasis on the organization and actions of the modern police. He has published scholarly manuscripts that address arrest practices, the use of force, how features of communities affect the actions of patrol officers, and terrorism. He has conducted two federally funded research projects dealing with the use of force by police officers—one on officer-involved shootings and the other on police special weapons and tactics (SWAT) teams.

JOHANNES KNUTSSON is a Professor of Police Research at the Norwegian Police University College, Oslo. Dr. Knutsson also has a part-time position as professor at the Swedish National Police Academy, Solna, and is a visiting professor at Jill Dando Institute of Crime Science, London University College. His research interest has primarily been crime prevention and evaluation of crime preventive measures. Other topics are problem-oriented policing, police use of firearms, uniformed police service, crowd management and control, and police investigative work.

JOSEPH B. KUHNS is an Assistant Professor in the Department of Criminal Justice and Criminology, University of North Carolina at Charlotte. Before joining the faculty, he served for eight years as a Senior Policy Analyst at the United States Department of Justice, Office of Community Oriented Policing Services. Dr. Kuhns has worked on dozens of research and evaluation projects that focused on reducing harms associated with prostitution, community policing and problem solving, police use of force, and drug and violent crime relationships.

EDWARD R. MAGUIRE is Associate Professor of Justice, Law, and Society in the School of Public Affairs at American University. He received his Ph.D. in Criminal Justice from the State University of New York at Albany in 1997. He has held previous positions at George Mason University, the University of

Nebraska, the U.S. Department of Justice, and the United Nations. Professor Maguire's professional interests cover a wide range, but most of his work focuses on three topics: police organizations, violent crime, and social science measurement.

GREGORY B. MORRISON is Associate Professor of Criminal Justice and Criminology at Ball State University. He has spent time as a police officer and as a firearm and deadly force instructor in both the public and private sectors. He combines his police and training backgrounds as an academic to critically examine the history and development of U.S. police firearm training, document contemporary training policies and practices, and explore officer performance in high-risk encounters. His current projects include the latitude that departments exercise in the content and delivery of deadly force training, changes in officer safety over that past half-century, and the development of a metric for measuring the difficulty of deadly force encounters and officer performance.

TOR-GEIR MYHRER is Professor in Police Law and head of the research department at the Norwegian Police University College. Before joining the Police University College he had 23 years of experience as a prosecutor (among these 15 years at the Office of the Director of Public Prosecutions), and legal advisor in the law department of the Norwegian Ministry of Justice and the police. He is also a part-time professor in criminal law and criminal procedure at the faculty of law, University of Oslo, from 2005. His area of expertise is criminal procedure, confidentiality obligation within the police and public prosecutor authorities, police powers and use of same, police and prosecution ethics.

ANNIKA NORÉE is an Associate Professor of Criminal Law at the Faculty of Law at Stockholm University. In addition to her work as a Senior Lecturer in Criminal Law at the university, she teaches at the Police Academy in Solna. Her research interests are in criminal law and police law (especially the right of the police to use force to carry out their duties and in self-defense). Dr. Norée has published several books and articles in her research field.

IZABELA NOWICKA is a Director of the Institute of Law in the Higher Policy School in Szczytno (Poland), doctor of law (LLD), younger inspector of the Policy, and a research and didactic worker of the Warminsko-Mazurski University in Olsztyn. Dr. Nowicka has been the manager of many important research and evaluation projects concerning national security. Dr. Nowicka is also the editor-in-chief of the nationwide quarterly *Policy* and author of many publications on criminal law and transgressions.

EUGENE A. PAOLINE, III is an Associate Professor in the Department of Criminal Justice and Legal Studies at the University of Central Florida. He holds a Ph.D. in criminal justice from the University at Albany, State University of

New York. His research interests include police culture and the use of coercion, occupational attitudes of criminal justice practitioners, and theoretical development in criminal justice. Dr. Paoline is the author of *Rethinking Police Culture* (2001), and he is currently working on a National Institute of Justice grant geared toward examining the variation in American less-than-lethal use-of-force policies and the various outcomes associated with the different policies.

EMIL W. PŁYWACZEWSKI is a Full Professor of Criminal Law and Criminology of the Faculty of Law at University of Bialystok, Director of the Chair of Criminal Law and Head of Department of Substantive Penal Law and Criminology. His literary output comprises over 300 publications, printed in Poland and abroad. In 1997 he won the Distinguished International Scholar Award of the International Division American Society of Criminology. He also lectures at the Polish National Police Academy in Szczytno and the Central European Police Academy where, since 1994, he has been a representative of Poland in the International Examination Board of that Academy. Since 2005 he has been a Chief Coordinator of the Polish Platform for Homeland Security (PPHS). Besides the 580 members of research teams, the list of participants of the PPHS includes representatives of the police, law enforcement, and administration of justice.

JUSTIN READY is an Assistant Professor in the School of Criminology and Criminal Justice at Arizona State University. He has conducted research on crime displacement, hot-spot policing strategies, victimology, and surveillance cameras. His published articles have appeared in *Justice Quarterly, Crime and Delinquency, Criminology,* and *Police Quarterly.*

ALLISON REDLICH is an Assistant Professor in the School of Criminal Justice, University at Albany, State University of New York. Before joining the faculty, she was a Senior Research Associate at Policy Research Associates and a Research Scientist at the Stanford University School of Medicine. Dr. Redlich has two research foci. One focus is on police interrogations, false confessions, and false guilty pleas. The second focus is on mental health courts and other forms of mandated treatment for offenders with mental illness.

JON STRYPE is an associate professor at the Norwegian Police University College. He has a background in psychology and statistics. Together with Professor Johannes Knutsson, Jon Strype has investigated police use of guns in Norway and Sweden. Further, he has been working on various survey studies in the field of police research, and is also teaching statistics and quantitative methodology.

DIANA L. SUMMERS is a doctoral student in Criminology and Justice Policy at Northeastern University. Ms. Summers has participated in various research and analyses projects that focused on police use of force, international drug trafficking, prescription drug abuse, and Central and Eastern European methods of policing.

WILLIAM TERRILL is an Associate Professor in the School of Criminal Justice at Michigan State University. He is currently directing a nationally funded research project on police use of force and has published numerous scholarly articles on policing, crime in public housing, and systematic social observation. He earned his Ph.D. in 2000 from the School of Criminal Justice at Rutgers University, Newark.

P.A.J. WADDINGTON is Professor of Social Policy in the School of Law, Social Science and Communications, University of Wolverhampton, U.K. He is the author of seven books and numerous articles on aspects of policing, especially riot control and the police use of firearms. He has been consulted by official bodies in the United Kingdom and overseas, most notably leading an international inquiry into the policing of the Boipatong massacre in South Africa in 1992. He recently was a member of a panel reviewing police and emergency service training in Kosovo, former Yugoslavia, on behalf of the Organisation for Security and Cooperation in Europe. He is currently a member of the Independent Advisory Group for Her Majesty's Chief Inspector of Constabulary's report into the policing of the G20 protests in London during April 2009.

MICHAEL D. WHITE is an Associate Professor in the School of Criminology and Criminal Justice at Arizona State University. Dr. White's primary research interests involve program evaluation and the police, including use of force, training, and performance measurement. Dr. White's recent work has been published in *Criminology and Public Policy, Journal of Research in Crime and Delinquency, Journal of Experimental Criminology,* and *Crime and Delinquency.*

KAM C. WONG is an Associate Professor at Xavier University. He earned his Ph.D. in criminal justice from the University at Albany, serves as the Vice Chair of the Hong Kong Society of Criminology, the Vice President/Associate Fellow for the Center of Criminology, University of Hong Kong, and Vice President, President AAPS (Asian Association of Police Studies). He has published three books and 95 peer-reviewed articles, book chapters, and law reviews on various aspects of Chinese policing, terrorism, and public law. He is an expert consultant to Hong Kong Police and Ministry of Public Security, China.

MARTIN WRIGHT works at the University of Wolverhampton and is the award leader for the BSc Policing degree. Dr. Wright is a retired police officer and is the creator of the Radio Links Program. He is currently engaged in research on community perceptions of violent extremism as well as public confidence in policing.